Split/Vision

Split/Vision

John S. Wilbur Jr.

iUniverse, Inc.
New York Lincoln Shanghai

Split/Vision

iUniverse, Inc.

For information address:
iUniverse, Inc.
2021 Pine Lake Road, Suite 100
Lincoln, NE 68512
www.iuniverse.com

ISBN: 0-595-31952-1

Printed in the United States of America

PARABLE
<u>Two Monks and the Maiden</u>

Two Monks, an elder and an apprentice, set out on a journey to a distant monastery. After many hours of walking they come to a fast moving river. There, they see a beautiful maiden standing by the river bank, weeping.

"Kind Sirs", she says with tears in her eyes. "My mother is very sick and I have to reach her bedside as soon as I can. I cannot ford the river. I cannot swim. Is it possible for one of you to carry me across?

Without a moments hesitation the elder monk lifts up the woman and carefully carries her across the river to the other side. After setting her down the monks set out again on their journey.

The two monks continue to walk in silence for many hours. The younger monk appears perplexed and angry. After much agitation he stops the elder Monk and remonstrates with him. "You know that it is a sin of our order to touch a woman!", he scolds, Let alone to pick one up and carry her! "Why would you do such a thing?"

"Oh, her," the elder monk replies with a twinkle in his eye. I put that young lady down back by the river. It is you who are still carrying her around on your shoulders."

(Buddhist tale, unknown)

To my lovely wife, Beverly,
and all those who provided support and encouragement in the long education and process of writing
Split/Vision.

Long ago there was a young soldier
Wearing a conical hat,
Yellow bag over his back,
Long gun on his shoulder,
His hands grasp rifle and lance.
When the order comes
He steps up to the boat,
The drums thunder:
He steps down into the boat,
Tears wetting his face like rain.

(Vietnamese, anonymous)

Contents

ACKNOWLEDGEMENTS

1. Understanding Vietnam
    Neil Jamieson,
    University of California Press
    ISBN, 0-520-20157 (pp-428)

2. The Birth of Vietnam
    Keith Weller Taylor,
    University of California Press
    ISBN 0-520-07419 (pp391)

3. The Mekong,
    Milton Osborne,
    Grove Press, New York
    ISBN-0-8021-3802 (pp 294)

4. Dragon Ascending
    Henry Kamm
    Arcade Publishing, N.Y.
    ISBN-1-55970-306-7 (pp 303)

5. An Anthology of Vietnamese Poems
    Huynh Sanh Thong
    Yale University Press
    ISBN-0-300-06410-1 (pp 429)

6. Vietnam, Anatomy of a Peace
   Gabriel Kolko
   Routledge, London
   ISBN-00415-15989 (pp190)

7. Shadows and Wind
   Robert Templer
   Penguin Books
   ISBN-0-140-285-970 (pp 400)

8. Going Back
   W.D. Ehrhart
   McFarland& Co.
   ISBN-0-89950-278-4 (pp 186)

9. Spring Essence,
   John Balaban
   Copper Canyon Press
   ISBN-1-55659-148-9 (pp134)

10. Vietnam, Short Stories
    John Balaban& Nguyen Qui Duc
    Whereabouts Press, ISBN-1883513-02-2 (pp239)

11. Memories of a Pure Spring
    Duong Thu Huong
    Hyperion East Press
    ISBN-0-7868-6581-4

12. The Sorrow of War

Bao Ninh

Writers Association Publishing House

ISBN-0-436-31042-2 (pp212)

13. The Quiet American

Graham Greene

Penguin Books

PART I
ARRIVAL

1

"LOCK AND LOAD"

It's a beautiful day. From twenty thousand feet, fresh white clouds of a new morning sit calmly in the sky looking down at Vietnam with me. Dark green, almost blue, mountains unfold gracefully into a plain of fields quilted with the careful geometric sense of order imposed by the country's ancient rice culture. Broad brown rivers the same milk chocolate color, lazily uncoil toward the sea, like dragons' tails in a world where dragons were born.

Everything is so peaceful. I remember thinking the same 30 years before, when I looked down from a US Navy C-130 headed "in country" going to war. Now, on final approach, I watch for signs of life below, sampans on the water, thatched roofs, water buffalo in the fields. As the land comes closer, random memories slip out from the errant corners of a former life faded pale with years. With them comes a feeling somewhere between a catch in my breath and a lump in the throat.

As the plane cuts back its power into its final glide for landing and hovers between flying and floating, I find myself somewhere between the past and present, the east and the west, war and peace, a question and an answer. I am holding my breath.

Touch down. Here I am. Trying to understand why, I recall a lot of little things, stray reminders here and there mixed with time. I remember when I was living in southern Florida and driving back from some small town courthouse on a late afternoon and catching the sun hammering on the hot sprawling land, flat as an anvil. It was then I could sometimes imagine that instead of the sugar fields and cattle grazing there would be rice paddies with the brown water of the Mekong Delta in canals, and the neat rows of thatch roofed hamlets and I would forget all the other things, remembering instead the rhythmic cycle of planting and harvesting, the wet rot of Monsoon rains, the busy passage of river life, the nimble movement of small wiry people, the quick sing-song yammer of an incomprehensible tongue. At such moments I could think about going back without ever having to do again what I thought I had to do before.

The plane door is unsealed and opens. The few passengers are already filing out, leaving me huddled in my seat staring out the window. There beyond the concrete runaway are rice-fields. I can see a farmer trailing a water buffalo. It is real. I'm back. I'm not sure I want to get up, not sure about anything at all, except that I am alone. Hot moist air brings the scent of another world of yesterday. Slowly I get up and shuffle to the door recalling the airborne chant, "Step right up and shuffle to the door. Jump right out and count to four…".

Back then I was a young hard charger. Today I'm a middle age man, actually somewhat beyond middle age. I've been a Vietnam veteran for more years than I had when we first arrived back in early 1967, a cocky hero to be. Now I'm sweating as only a new tourist can in a tropical third world airport.

Standing in Tan Son Nhut Airport in 1999 is like arriving at an empty stage, after the show is over, the crowd is gone, and the set has been dismantled. The one-time busiest airport of the world has disappeared. In 1968, if there was ever a location that was a perfect backdrop for the swarming spectacle of our Vietnam War, it was Ton Son Nhut, the hive of the queen bee. "Showtime", 24 hours a day for how long? Six years? It was where the air festered with helicopters thumpa-thumping the mantra of vertical assault, and jet fighters, bristling with killing ordnance, swarming like so many angry hornets, "Spooky", the stubby DC-3's fat as cigars spiked with electrically powered 50 caliber Gatling guns patiently wheeling around Ton Son Nhut's perimeter and waiting to rain death on any menace. Under this protection, air transports of every serviceable generation disgorged the banquet of goods and tools of war, as commercial jets ferried in the hapless and flew home the lucky on a warehouse delivery routine. Nobody messed with the business of Ton Son Nhut AFB, nobody, not even during the TET Offensive of 1968.

That was then. Today the vast concrete expanse of runway and air taxi space looks like an immense and vacant car lot. Tufts of grass sprout where the surface is split and cracked. Workers with long scythes wander about cutting back the growth. We are the first and, by all indications the only, flight of the morning. The airport is almost asleep, as if abandoned to itself. Concrete revetments blackened with mildew still huddle where yesterday's deadly F-4 Phantoms and F-102 & 4s used to sleep. There is nothing unintentional about this. Carelessness is the least prominent of Vietnamese traits. For accentuation, off to the side are five or six helicopters of different generations, colors, and types parked disheveled and neglected like old people no longer useful-A subtle communist message: who needs them anymore? Our manifest is approximately 40 passengers; barely one third capacity: an assortment of family members returning from Hong Kong shopping, some consulting "experts" of the too little too late government modernization projects, visiting Asian businessmen, and a few like myself without portfolio. There are equally as many airport "officials", the usual customs-immigration types, janitors, baggage men and airline employees. Beyond a few perfunctory arm signals beckoning people to get in line, there are no greetings, no directions, no gestures of guidance, not even stares, as if we were almost extraneous to their jobs. We enter the building. Its interior reveals a vacancy similar to an empty airplane hangar. The actual airport facility itself reminds me, in size, of the one on St. Croix, U.S. Virgin Islands. So little for a city of now more than 6 million in a country that is thirteenth in world population. What does that say?

The walls are institutional white; the flooring is dully-polished cement. A row of slow moving fans circle lazily from the steel rafters. Stale warm air joins the gloom of dim lighting, subduing our group. There is little talk. We are lined up behind a painted white line approximately 20 feet in front of the immigration booths. There is no sign or written instruction, at least not in English. As I move up for my turn, I mistakenly cross it. The uniformed official looks up; black, ice-cold eyes freeze me. He stops his work, comes around his booth and advances pointing to the line commanding retreat. I obey.

Like a whiff of smoke and the shout of "Fire!." The "enemy" flashes before me, the urge to kill him springs from its grave, alive again, the adamantine face of war, up close, ugly and personal. Blood in my eyes.

Until now, the journey of returning has been an abstract conception. All my conscious efforts have involved just getting here. I had thought the war was mostly over for me after the day I left, 30 years before. I saw myself as neither its avenger, nor its victim. Long ago, the war had been deconstructed, broken down like a weapon, laid apart, and set aside: the gun and the boots, the knife and the compass, the strobe and the flare, are there in the trunk in the attic with the old feelings in deep sleep like ghosts now almost too old to fight again. I hadn't thought through my arrival. Its moment was always a safe distance away. Now it is upright and standing behind a white line on the immigration floor. "Lock and load" again. Welcome back, Vietnam! "High Port and Cross Over", before I knew it

Eventually, I'm summoned to present my documents. We avoid looking at each other. We both know the score as he motions me through. The faces of the baggage handlers are expressionless. Despite the fact that it is the only morning plane and less than a third full, they make no effort to sort out the few bags. I'm starting to wonder if this trip is going to be a bad idea.

The last time I arrived here I saw myself as a hard ass warrior, committed to a task, sure of direction, and eager to get it on. I was met by an employee of the US government, driven to an Air America compound (the CIA's carrier of choice) and flown off to somewhere in the war with a defined sense of mission. Now I'm flying completely solo and my only mission is to find a reasonably graceful way to get out of the airport. I have a duffel bag, a daypack and a two-day reservation at a hotel. The only person who knows I am here is my wife. I know no one in the country. I have only vague plans, undetermined means and not even a very good reason for being here. Before I was lucky to leave in one piece and now I seem to be coming back in several.

I hoist my duffel and daypack and move out to the exit platform from the dim confines of the terminal. Sunlight dazzles me with the glare of reality. Outside are some pedestrian barricades where small crowds of people stand waiting. There they are, the Vietnamese people, the same as ever, sweating and jostling in the mid-morning heat. Their faces still shine and ripple with that furtive look of anxiety, darting expressions, and piercing eyes. The air is sticky with moisture cloying with the sweet-sour odor of unwashed bodies, so instantly familiar. After the impersonal and sterile arrival process, I feel released into a different world that seems the same but not the same, just as I am the same and not the same. I stop to gather it in, stupid and slow in recognition, a blurred lens waiting for the aperture to find its focus.

There is little time. Inevitably, the hawkers are approaching sniffing out the tourist, shouting phrases for "Taxi" "Bags", the usual. The hotel had faxed my confirmation with the assurance that someone would meet me at the airport, so I'm hopeful to avoid airport haggling. With great relief, I catch sight of a slight, older man dressed formally in a rumpled gray suit holding up a card saying "Mr. Wilbur" like a life raft. There I am. I'm "Mr. Wilbur", a tourist. Before, I had been something else.

At least this time I'm better prepared. For the past two months I crammed for the first time to learn what I never had before: about the country its history and origins, a bit about its culture and society, its post war economics and regional politics. I even took a stab at trying to re-acquaint myself with the language. For the length and intensity of America's exposure to Vietnam, it was surprising how little historical and academic information was available. Clearly 90% of all books on the shelves under the title "Vietnam" were about the war. That I already knew.

Homework in early 1967 was another story in another world. Graduating from college in 1964 I elected to enter the US Navy to be commissioned in its active reserve under a 4-year commitment. Such a decision was not at all unusual for that time. Even though my college years were 1960-64, we were dyed in the fabric of the Fifties generation with no premonition of the future as the Sixties turned out to be. The Cuban Missile Crisis and racial civil rights said it all for the major issues of our day. Entering the military to become an officer was as natural a post-graduate opportunity as graduate school is today. Other than Law and Medicine, Business schools could be counted on two hands. The military was a convenient and reliable tool to shake out adolescence and absorb the practical- ities of responsibility and character before marriage and career intruded with lifelong commitments and obligations. Besides, most of the older guys who were my role models went in, so I followed them.

I was a water person; a swimmer from the age of three and fascinated with scuba diving since age 13 when it was a rare oddity, so I fantasized about becoming a Frogman. It was easier imagined than done. The first two years were consumed with constant specialized training in the Under- water Demolition Teams swimming on beaches and "locking out" of sub- merged submarines at night; intense and exciting, but not quite enough for me. War drums began sounding out of Southeast Asia. The Marines were landing in South Vietnam. Army units were flown in to establish a ground force there. So what about us?

I bitched about it to my best friend in the Navy and senior officer, Rick Trani, as we sweated in the haze of a late sultry afternoon doing PT on the helo deck of the US Navy LSD (Landing Ship, Dock) somewhere off the coast of Haiti sometime in the summer of 1966. Recalling that seminal afternoon now, it is hard to recall how fretful we were to be missing out on the "real" action happening on the other side of the world. Looking out impatiently over the flat plate of the ocean as if looking for the shimmer- ing path leading to war's bright fortunes, we feared that we would never get there before it was over, all the while failing to imagine that in less than two years only one of us would make it back alive.

Without being careful of what we wished for, within two weeks of our return to Little Creek, Virginia, I was notified that I had been transferred to SEAL Team Two, Rick to follow six months later. The SEAL Teams (Sea Air Land) were outgrowths of the UDT's and the Navy response to the development of the Army's Special Forces-never underestimate the force behind inter-service rivalries. We were thrilled. Since their inception in 1962, the SEALS (there were only two—one in the Pacific and one in the Atlantic) were very small and very secret.

Off we were sent to all the Army misery schools in crash courses of jun- gle warfare in Panama and Ranger school in the winter mountains of Georgia. Back to Base, off we went through six weeks of special unit riverine tactics and intensive small arms and demolition practice. By the time the fifteen of us boarded our specially routed C-130 transport in early March 1967 swollen with gear, we knew, or thought we knew, how to ambush, search and destroy, sneak and peek, and kill the enemy whoever, whenever, and wherever he was. Since we were the second platoon in cycle, with the first still in country for only four months, there was little operational or organizational history on what we were going to encounter, which is to say that other than spare tactical reports and broad overviews, as for actual knowledge of Vietnam, the country, we could have been going to the moon. Circa 1967, Uncle Sam was in a mighty hurry to get us there.

So was I. Hurry had dogged me all my conscious life, and maybe in the other parts as well. Ever since I could remember, the grass was greener, the sky bluer, and the air fresher somewhere else with something else. The here and now to me never quite caught up with the there and then. Not only was I to find out what there turned out to be, but also how long it would be there. It wasn't until I had finished law school afterwards and was three years a prosecutor with the U.S. Justice Department that I read the news of the South Vietnamese final collapse that sighed out its exhaustive aftermath in 1975. Some hurry! By then it was with far more relief than concern, and who knows what shame, that America turned its broad back, walked away and all but slammed the door on anything to do or think about "Nam". As we settled back, finally unburdened to enjoy the endless promise of our future, as ravaged Indo—China's revolutionary rancor disemboweled itself in an odious stew of political, social and cultural retribution. With this spectacle in our rear-view mirror, no wonder we drove on for distance, almost refusing to look back.

In the power vacuum that resulted from our abandonment, Cambodia slid into an abattoir of mass murder and cultural debasement. This infamy provided a cover for Vietnam's less genocidal repression, as its Marxist-Stalinist leadership replicated an Orwellian "Animal Farm" on an exhausted population. Those who were winners were believers sold on Socialist illusions as bankrupt as the government's coinage; bought off in a rough exchange for down home graft and corruption that served as a crude

method of regressive wealth distribution. The losers were both dispossessed and terrorized by the gun of "re-education" pointed at their heads.
Nothing the Politburo touched in the economic sector worked and in
order to hide its failure, it simply buried any alternative thinking that
could. In 25 years of absolute rule, Vietnam was to become, if not to
remain, one of the poorest and most populous in the world. It was a classic
Phyrrhic victory, and of course, we helped.

Back home, having failed to "win" the war, we settled on revenge in the
form of diplomatic isolation and economic strangulation allowing the
acids of our bitterness to leach into their economic ruin. This, in effect,
held any form of post-war reconstructive aid hostage to the gruesome bar-
ter of dumping bastard war orphans in the Philippines for the grisly recovery of un-certifiable MIA bones rotting among unknown jungle hills, a,
truly priceless exchange. In the end super-power politics of peace proved
better muscle than our guns and ordnance and Vietnam was essentially
blipped off the international radar screen.

So instead of remaining an obscure country out of sight and wishfully
out of mind, Vietnam became, for Americans, a convenient pariah, a name
and a memory rarely mentioned, avoided like a death or mental illness in
the family, lingering somewhere between a scab and a scar. Given this
charnel house of burned out feelings and awkward memories, it was not
unusual to encounter surprise among those who heard of my plan to
return. "Why would you want to go back there?" was always a good question, hard to translate into a concise answer.

I settled on "curiosity". It worked better in conversation. Besides I was
curious, about many things. Interestingly enough, so was almost everyone
else. "What is that place like, what are those people like, what's happening
over there?" Who better to seek these little known answers than one who
had at the least a reason and a starting place to find them.

2

HO CHI MINH CITY, BUT STILL SAIGON TO ME

Any sense of familiarity fades fast as we pass the gates of the airport. We are immediately engulfed in a swarm of motorized "cyclos" (motorbikes), the new monsters of the Third World. They flow around the car like ants around a beetle in a snarling staccato and spewing blue bilious exhaust of crude gasoline. At each intersection they pile into and around each other in dense restless thickets, only to speed off in an incessant chase towards some unknowable urgency. Almost all are young, the most prominent feature on the face of Vietnam today. My immediate favorites are the young women with facemasks and long sleeve armbands as protection from the sun and exhaust. They resemble fragile bandits with their Ao Dais panels flying behind them like magic carpets.

Although we follow what must have been the same route that I had driven countless times years before, there are only a few vague features of familiarity to grab at. The boulevard has been widened and the building construction on both sides seems more dense and higher. But it is the absence of things so prominently etched on images from the past that have disappeared, just as in the case of Ton Son Nhut, not only different, but changed, as in no more.

There is no barbed wire, no barricades or sandbags anywhere, no flags, banners, signs, or emblems and badges; nor uniforms, or automatic rifles, side arms, bayonets, machine guns, artillery, jeeps, tanks, half-tracks or trucks anymore. Everything that reminded or forewarned of a state of war has disappeared from view, as if a great broom has simply swept away it all away into the dustbin of minor history.

Anyone who was in and around the city of Saigon in the sixties knew of or about the Continental Palace hotel. It was never a remarkable edifice architecturally, but it was nonetheless a handsome, sturdy, rectangular structure of five floors with prominent mahogany balconies, a building that commanded an impressive corner in the epicenter of the French developed city. In my day, it was where the action was, the hub of where to meet and greet. Its centerpiece was the open high arched veranda, or *terrasse*, on the corner fronting with a broad and open view of Municipal Theatre-Opera house adjacent to the hotel and the beginning of the spacious Le Loi Boulevard. There, one would find regal rattan fan chairs and tables covered with white cloth often decorated with flower arrangements, white liveried waiters, and sometimes a modest orchestral quartet, and one could look around and sense the "Raj" of being there. Sitting there enjoying a "33" beer, a gin and tonic, or high tea one could observe the whole panoply of the American imperium: journalists in safari jackets and their stringer-handlers concocting story lines or swapping hearsay scoops, staff-colonels patronizing their ARVN military counterparts, the broad-swath of GS civilians from the alphabet soup of agencies like USAI, USIS, DOA, US Medical Service, CIA, etc., etc., discussing plans, operations and the pettifoggery of Headquarters and Washington. Then there were the "extras", young footloose junior officers on R&R like me looking around, trying to get a buzz on and hoping to get laid. The location favored both, if not invited it, since across the square and down side street was Tu Do Street (now renamed Dong Khoi St.), Saigon's red light version of Hong Kong's famous Wang Chai district.

Although the clean geometry of the hotel's lines still reminds one of a cross between a bank and fort, gone for sure is its old panache and élan. Today's Continental Palace has been humbled but kept in service. Considering its former reputation it's not surprising that the conquering "Peoples Party" found it distastefully symbolic of an imperialist past. As an example of their ambivalence about sanctioning capitalistic endeavors that might offend their socialist prudery, the *terrasse* has been sealed up behind the glass and mortar of converted offices for various southeast Asian airlines even though the effect of the "renovation" significantly devalues the profitable potential of one of Saigon's more attractive tourist venues. The result is that now the Continental no longer commands anything.

The Continental, with only 50 or so rooms, is not a big hotel by modern standards. With the onset of Monsoon season, roughly June through September approximating our summer, there are few guests. When I close the door to my room, the continual motion of the 48-hour journey suddenly ceases. I look around at the high ceiling with dark polished mahogany moldings. With the exception of a television set, and a sleek European wall air conditioner, it could be the same interior of the days of French colonialism, or maybe the Japanese occupation, or even me at age 26, 1967 (featured in the opening scenes of the movie Apacolyspse Now) But it isn't. There is just me at 59 with my bags in an empty room and the mirror confirming that I am no longer young. Going to the window I stare down at the street only two floors below. Across is a busy shop of some sort. People are going in and out. A few women are wearing traditional Ao Dais, but then I see they are the shop clerks and everyone else is in the casual open short sleeve shirts and pants. Everyone is young. It's noontime. Street vendors are roaming the sidewalk plying their traditional wares: combs, cigarettes and lighters, some traditional snacks. There is a short alleyway perpendicular to the street used as a parking lot stuffed with moto-cyclos. At close range, I can see their expressions, track their exchanges, and watch their movements while I try to feel some connection touched by memory in the confusion of being close but distant, here now and here then but all I can summon are faint outlines of faded faces, dim recollections and vague feelings in an empty hotel room. Now what? The question hangs in the air, turning slowly with the overhead fan.

Hunger gets me going. Leaving the hotel, I stop at the corner where the former veranda had been. I know this corner. I'm oriented. Across the side street the long mothballed Municipal Theatre/Opera house appears closed up, inoperative, or still under reconstruction after thirty years? I wonder when the last performance occurred. Beyond the Opera House is another former landmark for Americans: the Caravelle Hotel or the "Pink Palace". Considering the humbling of the Continental I am surprised that they allowed it to remain pink.

Once it was the designated lair of jet-set journalists, the network TV news and national and international magazine guys who routinely jetted in and out, first as anxious courtiers of the war, but quickly converting to its morticians after the post TET mood swing, playing critics to the movie they found themselves producing. They ate well, drank well and grabbed anything they wanted; helicopters, boats, and jeeps often with generals holding open the doors as if they were a livery service to their capricious needs. Given this stigma, I wonder not only why the Caravelle is still pink, but also why they are putting the finishing touches on a 15-story pink annex.

From the corner I stare at the river of cyclo traffic and recognize major pedestrian obstacles. Watching carefully how others maneuver, I grasp its central reality. "He who hesitates is lost". Beyond this and the acuteness of need, I have no other ideas about how to negotiate the chaos. Even so, in order to reduce the probability of early error, I walk around the square instead of across it. This leads me to another fixture of American "occupation".

The Rex is another older hotel from the French colonial days that was requisitioned and converted into a senior Army Basic Officers Quarters (BOQ). Though one of many, its location made it the most prominent, or at least the best known. Together with the Continental Palace and the Caravelle they comprised a triumvirate of American tenancy in Saigon. While the Continental *terrasse* represented the more cosmopolitan collage of wartime society, the Rex was strictly the venue for the military version of the checkered cloth steak-house crowd. Its twelfth story rooftop deck served as the Officers' Club home-away-from-home. Every night had a happy hour with charcoal grill cookout. There the tactics, strategies, and SNAFUs of the day were loudly cursed, mocked, or defended, fueled by the octane of beer kegs and liquor. From the balustrades one had the best view and appreciation of the French designed city featuring broad boulevards, squares and the nearby Saigon River port. And there, as if behind a fortress with a moat, we could eat and drink away the nights in splendid insulation from the war and the confusing if not confounding Vietnamese sea around us. In 1967-68 the Rex was conspicuously defended by barricades of cement-filled 55-gallon drum barrels, mounded with sand bags, snarled with barbed wire and guarded by well-armed American MPs. Today I am welcomed by silk turbaned doormen dressed in bright Mandarin costumes standing as guards with fake pikes and phony daggers, a strange wake-up call. They escort me politely to a desk receptionist arrayed in a flowing embroidered traditional gown and wearing a costume-jeweled headdress. She graciously accompanies me to the rooftop bar restaurant. "Where are you from?" she asked in slow and careful English. "The United States" I said. Surprise shows on her face.

I am the only customer, attended by three costumed waiters. Thinking it would be a good time to try out my newly acquired Vietnamese phraseology, I tell the nearest waiter I'm hungry and thirsty. It doesn't work. Whatever came out made no sense. I try again, getting the same blank stare. I give up and reach for the menu. This he understood. He also understood English.

I worked hard trying to master my phrases, doggedly repeating them from the tapes I got at the Public Library and listened to while driving to and from work. Vietnamese is very difficult and an unusual challenge principally because of its tonal quality. To the best of my limited knowledge there may be approximately six tonal sounds to a given word with each tone capable of conveying different meanings. A tone sounding almost the same may mean something either unintelligible in the context of what one is trying to say, or something possibly embarrassing. This renders the "phrase book" of dubious assistance. As a further dis-incentive a surprising number of Vietnamese speak some English, and manage to speak it far better than foreigners do Vietnamese.

I order steak and frites for the sake of simplicity along with the national beer "33 Ba mui Ba". The heat of the day is lifting. The dynamic of monsoon season unwinds in the slow upward spiraling of white thunderheads into a forever-blue sky speckled with the ubiquitous crowd of black turkey buzzards working the physics of the heated air in a lazy swoon. From twelve stories up Nyugen Hue Boulevard grandly presents the Saigon River Quay and beyond it, across the Saigon River, the flat swamplands of the Rung Sat extending south to the South China Sea 40 miles away. To the west the tree shaded Le Loi Boulevard stretches toward Cholon, the largest Chinese quarter in the country. Below the streams of cyclos and vehicles rush forward and damn up like a watercourse. Gratefully, the restaurant is high enough to mute, the traffic below.

Leaning out over the balustrade, trying to take it all in reminds me of that momentary dislocation of reality that comes when hanging from a parachute, and it dawns on me that I am seeing everything from two different angles at once, a kind of split vision of today and its yesterday, the now and the then blurring as I try to focus on both

Turning around, I notice a western couple has come in. They are American. With a first glance, I'm glad that I hadn't urged my wife to come with me. He was a Vet for sure. She was the dutiful wife following some itinerary obviously not her own. They are both hot and look in need of regrouping. We barely acknowledge each other, though I don't know why. We are the only customers.

Here we are, with perhaps much, or at least a little, in common. We live in the same country, possibly across town, speak the same language, and perhaps cheer for the same team. We have traveled far and expensively to get here. Now we are standing in the same spot probably for the same reasons, call it nostalgia, going back in time, looking backward, all those impulses that grab and twist and turn in search of something no longer there like a dog turning in circles in the hunt for his tail. Who knows? Probably neither of us.

I can't remember if we even look at each other. It's as if we are standing on a river's bank waiting for the other to cross. If I had walked over and talked to them we would most likely connect, possibly share a beer, exchange itineraries, at least establish the courtesy of nodding or greeting in passing the next time. But our mutual disinclination speaks volumes about our predicament and the peculiarity of our war, in the sense that it has failed to bind us enough to share our experiences. Maybe it is because we lost it and have assumed its shame? or because we were in different outfits, at different times, or more simply that both of us at this moment are off our social feed? The answer is probably yes to all of them. The fact is that the Vietnam War fostered little cohesion among us, socially or otherwise. We won no victories, found little glory, and heard few cheers. There will be no books proclaiming we were exemplars of the "Greatest Generation" or the "Best and the Brightest". For the most part, we were "Tweeners", or maybe "Middlers", an amalgam of middle road smarts, average talents, or dim horizons. We might not have been smart enough to know just what else we should have been doing, where we should have been going out of college or high school, or what choices if any presented themselves at the time. Maybe we were not driven enough by our perceived ends to justify avoiding the draft.

Our shaved heads, and the drill instructor's obscenities, removed us from society overnight. Boot camp forced us to develop our own. We cohabited with every shade, accent, odor, brain, body, fear and want forging a composite material that if nothing more, made flesh and sinew of the name "American". Even so, with this new and often surprising recognition, we were soon scattered among different units with all the planning of throwing seed on a field. Wherever we landed, most became spare parts to be installed and replaced in programmed wear and tear cycles of necessary inventory. If the ingress to war was haphazard, so was its escape. When our time came to be sent back it carried all the sentiment of a punch clock scheduled as carelessly as we had come. Bussed to the tarmac, handed tickets and lined up for the thousandth time we filed off in random groups disappearing into the diasporas of our tomorrows, rarely, if ever, to assemble again.

The last time I was in the midst of Vietnam vets was on just such a return. We boarded a Braniff flight, an orange disco job that sat on the runway like a dream come true filled with happy but tired faces going back to the "World", as home was then called. When we got to altitude, we could soon see the approaching coast with its string of beaches like white ribbons cutting the land of dark jungle-green from a beautiful deep blue sea. For the new "Vets" going home at last it may have been the most important goal line of their lives and soaring over it, for many, the greatest victory of all.

On perfect cue, the Captain came on the PA and graciously congratulated us "on behalf of the American people for a job well done". "Wow", that was a first! With that he pulled the plane into a steep bank and away we hurtled into the wild blue yonder. Cheers went up and faces spilled out with pure joy. For the next hour or so the men "grab-assed" around joking and visiting up and down the aisle until the euphoria wore off and fatigue wore on. Before long, most of the guys were sleeping while some of us stared at the overhead into the suddenly blank sheet of our futures. Unable to sleep, I stood up and paced the aisles as if by the instinct that I was still "On Watch".

Watching their faces, I saw how young they all were. Even at 27, I was an old guy to most of them. Still an officer in their midst, I retained the presumption of age and wisdom even though its facade would soon crumble. Back in the "world" we would all be suddenly different again, like we were before, all different again but never the same. After four years, I knew my way around them, had a place among them and with them absorbed the muddy lessons of their humanity and mine. Together we had seen how frailty and strength wrestled with each other, wounding both winner and loser, and how a clear winner rarely emerged.

It would take distance and time before our new forms would reveal their shapes, whether to find coherence or lose it. We were so freshly departed from the war and harm's way that we probably thought we were going to be free of its future, and that since the only reality was in leaving; the arriving would take care of itself. Suspended between the past and the future, we did not understand that we were just part of another file in another column of another army turning its back on another war and destined to repeat the same litanies of our forebears, who in returning home to put their former lives together found pieces missing, left somewhere back on the trail.

Nothing awaited us on arrival at Andrews AFB except a line of empty gray buses. No bands played, no "Tunes of Glory". The only greeting was the officious barking of the personnel Yeoman types. "Listen Up" followed with a bored but meticulous recitation of bus transfers and flight schedules. They ushered us on to the alphabetized rows to be processed, then bundled us into groups for our destination transports. No longer were we the hero/survivors of the take-off 48 hours before, just the daily commuter flights of young men trickling out of a war and into a world that preferred to ignore us.

On arriving at the San Francisco airport, we stood around with our duffels, trying to get our bearings. There wasn't much to say as we looked around, wondering how and where to fit in, how to join the hurrying seemingly purposeful lives that swarmed around, close enough to touch, but faraway from reach. Was it this that we wanted to get back to or was it only where we had been that we wanted to get away from? Replacing one reality with another suddenly seemed hard, a lot harder than when it was just a dream.

Being in civvies shielded us from the discomfort of uniforms as undesirable reminders of someone else's problem. Little could we grasp the irony that we believed in the people at home far more than they believed in us. So we broke away quickly, choosing to lose ourselves in the crowd, and because we scarcely knew each other, with hardly a goodbye, never to see one another again, and, as most discovered, never really wanting to.

Not all of us disappeared though. I still see and catch glimpses of our random standard bearers on TV, at Memorial Day and at Veterans' Day functions. The other veteran groups from WW II and Korea, almost without exception, pass the inspection of dress uniforms and march proudly with flags held upright, chests full, eyes front. And then there are our guys, usually off to the side looking slightly homeless. They always seem to slouch in the scrambled eggs of various field dress of different units, tattered epaulets, hair sticking out from the soft hats embossed with a lot of macho bullshit as if they are stragglers of a retreating army, and it makes me want to cry.

3

"GIVE PEACE A CHANCE"

When I turn around from the balustrade, the "Vet" couple has left. We have tacitly accepted our mutual estrangement. I feel ashamed of myself and a little depressed, so I set about to get on with it. I had a new/old city to visit, the freedom to wander, and all the time in the world.

I find myself on what used to be on "Tu Do" street, just across from the Caravelle formerly the best-known "Red Light" district in Vietnam in wartime, the honey pot for macho American libidos tantalized by the bait of the doll-like Asian woman and fueled with a careless exuberance of life in Saigon's fast lane.

Its sidewalks used to host a string of euphemistically named "Tea Shops". In these cave-dark recesses tiny (but not fragile) Asian women/girls dressed in the tight bodice silk Ao Dais would sit and flirt for dollar bills in seduction of the war bored or weary Americans, farther from home than any could imagine and in a world stranger and more exotic than we knew how to deal with in any other way. And so got up the ditty, "Saigon Tea, Saigon Tea, Whatcha doing to me, with one hand in my pocket and the other on my knee."

With the same revanchist zeal that sealed up the Continental Palace's imperialist *terrasse*, Tu Do St. is now renamed as "Dong Khoi" St. and is remarkable with its apparent sanitization. Gone without a trace, of course, are the "Tea Houses" and the "Tea Girls" (sent to "re-education" camps often in the hinterlands and forcibly separated from their children, many of whom were Amerasian war orphans (segregated and raised in state run orphanages). Today it features attractive and tasteful antique and fine arts shops presenting Vietnamese art and lacquer work and undergoing renovation to house a strip of high-end western chain boutiques. Before long, and if the renovation and the tourist trade can keep going, it will regain its original status as the tourist shopping avenue of the city.

There are only a few pockets of commercial prosperity apparent in downtown Saigon but turn any corner off the main streets or boulevards and there amid the warren of back streets/alleys/walkways is where the real commerce of life ebbs and flows.

I follow one of them, threading my way through the multi-storied tenements crammed between the side streets, letting the current of movement steer me. The walls are flaked with worn paint streaked with stains from various discharges. Narrow cramped iron balconies seem to burst open from the mildewed walls behind which the city dwellers live out their cramped crowded lives. Plants, birdcages, bicycles and sundry other possessions hang or dangle from the balconies, garnering a few more precious inches of space. Cats' cradles of clotheslines draped with drying clothes create a checkerboard of light and dark shadow below.

Porters lug their sacks of rice and merchandise, balanced on their heads. Construction workers thread their wheelbarrows of sand and cement throughout the city, engaged in constant patching and repair jobs. Odd vendors tucked here and there in corners sit amid their baskets of goods or sundries hawking their wares. Some are selling Pho soups, others cigarettes either in pack or in ones and twos with matches. Jack hammers, car horns, the rattle and exhaust of the cyclos penetrate from the surrounding side streets and avenues, competing with the jabber among neighbors overhead, the bartering among customers below. Everywhere there is movement, mixing and stirring the odors of sweat, low-grade diesel exhaust, charcoal braziers, steaming cooking oils, tobacco, slop and refuse into the rich brew of the Orient.

Monsoon thunderheads mass together like a deep bruise. At the threat of rain, I find a backseat in a corner café. The air flushes with coolness. A rumble of wind hurries toward us, sweeping a gray wall of rain like a giant broom chasing the crowded traffic off the streets into the doorways and under the nearest shop awnings. The café is packed. For the first time I am completely surrounded by Vietnamese. All are young. In the shadow-light their faces glisten like olives in a jar framed in the black luster of hair. Dark marble eyes watch the rain as I watch them.

The view from behind another's eye is always a mystery. Between different cultures and races at war, the mystery is deepened by misperception and suspicion. But that was then. This is now. Now a Westerner seems converted into an item of curiosity rather than an object of mistrust and the same is true with my lens as well. The evidence has been there since I arrived. It has just taken awhile to assimilate: the absence of things expected, the signposts no longer there, bits and pieces of old thoughts have fallen away, worn out images have faded, the outlines of the war have dissolved. Vietnam is no longer at war. Here I have been looking out at them dragging along the past while they are looking out and seeing the present flowing into the future. One holds the shards of war, the other the vessel of peace. I wonder what that means to them other than waking up in the morning and feeling different at long last. Back in the Sixties and Seventies, young Americans who had chanted and swayed to it at anti-war inspired rock concerts had no idea what "Peace" was, unless accompanied by the melody of a song, a hand painted placard or tie-dyed in a tee shirt. Peace was simply something we had in our lives, taken for granted like the air we breathe. As for war, all we knew about it was that it happened somewhere else, screwing up someone else's world. Until it snuck up on us, the word "Peace" meant to me little more than a rhetorical flourish applied to a political speech. Other than that it was never really objectified. The Cold War was frozen in place with no thaw in sight. Glasnost was to be born only to the graduates in the following generation. The Vietnam "conflict" was just starting; we had not talked ourselves into an all-out war. We were just oiling up our weapons and getting ready to lock and load when a bunch of hirsute and intellectually disjointed professors at, where else?, Berkeley, California, decided to steal the march and make an announcement about peace on the steps of Sproul Hall at noon on a day in early April 1967. Strangely enough I happened to be there, visiting a girl-friend, three days from boarding a C-130 flying one way to Vietnam. Did someone mention "Peace"?

I'd flown up from San Diego on two-days leave to see for the first time if it was true that San Francisco was all it was said to be, the Elysian field of platitudinous liberty, do-what-you-want freedom and loosy-goosy fun. At that time it was the coolest place in the American Universe for anyone between pubescence and marriage. My friend was a resident/student who brought me to the event. It featured the music of the Beatles. How was I to know that it was going to be the first "peace" protest of the new 60's era until I read it many years later. The clear California afternoon provided brilliant theatre. Everyone who didn't work for a living and could blow off a class was present (with their dogs) trying to look poor, cornfield plain, and fake dirty. And, oh yes, there was some harsh smoke cutting the air and a lot of dizzy smiles.

A long line of indistinguishable men in scruffy clothes followed each other reading speeches from sheets of paper, talking up peace and unity and talking down empire and power, scolding the arrogance of our leadership, and to give it a New Testament ring, bearing witness to the yearnings of the unseen and unrepresented peasant poor. It was a confusing and awkward performance, made especially hard to hear because of nearby construction workers purposefully leaning on their jack hammers, in conspiracy with someone cutting off the mike, not to mention the student dogs wearing colorful bandanas barking and romping among the fountains on the plaza.

It was a wonderful day for peace, or to American youth, just another day, especially since no one had ever lived without it. Did I want to join them? Yes I did. I liked the music, the dizzy smiles, the unbuttoned shirts opening up the world of unrestrained milk white tits and the generous promise of something more after wine and candle light. Oh Yes! I had been missing something, if only to find it too late.

My friend kept her distance, including her dog. Later there was wine and candlelight. Her friends came over to help. Word had got out. Here I was, all ready to smoke a joint for the first time in my life, but the long haired guys gave me the direct impression that they thought I was an asshole and their ladies didn't come over to help. I slept alone.

The next day she drove me to the airport. There may have been some small talk but I remember it as a largely silent drive. She didn't dislike me, but I didn't exactly help her out. She was nice enough to walk me to the gate. "I think I should wish you good luck" she said, "but frankly I think what you're doing is the dumbest thing I can think of." Food for thought!

On the flight over to Vietnam I wrote and re-wrote her a soulful letter. There was no reply. Later on I wrote her again and then a couple others whose addresses I had saved and got the same response. I wasn't too sharp at picking up on things but "Hey, I had a war to fight".

The issues were being defined, the conditions ripening, the social elements grouping like freight cars waiting on the siding. All they needed to get on track was the engine. Vietnam and its call to arms for American boys to be killed 12,000 miles away provided the coupling, but it was the threat of the DRAFT that pulled the train—the "Peace Train".

Rain roars upon the awning and bounces off the pavement, gathering into rivulets rushing towards the already overwhelmed gutters, forming confused pools choked with the refuse and detritus of an overcrowded and under-managed city. Before long the storm's energy is spent, and with the cool, freshened air comes a momentary silence without the din of traffic, punctuated only by the patter of water from the dripping awnings, and balconies. Soon the first and then the rest of the shelter seekers are off, like messengers in a hurry with unknown news. I linger awhile longer sipping my hot tea as the world changes utterly back into the bright sunlight like the promise of a new day.

There are only two or three customers left in café/tea shop. As I am paying for the tea, the proprietor approaches and points at me, "Where you from?" he asks in English. Somewhat surprised, I answer, "American" and then add "United States" for clarity.

"Oh, really" he beams and turns to the others with some excitement and announces "American, United States." Looking back he says with a big smile "We think you maybe Russian!"

Shaking my hand vigorously and signaling for the others to do so, we stand around somewhat stupidly not knowing what to do next except nod back and forth and keep smiling (always a good fall back).

Later that day I return to my hotel to sort out my travel arrangements. The Continental Palace's hotel staff was as helpful and accommodating, as it knew how to be. The young lady at the concierge desk is a law graduate hoping for a position in some government ministry. In the meantime she is using the job to improve her English. I'm surprised to learn that English is considered as a major skill requirement for the young and is the only foreign language study that the government encourages and is willing to subsidize.

Other than air travel, which is restricted to the major regional cities (only a handful in number) there is a short menu of options. Vietnam has only recently renovated the Hanoi-Saigon railway for passenger service, but this only amounts to a trunk line with limited service. Moreover, while there are buses everywhere, there is no national bus "system" in any interregional sense and its general service remains a patchwork of local routes. This leaves the private car as the only sensible mode of travel for the tourist.

I have a card for a "travel consultant" given to me by my only US business contact familiar with Vietnam. When I go to see this "consultant" he speaks great English business jargon, describing his transportation assets, capabilities and terms, but indicates that there will be a significant surcharge for the government-required guide in addition to the driver, the same whitewash. He apologizes for the government rules and regulations but states he would lose his license if he did not comply.

After this less than satisfactory encounter, my pretty concierge friend, seeing my frustration, earnestly re-explains the official line and finishes with an "I'm so sorry" smile, reminding me that Vietnamese were always careful to accompany disagreeable news with great shows of empathy. I also remember that after every "No" there often lingers a "But", and soon she suggests, in a conspiratorial whisper, that I talk to the Saigon Tourist agent at the hotel. He "happens" to be lurking around the lobby. Her suggestion at first seems an invitation into the jaws of the wrong animal.

Saigon Tourist is an "SOE" (State Owned Enterprise.)—a copycat version of the infamous "In-Tourist" of Soviet Russia. It controls the key syndicate of premier hotels such as the Continental Palace, the Caravelle and the Rex, as well as most car-for-hire outlets and dominates just enough of the terms and pricing to control any unofficial competition.

After a long sympathetic introduction by the concierge, the young man, far from being an officious bureaucrat asserting dogmatic rules to frustrate the Yankee tourist, acts as if he could care less if I took off for Cambodia as long as I rented one of his cars. "Yes, no problem, you can hire a car for as long as you like and go wherever it can take you." "No, no problem, you do not need to have a guide, you can stay anywhere you want; and yes, there are roads to get you there. No you need no documents, and yes, we take credit cards. You can pay upon return. The only charge is a per-kilometer charge and a small stipend for the over night of the driver." "No problem".

"No Problem" is music to my eager ears. If it is no problem to him, it is no problem to me, nothing like the comfort of bland assurances for the anxious foreign tourist.

Having a car with a driver to travel where I want means the keys to the kingdom to me. It was more than I had expected to bargain for. This leap-frog over the bureaucratic briar patch is the first signal in a trail of signs that the Central Government at many levels has become a toothless watchdog. With their rigid penchant for control, far too many manifestoes are issued for too few watchdogs who, in addition to wearing out their bite, are also losing their bark and becoming plump and complacent in the process.

4

FIRST NIGHT ON THE TOWN

Buoyed by this open door, I treat myself to an excellent meal at a trendy new restaurant called The Lemon Grass, recommended by the young concierge. It is modern Vietnamese, clean, tastefully decorated and specializing in cross-cultural cuisine California style. I am not surprised when I find out that it is owned and operated by a Viet Kieu (a South Vietnamese refugee/ex-patriot, many of whom settled in California). The clientele is predominantly western, but not tourists, mostly worker-traveler "ex-pat" types who seem to be repeat customers.

After dinner I'm primed for a stroll and so are the Saigonese. The ghosts of wartime curfew and the anxious furtive hurry to get home behind the security of their doors and walls are long gone. The street is jammed with the moto-cyclo crowd, young people taking their family or girl-friends on a "wheely" along the sight seeing esplanades where everyone can escape from the condensed heat of their cramped quarters. They are the new middle-class; their first capitalistic ambition seems to translate into getting wheels and whizzing out of the family compound.

Without the nightlife of the "Tea shops", née Girlie bars, the former Tu Do St. is subdued and dark. If Vietnamese Communists have their infamous faults and deserve their ashes in history, something should be said about their virtues. While Ho Chi Minh looked the other way at mass murder, institutionalized bullying, and pious thievery, he and his followers were at least devout prudes. Among the "undesirable" aspects of life they vacuumed out of Saigon, prostitution and commercial licentiousness were among the first to disappear. By any comparative standards, at least in

1967-73, Saigon was auditioning for Sodom if not also Gomorrah. Cleaning it up was a praiseworthy improvement. The human damage in doing so by forcible expulsion "re-education", and hard labor among jungle hills was arguably no worse than allowing further degradation of Vietnamese women. This evening, none of that is present at first.

The headlight of a cyclo comes off the street onto the sidewalk shining directly into my face, and stops alongside me. "You come with me, make love sucky sucky!" spits a hard feminine voice. No question, just a command. I couldn't see from the headlight but I could feel a small strong hand grab me. Shielding my eyes, I can see her Ao Dais spread over the bike and brushing against the ground. She has a conical hat slung behind her head. "You come, we make love", she repeated, tugging my arm.

So the squeaky clean up has lost its grip, I see. Some things never change. I pulled, or tried to pull my arm away, but she held on. The set-up is obvious. The new generation simply picking up on the tactics of the old—GI gets on bike thinking cheap blow-job, girl turns the corner into the alley where the pimp's gang waits with knives. End of story. I shake her off as gently as necessary only to hear her spit out "You fuck-off, cocksucker!" Oh my, just as I remembered it.

I'm hardly a hundred yards own the street when something unseen pulls at my leg. Wheeling around, I see that this time it's a tiny hand belonging to a little girl not more than eight to ten years old. She stares up at me, putting her hand to her mouth and then points to a sleeping infant dangling from her hip, like a rag doll, but it's real. People are passing by without a glance. There isn't a parent about. I start to walk again, but the little hand keeps its grasp. It's a perfect shake down. Part of me wants to force some money in her hand but then another part doesn't. There is "face" to consider, a compelling, if not fateful, value in the East. I wave her off and pick up the pace. It doesn't work. She doggedly matches my stride, the baby's head bouncing along almost hitting the pavement. Before us is Ton Duc Thoung, the major avenue along the river. Across its six lanes are the river quay and a promenade park overlooking the water. A tactical maneuver is going to be necessary for extraction. Stepping off the curb into the stream of headlights I resolve to make it halfway across before my nerve runs out. Here I have to face up for the opposite traffic. In that moment of hesitation the little hand catches up to me. I can't believe she made it, but then this is more her turf than mine. We are surrounded by a river of headlights that part around us without slowing in the least as if we stand like a boulder in the stream. I'm the only one who is afraid. There are no traffic lights to assist our crossing. I reach down and grab her hand as much for my comfort as for hers. The baby still hangs at a dangerous angle. With my other hand I lift it up and stand there waiting for a gap in the traffic.

Somehow we make it to the other side. In surrender, I shove a handful of Dong into her hand (the Vietnamese slang for money). Wasting no time she grabs the baby and disappears into the night. I look around suspiciously. No one seems to notice, but then the Vietnamese are masters of un-noticed noticing.

Leaning against the balustrade along the river I stare at the scene. Tonight the bright yellows, reds, purples, greens, and blues of elaborate Asian advertising shine against the night sky, backlighting the cargo ships lined alongside the quay. Fuji Film, Honda Motos, 333 and Tiger Beer, Coca Cola signs and others undulate off the marbled water all promising a better life full of modern things in the future. In 1967-68 the Saigon River was a dangerous place and the scene of sporadic violence of both criminal and guerrilla VC activity. Behind me across the avenue sits the venerable Majestic Hotel that figured as an urban centerpiece for Graham Greene's well-known novel in the "fifties", "The Quiet American", that described the roiling internal politics that presaged the future American Involvement. No longer a scabbed, stained, and worn down colonial relic surrounded by cement barrels, barbed wire and heavily grated windows to deflect hurled grenades or the home made bombs, the Majestic seems to be enjoying yet another commercial renaissance, now floodlit, repainted, and marbleized with glistening golden entrance pillars. I wonder whatever happened to its legendary bar, which was off limits after curfew, and recall spending a boozy night listening to the tales of a white-haired Swedish sailor who in answer to my question if it was the first time he was in Saigon said, "Sonny, the first time I saw Saigon was coming up river on a four-masted schooner in 1921." That sounded like a good one, so I listened to him and his friend talk of ships and ports, docks and cargoes, opium dens and mama-sans, the fucked up politics, what with the commies getting to all the wogs, how Asia was going to Hell! Tonight there is no curfew or barbed wire or even much darkness. The Promenade Park is filled with people for whom the recollection of the past has been displaced by a welcome forgetfulness. Lovers fill the benches entwined and blissfully whispering the sweet nothings of promised love forever. Everywhere, children are playing various games and laughing under watchful parental eyes. A family of five almost impossibly heaped on a single cyclo creeps slowly along the walkway, chattering excitedly. The night is alive and well. Peace is abroad in the land; a promise of a better life is in the air, if not exactly a guarantee that there will be an era of good will among men. No matter, it's a sight well worth the journey. I wonder what the old Swede would say?

5

THE FLOWER PEOPLE OF SAIGON INVITE YOU TO WITNESS "THE LIGHT AT THE END OF THE TUNNEL…"

My plan is to travel to the Mekong Delta the next day. I feel buoyed up by the excitement of seeing the great rivers once again. I never really liked Saigon except as an R&R respite, but the tight window of time energized me to do as much as I could.

I have one possible contact. It is a "friend of a friend of a friend" kind of thing. All I know is that she is a young Vietnamese who was educated in the US and is married to an American. Although I feel awkward about offering such a tenuous introduction, given the alternative of a big and complicated city without any reliable guideposts or direction finders save a 30-year-old memory, I don't hesitate for long. I call her at her office number.

Her name is Hoang Thi Mai Huong. Fortunately her secretary speaks good English and puts me right through. Before my multi-part introduction concludes, she says that any friend of her friend is her friend and she would be happy to meet me during the day, but why not come to their house for an informal dinner. Why not? She will send their driver to pick me up, if that is OK? Why not, I agree. Around 8:00 p.m., is that a good time? Why not, I repeat.

Traveling alone is a constant roller coaster, a series of highs and lows that seem to either overlook or skip the plateaus. It magnifies so many things that are unconsciously taken for granted with the variety of fall-backs and options at hand or within reach. Take away human companionship, a communicable tongue, familiar financial arrangements, food you know how to eat, and pretty soon you can actually count your blessings. There is also the daily wear and tear of being with yourself and its limitations. It's easier to hide and get a breather with company, and you learn a hell of a lot more.

Having something to look forward to helps the day pass quickly. Thanks to hooking up with Kim, one of the pedi-cyclo riders hanging around the hotel (traditionally called "Cyclos"), it is also a great success. The pedi-cyclo is the pedaled successor to the Rickshaw, all but replaced by the motorbike that has assumed the mantle of "Cyclo". Kim's foot pedal contraption is relegated to only occasional touring for the hotel tourist. On the other hand, there are hundreds if not thousands of moto-cyclos for hire by almost everyone, mostly by those trying to pay off the loans on their machines. I don't want a (motorized) cyclo or a car. I want a leisurely open-air pedi-cab and Kim is my man. Recommended by my little concierge friend, he has three major assets: he can talk understandable English better than most; he is a knowledgeable guide, and—most importantly—a good guy. Oh yes—the price is right, about .75 cents an hour not including tip!

Surrendering my body to a worn rattan converted lawn chair and submitting to the "go with the flow" strategy of its urban navigation, I sit back in my broad open-air seat and watch Kim struggle to get his gargantuan load out into the traffic. Once in the avenue we become the beetle among swarming hornets. Kim is undaunted, using every degree of leverage and angle of pavement grade to grab advantage amidst the torrent of motorbikes, very like a canoeist reading the eddies and back currents in order to maneuver among the rocks and whitewater.

Despite the fumes and roars of traffic, after a short time, I don't care if I can touch the truck, cab, van, or motorbike swiping by. It doesn't matter that I wipe my face with a handkerchief and come up with black grime, or feel my shirt pasted with sweat. Instead of the fast-forward blur from the internal combustion machines, I can feel a part of the scenes we are passing through, and notice the mélange of street life in its details and specifics: the designs in the architecture, the layering of the foliage, the small carefully potted gardens, the dappled shades and light, the variety among the people, the medley of their styles, expressions and looks otherwise unnoticeable. Before long, I'm hooked on the Cyclo as the only way a real tourist should go.

Kim is small, and gnarled, monkeylike and reddened like a chestnut by exposure to all extremes of weather and close to ground living. The first two things I learn to like about him is that he's tough and cheerful. When he hears I'm American from the war days, he's eager to show and tell all he knows, which turns out to be a surprising amount of information, and probably as much, if not more, than I would learn from a "guide". In a short time we settle in companionably and he gives me a pedaling commentary of his life: about the years after the Commies took over and how the police gendarmes had quickly changed from being hard asses on documentation and traffic regulations to lazy shake-down artists. During this phase he had been fortunate enough to be a houseboy for a Canadian businessman, which was how he learned his English, and also how he got by through the hard times after the war. When the Canadian's firm gave up and closed up, he stayed on with the house, which was assigned to a highly rewarded woman political cadre. About her, he said only that things were "not so good" and, uncharacteristically, declined to say more.

The concierge had given me the name of a well-known Pho restaurant for lunch and Kim knew it well. It is in a shady and quiet side street across from the Louis Pasteur Hospital (the only western name remaining in the city).

The place is crowded and animated, always a good sign if you're hungry and worry about the quality of the food. By the signs, ranging from two or three Mercedes outside along the curb to the book-bag carrying students inside, I know I was sent to the right place. It even has a touch of home. The walls are papered over with huge scenes from the Rocky Mountains in spring time, clear pristine streams meandering through sunlit meadows, back-dropped by the kind of snowy peaks that produce the runoff streams from which Coor's claims it makes its beer. It's almost as good as an air conditioner.

Looking about I try to figure out how to proceed. Pho is a kind of oriental fast food. It is essentially a broth noodle soup but its preparation and components are far more complicated than that. Steaming bowls are ladled from a large master kettle, prominently displayed in the front. Then the selected choice of prepared chicken, pork or beef strips are added, along with garnishes—sprouts and green onion, herbs and legumes. Next come the various sides—mostly greens, herbs and other presentations of meats, fruits, and legumes wrapped carefully in banana leaf packets or soft dough. Also included is a standing tray crowded with cloudy bottles of colored spicy sauces of varying octane. From this array one is then left to tailor-make his or her bowl, a feature that seems to explain much of its universal popularity.

After I get the picture and silently rehearse the procedure, I am ready to risk signaling one of the matrons. She quickly takes pity and brings me a bowl with chicken strips and supervises my selection of ingredients. It is delicious, nutritious and filling. I feel a joy of initiation and following the meal order another 33 beer, burping loudly and picking my teeth openly with the best of them.

There aren't many landmarks for me in Saigon I want to see for old time's sake. One for sure, though, was 47 Phan Tan Gian. Back in 1967, 47 Phan Tan Gian was a substantial residential estate by Saigon standards and in its toniest neighborhood. Around that time it was leased by the U.S. State Department and converted into a compound to house some of its young Foreign Service Officers, usually 5 or 6, who rotated in and out on assignment. It loosely functioned like a select Frat house. By the time I first visited in early 1967 it had developed the colorful reputation of being a sort of unofficial headquarters for the "Best and Brightest" of the young college grads doing their non-military government diplomatic service. Some of its illustrious tenants went on to become well known career diplomats and even ambassadors of note. One of them, an old college friend at Yale, T. McAdams Deford—"Mac"—was a principal personal aide to the then Ambassador Ellsworth Bunker, a plum assignment for someone just in his mid-twenties.

I had the good fortune to become a beneficiary of Mac's generous hospitality whenever I got to Saigon for debriefings, which was every month or so. It was always an exciting and memorable time when I found there a cot, sofa, or the rug for the night. Something was always going on and things were always done with great panache. On most occasions when I was visiting there would be dinner parties with many courses of Vietnamese cuisine prepared and served by a constantly growing staff comprised of the extended family of the "Houseboy" (a symptom of war time, when a Vietnamese hire would gradually and through a variety of inducements secure positions for his or her relatives, many of whom were, or represented themselves to be, refugees from the contested countryside.)

The evenings were enlivened by running commentaries on the war, anecdotes and tale-telling; in general the dinner parties served as unofficial debriefings of whoever had just returned from some event or place of current interest. Casting one's nugget of random information on the common table was a contribution to a passionate debate, which led to fierce argument and often eloquently inebriate speeches. Usually present was an eclectic mix of people drawn from the menagerie of U.S. Government services, agencies, and departments, as well as the representatives of humanitarian causes and charitable institutions. Also included were the informally vetted journalist, the less credentialed stringer, the visiting businessman, the occasional thrill-seeker whose means or madness attracted him or her to the lamp of war and anyone else on who had been invited at the last minute. The only requirements for admission were that you knew something interesting, had something to say, could drink late into the night, and would leave early in the morning.

For Vietnam was "The Show" of its day, our day. Screw the stateside sit-on-the-Dean's floor student pacifist. This was Real Time, no moot court here, where the empire of "Life, Liberty, and the Pursuit of Happiness" depended on our personal commitment to its unbounded glory. As an occasional guest from the boonies, one who had been secluded in the jungle with a highly focused and specialized military unit of little intellectual distinction, these evenings burned with a fierce brightness, the fire fed by unbounded zeal and old boy camaraderie.

And so it was to be befitting the *joie de vivre* of this singular crowd that it would imagine and set the stage for the one event that would, more than any other, epitomize the Time of our Time in Vietnam and draw a disconcertingly bright threshold that, in its way and in retrospect, signaled the end of the beginning, and the beginning of the end of the war.

In the late fall of 1967 Ambassador Bunker and General Westmoreland returned to Washington to address Congress. In his speech before Congress, Westmoreland stated that he saw a "Light at the End of the Tunnel", a phrase destined for ignominy, and one that stuck like a quivering dagger in the sand. It was an unfortunate metaphor. Shortly thereafter, following a questionably sober deliberation (confirmed by Mac and crowd, plus notable co-hostess Pooh Kuhn) The Phan Than Gian Gang promulgated its invitation to all their extended associations. It arrived in a light blue card on which was embossed in gold lettering, "The Flower People of Saigon cordially invite you to witness the 'Light at the End of the Tunnel' party, December 31st 1967". There was something about coming in your favorite 60s costume. Katie bar the door!

It quickly evolved into a monster bash, redolent of the tone and spirit of American energy, optimism—and a healthy dash of the sardonic for spice. None who attended will ever forget it for the rest of their lives.

It was one part New Years' Eve celebration, two parts multi-cultural Mardi Gras, and three parts Frat House Toga madness. The guest list started with the Ambassador and the Commander Military Assistance Command Vietnam and reached as far down as me, a mere LTJG (Lieutenant Junior Grade) USNR, and everyone else who was of interest or enjoyment to a youthful group of ex-Ivy Leaguers. These included many wealthy and, therefore, connected Saigonese with their pretty, and even luscious debutante age daughters all the more remarkable for their arrival bearing three to four varying outfits of dress: one for the formal entrance show, the second and third for the sweaty rounds of dancing frenzy and the fourth for bathing or seduction afterward. Anyway, they knew how to party, having prepared for most of their young lives to do so.

Bunker and Westmoreland's designates showed up good-naturedly and left on schedule along with others of senior rank whose preservation of their dignity and decorum required an early departure. Three or four rock and roll bands made up of GIs and the "hot" Saigonese rocker groups rotated to insure that the hearth of booze and noise remained sufficiently stoked, aided by the disorientation of strobe lights with multi-colored flares. But then there was the hard-core, awash in rum, gin and beer of endless supply from the PX and further liberated by carefully disguised incognito costumes. We weaved and stomped the night away drenched in the exertion of revelry half way around the world from our homes and inhibitions. Casualties of excess occurred early and often. Here and there inert figures were slouched or toppled about. Surprisingly, only one or two ambulances were called but no violence was reported. It was, after all, a high caste affair. By the ragged dawn most of the diehards had been vanquished, and at the end there were few left to muster. Those left standing were unable to file a proper "after action" field report. I can't say I was among them, but I can remember something about morning.

Thirty-three days later in the same pre-dawn hours during our sterling crowd's deep sleep, the infamous TET Offensive was launched as a reinforced Viet Cong regiment stormed over the Dien Bien Phu bridge bordering the compound and occupied it as their command post for the overall assault of the city proper. So much for the "Light at the End of the Tunnel"!

Looking back, I have always clung to that night's marvelous irony holding in one frame a mélange of all its theatrical, almost operatic elements etched against the gathering portents of the future, imagining it as a final scene in a film with the camera panning the riot of joyously mindless bodies as it gradually pulls back, into the night. As the party grows more distant and the music fades, it reduces to an abstract circle of light in the darkness taking on the image of an isolated boat in a rising sea, or maybe just a circle of wagons alone in a comfortless frontier. But then maybe it should be less elegiac, for nothing could be as poignant as the contrast of those memories and with the reality of what presents itself when Kim's cyclo comes to a stop at the old gate, 30 years later.

It is still there, but the once impressive wrought iron and brick colum-
nar fencing, that had allowed an aesthetic view into the compound's once
garden and grounds is now barricaded by large sections of rusting corru-
gated steel sheets resembling warehouse doors. Above them I can make out
the elegant oriental peaks of the old tile roof, now mottled with mildew
and grime. I walk around to the Phan Tan Gian street side and find a gap
in the driveway gates through which I can glimpse the main entrance. It is
the same place, but without its former life's panache and activity has aged
and is now disheveled and neglected like a fond acquaintance who has not
weathered well. Now, it is most likely the property of a wealthy, well-connected official (who else?), but there is no light or activity to confirm residence, just an older Mercedes Benz spattered with leaf and nut droppings
from the large ficus tree that overshadows the driveway round-about. The
car's condition confirms indifferent use and maintenance. Gone is the
stage upon which we once unknowingly argued laughed and swayed-in the
cusp of great change and shift of fortune foretold.

It has gone on to another life, or coming to the end of its own, as have
all of its former tenants, owners, and the present observer, who turns away,
having concluded that there is really nothing to see. Besides, it is going to
rain.

There never does seem much to see when revisiting scenes from the
past. Whatever remains invariably tells us little, like grave markers that try
to describe someone who is no longer there.

The afternoon rain is soon to come; the air welcomes it with cool sweet-
ness. Kim insists that I wrap myself in a rubber poncho, while he dons his
bright yellow plastic. Off we go, rain banging against our waterproofing
and popping off the shining pavement. Dry beneath we bounce along with
others, undeterred. The streetscape is vivid, with glistening ponchos of yellows, oranges, blues, and greens, bringing to mind "The Umbrellas of
Cherbourg". All of the visible dirt and grime washes away. The traffic of
the side streets becomes scarce. For a few moments the city sounds are
muted and I have the Orient all to myself.

6

PARTNERS IN A BRAVE NEW WORLD

Waiting in the lobby for the Vietnamese woman's driver to pick me up for dinner, a young American man wearing shorts, a tee shirt and sandals wanders in. There are only two of us. After a pregnant pause he looks down at a piece of paper then over at me and says. "I'm looking for a John Wilbur." Making contact with a welcoming face in an otherwise anonymous and very foreign city is one of travel's more pleasant moments.

"I'm Steve Reid, Mai's husband," he tells me. "Mai had to work late and needed the driver." Since he had nothing to do, he came to pick me up. They live only ten minutes away and it's no trouble. As we drive, he tells me that he comes originally from Alexandria, Virginia, and is the son of military/government beltway careerists. While at the Harvard Business School he met Mai, who was studying at the Kennedy School of Public Administration. After getting his MBA, he decided to travel for a year and, drawn to the East, wandered around a bit until he made a connection with an Australian construction materials firm that marketed its wares in Vietnam and Thailand. In this venture Steve took the opportunity to renew his friendship with Mai, who had returned to Vietnam post-degree and was engaged in government business liaison and consulting. They married just about the time Vietnam opened its door more than a crack to international ventures and allowed capitalistic forces to operate with some free market liberty. It was called "Doi Moi"—"The New Beginning"—a policy dating back to 1995 and 1996.

Their home is in an urban/suburban sector about 10 minutes from the Continental. It is in the city's residential area but zoning distinctions are so blurred or indefinite that practically every area is essentially mixed-use. By Vietnam standards it is both spacious and modern. Like many upper-middle class Vietnamese homes, it is configured in a compound, confined behind high walls and consisting of a main living quarters, with small and separate out-structures for different functions—maid's quarters, a washing and cooking area and an outdoor eating pavilion. Steve told me on the way out that their landlord was one of the highest-ranking female political cadres of the "Ho Chi Minh City" district. She lived next door and owned other properties adjacent to it. It was left unsaid as to how she, a communist Northerner, earned the means to amass this relatively conspicuous wealth.

Mai comes to meet us and we sit out in the dining pavilion with the one-year-old daughter and her nanny. With her quick, gay laugh, she instantly makes me feel at home. Small, expressive and animated, she recalls at first a young girl who must have been a tomboy, open, frank, and having fun meeting someone and something new. I find almost instantly that it is impossible not to like her.

Soon the cook presents a full Vietnamese meal with several courses and a very welcome cold bottle of white wine, never mind the vintage, and over the meal we begin a long and animated conversation almost as if I was the neighbor next door, forget about the 12,000 miles. Mai is a true North Vietnamese type, calling to mind all that I remember from years before. I learned then that there is important differentiation among and between those of the Vietnamese North and the South. Those who left the North as political refugees in the 1954 exodus developed the reputation for being more aggressive, with stronger convictions and more determined industry than attributable to most southerners, a characteristic of the immigrants who endured the hardships of resettlement, and a commitment to start a new life. During the war we developed a pronounced preference and admiration for the Northern types. They fought harder, probably because they had more to lose.

Mai is the first true Hanoian I've ever met. She is from a politically well-connected family; she mentions that her uncle has been Ho Chi Minh's personal secretary all his life and is still alive as a sort of venerated keeper of that almost sacred flame. She was born well after the war and because Hanoi was conspicuously exempted from wartime destruction, while the surrounding countryside was not, she doesn't claim the traumatic memories of those times. Nonetheless, she grew up indoctrinated into its rhetorical history. Because she was from a privileged family of the political elite, she was assured a good education and a sophisticated view of her world. This enabled her to obtain a degree from the University of Moscow followed at some point by a degree from the Harvard Kennedy School of Public Administration.

With such a resume, she became highly useful to the government in the commercial diplomacy of attracting and handling foreign interests. She is now the General Manager of the Saatchi & Saatchi advertising and public relations firm and heavily involved in trouble shooting the intercultural business "snafus" that constantly occur with a foreign corporation trying to do business in Vietnam.

By Steve's account and others I was to hear, this is a wearing battle. For one thing, he explained that the playing field is always shifting when the Central Government is the referee. This often reflects a classic "one-foot on the brake, the other on the accelerator" syndrome wherein the Politburo's internal struggles and conflicts project contradictory or uncoordinated signals. Such variance and ambiguity becomes close to fatal for the businessman, who relies on an agreement but finds it changed in midstream, shredding the careful profit equation on which the agreement was premised. Another is the collision of investor expectations with Vietnamese reality; much is promised but much less can be reliably delivered. Then there is the invariable abrasion of misunderstanding and mistrust between the different business cultures.

Listening to Mai and Steve discuss these issues, I am impressed with how vital they are for tomorrow's global economy. Each is highly intelligent, superbly educated, and rich in the perception and experience of the new commercial frontiers on the horizon. But the cost of their efforts and the weight of their challenges are bringing matters to a critical juncture. As they continue to live in Vietnam and build the basis for their family future (they hoped to have a second child soon) they are also approaching the moment when they must decide to stay or to leave. Steve has become dis-enchanted and pessimistic about the future economic climate in general and particularly the business environment. Will it become one in which he could function profitably? He reports that the outside competition from the Chinese (Singapore, Taiwan) Thais, and other Southeast Asian ele-ments is overwhelming in terms of developing viable financial projects. The revolving frustrations of government micro-management on the one hand and grasping corruption on the other excluded sound business sense from planning for the future. And then there was the "Southeast Asian Flu".

Having been in economic "lock-down" over the previous 30 years, Vietnam was unable to fuel itself on the high-octane (but eventually toxic) Southwestern Asian growth of the 80s and 90's. While in one respect the country was shielded from the severity of disruption in Indonesia and Thailand, the depression of the area was nevertheless a blow for a frail economy.

During the period of 1985-90, the disastrous effects of the Stalinist/Marxist experiment with theoretical socialism were producing the specter of famine. Disgraced by this denouement, the Politburo was sufficiently threatened to face up to their dogmatic economic ignorance and recognize the necessity for a more market-oriented economy. In fact this policy reversal was a precondition mandated by the World Bank and Interna-tional Monetary Fund for bailing Vietnam out of its banking system's imminent collapse. The result was a fundamental sea change in the per-spective of foreign interests doing business. These expectations fostered an exuberance of optimism among the foreign commercial elements that lusted after Vietnam's potential market for almost everything. Among those attracted was a new breed of young, academically trained, and entre-preneurial "20 Something's" to whom Steve and Mai belonged.

Independent, unattached western business adventurers traveling light, they were either unafraid to experiment, or poor enough to see risk only as opportunity. They embraced the label of "ex-pat" as a badge that identi-fied them as gutsy path makers marching to a drum most others dared not heed. By Steve's account, when the financial bubble burst in Singapore,

Jakarta and Bangkok, there were few soft landings for this crowd in Vietnam. Of those who bottomed out, many quickly departed, and those who were survivors were seriously reconsidering the wisdom of remaining.

The second bottle of wine was coming to an end. Under the veranda, the night air was warm and moist, throbbing with cicadas while motionless geckos throw dark shadows on the rough mottled stucco wall, waiting for their insect prey to be drawn to the lone cone of light against the blackened night.

The "Asian Flu" had thinned the ranks of their friends and compatriots, casting a slight melancholia on the Reids and making them reconsider some of their former assumptions about continuing to build their family life here. The disappearance of loose times with early success and the evaporation of supporting friendships has dampened their sense of the future and hinted at the prospect of isolation, notwithstanding Mai's Vietnamese roots.

Mai was not a child of the South. Despite her congeniality and winsome friendliness, she had made few friendships among the South Vietnamese beyond those developed through business. Since she travels to Hanoi almost weekly on business, her frequent visits with her family and friends keep her far from isolated—and the Reids are hardly friendless. Nonetheless, Hanoi is 900 miles to the North and the U.S. is halfway around the world.

A cab took me back to the hotel. One of the maxims of foreign travel is to watch out for the cab drivers of the world and be sure to choose one with a meter. Arriving at the hotel, I grope in the darkness for the right denominations to pay the fare. When I reach the steps of the hotel, the driver runs up waving the money. Knowing no English he calls for the doorman. I am embarrassed by the complication until it is explained that I had overpaid the fare and he wants to return the small tip (wow!). I assure him there is no mistake. The driver bows shakes my hand. Not a bad ending for a first day a long way from paradise.

PART II
PASSAGE

7

THE TIME OF OUR TIME

My driver's name is Houng. He is not from the Delta nor can he speak much English, two things that I had been promised by my Saigon tourist agent. But at the least he is present, ready, and presumably able to drive. The car is an elderly but still dignified Mercedes. Its greatest asset is that it would "hold the road" against the hordes of smaller vehicles. It is early when we leave and I'm excited. Next stop will be on the banks of the Muddy Mekong 60 miles away.

The outskirts of Saigon reflect the urbanizing demographics of today, an anarchic jumble of everything huddled cheek to jowl and mud ugly. Here a rice field, a thatch hut, a mud enclosure with chickens and ducks under foot, there a three-story cement-brick-stucco home-business of a merchant, first floor given over to the shop, or beauty salon, or pharmacy, or electrical appliances, even a noodle shop. Above it are living quarters, and from the roof fly the clotheslines of the multi-generation family like nautical pennants. Next to it is a truck/car/cyclo engine repair business with a junk heap of cannibalized parts and discarded motors of the last 30 years. Or a construction supply yard, maybe a gas station, and then back to the field again with the water buffalo and of course people everywhere, with all the endeavors and struggles of their existence squeezed in between the next field or ditch or canal, a snapshot of the third world making do wherever and however with whatever, bereft of planning, management or control. With the same indefatigable energy that drove them to dig elaborate tunnel complexes, endlessly repair bridges, survive bombings, and literally carry the war on their backs, today's Vietnamese are still digging, still with picks and shovels as during the war years but instead, now thirty years later, trying to dig out of the Communist ruins.

It is only 60 miles or so to My Tho, the river port town that serves as the main gateway to the Mekong Delta. The road we are traveling south is commonly called Highway 1 (and there aren't many more with numbers). Not much has improved since my first trip on an armored convoy my first week "in country" in March 1967. In many respects it is still a two-lane country road of various impervious surfaces under constant repair with use and development occupying the same space simultaneously. It is just now undergoing the initial stages of enlargement to three-lanes; a dramatic reminder of how inept and impoverished the Vietnamese government is in providing basic infrastructure.

Lurking behind these obvious deficiencies, however, is an environmental time bomb. From all of its seams, edges and gaps of commercial enterprise and human habitation the effluent of waste oozes, leaks, and festers. Unchecked and ignored, it clogs the sewer pools and drainage ditches in a sinister toxic stew of refuse, offal, garbage, petroleum and acids. There it slowly leaches its venom into the nurturing earth and tomorrow's streams, rivers, and tidal sluices. With the constant agitation of an increasingly dense population just now awakening to the needs and wants of industrial products, ignored concerns like basic health and hygiene loom darkly, a perpetual crisis with God knows what consequences. In Vietnam's world of today, however, this hangs well in the back of the long line of more immediate problems if not more dramatic concerns.

Just as these scenes and images of industrial exurbia make one grow despondent, the heaping congestion finally begins to thin. Beyond the road's edge at first in gaps and then unobstructed, the field of view opens as if a tattered curtain has been pushed aside, and the ancient rice culture begins to re-assert itself and assure the anxious traveler that maybe, the natural earth still rules.

Historically and culturally, Vietnam would not exist without its ancestral marriage to the rhythms and methods of rice cultivation. Watching an unbroken scene of myriad fields drawn by carefully fabricated mud dykes into its design, one can imagine a massive multihued quilt stitched together by communal hands. There, compressed between an endless sun and ocean blue sky against the green and brown earth, clusters of peasants timelessly work their paddies with hoe and plow behind water buffaloes plodding dumbly in their yokes. In such a scene Vietnam's peasant world presents itself as in a still life painting that frames their existence.

Imagine Vietnam as the barbell it roughly resembles lying on a North/ South axis-roughly the shape and length of California. At the northern end is the ancient Red River Delta bulging between southern "Cochin" China and the Gulf of Tonkin. Likewise at the southern end is the large bulge of the Mekong Delta formed by what was once called Cambodia (historically known as Khmer) and the Gulf of Thailand. The two are connected by a long north-south cordillera of rugged mountains on the west and a coastline (along the South China Sea) to the east that is longer than the state of California. It is essentially the two deltas that have dominated the economic and political culture of Vietnam.

Historically, Vietnam's people and culture are distinctive. It is a matter of great pride that their origins only closely post-date those of China, within which Vietnam was more that once forcibly included and by which it has been anciently influenced. The mutual histories of the two nations have been marked by several invasions, occupations, and expulsions over the many centuries. As a result Vietnamese culture has been strongly infused with Chinese learning, attitudes and values, while nevertheless fiercely asserting the autonomy and independence that exists to this day as a central tenet of national rule.

For most of its internal history, Vietnam has regarded itself almost exclusively as the "Northern Kingdom", a term essentially describing the Red River Delta and its ancillary regions, with Hanoi as the perpetual capital and the country's political and cultural center of gravity. In contrast, the cultural identity and sovereignty of the Mekong Delta region has been less clearly defined, since it has been heavily influenced by the neighboring Khmer kingdom, whose culture and influence, in turn, derived from the Indus influence of south-western Asia out of which the western term "Indo China"" applied. It was not until the 15th and 16th centuries that Vietnam came under unified national political control and the Khmer influence waned. Nevertheless, the national significance of the Mekong Delta became fully apparent only with the 19th century imperial incursion and domination of the French, whose western methods and means of development vastly expanded the region's economic potential.

With classic colonial intentions the French undertook extensive agricultural development by draining and canalizing the vast Delta wetlands, converting them to agricultural use for rice and hemp. On its northern reaches around Saigon, they introduced the plantation growing of rubber and coconut products. An influx of ethnic Chinese along the coast created a new economically powerful element, especially in the commercial lending and exporting areas. By the 1920s and 30s Saigon had become the trading and commercial center for exports, challenging Hanoi as an economic rival.

The complicated dynamic of the French colonial era was to have a profound effect on traditional Vietnamese culture and society. Its impact is best-described and explained in Neil Jamieson's "Understanding Vietnam". In it he comprehensively details how revolutionary western influences were to usher in the tempests of European 19th and 20th Century political thought and action, which initiated a breakdown of the fossilized Confucian mandarin model that had dictated the social mores and ethos for centuries. These influences gestated throughout the colonial era inclusive of World War II, the Japanese defeat of the French, and the French post-war re-occupation of 1945–53, producing a brew of diverse political ethnic and religious groups that simmered with social disarray and political turbulence.

With the post-WWII re-imposition of the French imperialist design, nationalism became the popular uniting social force and banner for what would be termed the "colonial" war of "French Indo China". Even though Communism's hold on the country was still nascent and fractional at its inception, it was Ho Chi Minh, who, with his organized and aggressive Viet Minh cadre (with its experience gathered during years of guerrilla warfare against occupying Japanese forces) seized the signal banner from a crowded and ineffectual field of other factions and leaders and emerged the de facto Commander in Chief.

Following the dramatic French defeat at Dien Bien Phu in 1954 ousting the French for good, Vietnam secured its territorial independence.

Nonetheless its political scene remained clouded and fragmented. Despite their military victory, the Communists did not become the dominant political party nor was Marxist Leninism the most popular political creed of the day. Because of its militancy and cohesive leadership, however, Ho and the Viet Minh nonetheless emerged from the war as the most organized and aggressive single force and soon were in charge of the North. In the South another story unfolded.

From the end of WWII, and in the hiatus of the French reoccupation and its withdrawal in 1954, the South had patched together a democratic republic that functioned ineffectively under the influences of various religious, ethnic and republican groups. Regardless of their several internal weaknesses and divisiveness, however, together they were able to forestall the Viet Minh from taking effectual national power and control.

Because the French/Vietnam peace process was negotiated in Europe under United Nation auspices, the active involvement of Russia and Western leadership inevitably sanctioned only Cold War solutions, and ultimately, Vietnam's division into two countries under the Geneva Accords. This provided unfettered control of the North to Ho and the Viet Minh while ceding political autonomy to the South. A principal resolution imposed by western participants was the provision and the assurance of unobstructed voluntary relocation of non-communist northerners to the South during the course of one year.

It was the feature of this "Repatriation" that sowed the enmity and resentment that preordained eventual war. It brought to the South a bitter and determined element of northern Vietnamese, mostly Catholic and educated bourgeoisie, whose values and attitudes were antithetical to the dogmatic communism of the North. This element eventually achieved a significant military and political leadership that was to become the backbone of defiant opposition to any communist concession or rapprochement. While before it was a country of different styles, habits and persuasions, Vietnam now found itself ranged apart into two halves with separately constituted governments and distinctly antagonistic beliefs, that mirrored in many ways the Korean situation, whose political bifurcation at this same period was fixed in an armed and divided coexistence.

In picturing this retrospective it is paramount to bear in mind that this was the decade when the Cold War lay frozen, deep in the hearts of the superpowers who saw in every conflict only surrogates to be used in their check-checkmate dreams. After the military stalemate of Korea, Vietnam became the favored board on which many of the same pieces came to play.

Ho Chi Minh had two goals that were both mutually supportive and interdependent: one, the final "reunification" of the entire nation and two, the implementation of Marxist/Stalinist socialism for the entire society. Following the Geneva Accords, he quickly set about tidying things up in his backyard. This initiated a brutal program borrowed from Stalin's blueprints that was to be copied (and exceeded) by the Pol Pot's madness 20 years later. The landowning, mandarin, and bourgeoisie elements of North Vietnam were in effect erased from society, eliminating its entire leadership structure and opposition. From afar, Ho directed the development of a tight clandestine organization in the South that engaged in agitation, subversion, and relentless propaganda in preparation for civil war.

In the events of the following ten years (1955-65), the South played into his hands. The South was roiling with the political fractiousness of an immature as well as insincere constitutional democracy. Among its symptoms were: disunity and dissension among fragmented groups, confusing and somewhat bizarre religious elements, vast social and material inequities, epidemic corruption, multiple coup attempts and leadership syndicates bordering on gangster-ism. Graham Greene's "The Quiet American" catches its depressing tone and presentiments of self-destruction. Meanwhile the people of the countryside had become ripe for conversion to Ho's ideology.

Against the tightly adherent society of the North with the rigid totalitarian leadership of a revered and feared leader, the South's fractured and disjointed society seemed predestined to become a military mismatch. Nevertheless, it was not going to be a pushover. Neither side, despite its strengths and failings, was politically or militarily potent enough to deliver a knockout blow. With the Soviets and Americans rushing in to support their client states like ring handlers in a prizefight, one urging victory, while the other promised no defeat; the imminence of civil war became unavoidable.

It was going to be bitter and bloody. Soon the indigenous struggle of a remote and otherwise inconspicuous country as far away as anyone could imagine would reach out, grab our television sets and wring our necks.

America's involvement in Vietnam was not so much a tragic mistake as it was a reasoned miscalculation. Most pundits, clairvoyant in retrospect, seem to overlook, or discount the ingrained Cold War mentality that was then served as the basic mooring of mid 20th Century reality for a world to be run by men who had won world wars. The domino mentality (if one nation falls to communism, its neighbor will be next) was not unrealistic paranoia. There was a drumbeat of evidence supporting the concern that the world was caught up in an armed political struggle to determine which political/economic soul was going to win it; the Communist Dogs or the Capitalistic Pigs. The accumulated experience of Greece, the Congo, Malaysia, Korea, Cuba, and Yemen may not have constituted proof beyond a reasonable doubt but it certainly constituted the greater weight of evidence of its time.

And it was our time too. My age group or generation was born out of WWII. Our early childhood saw our Dads leaving home in uniform, coming home in uniform, marching in parades, and everywhere and always flags waving in Red, White, and Blue. When we became old enough to follow the radio news, read magazines and go to the movies we had been fed a red meat diet on the "glory of war". After all, we had just won the biggest war in history, two enemies at once on both oceans. Every other movie that came out in the early 50's glorified it in some manner. There were Air Force movies, Marine movies, Navy movies, Army movies, and each Service out doing the other in "Derring Do". Who can forget "Battle Cry", "Bridge Over the River Kwai", "Run Silent Run Deep", "The Cruel Sea" etc.. Every male actor who became a star in the 1950s cut his acting teeth in one war movie or another: John Wayne, Audy Murphy, Jimmy Stewart, Burt Lancaster, Kirk Douglas, Richard Widmark, William Holden, and who can forget, Ronald Reagan? Each and all killed the bad guys, fought bravely, sacrificed courageously, was wounded often and

sometimes fatally. Such portrayals inspired endless imitation in the back-
yards, basements or wherever young boys found dugouts for their imagination.

Then came Communism and Stalin, the Darth Vader of a terrible
planet, endlessly distant and cold. It was "Us", the Free World, versus
"Them", the Iron Curtain. We were White and they were Black with a
giant mushroom cloud ranged between us, lest we forget to be reminded
by the fire alarms and sirens that inspired the classroom drills of hiding
under our desks.

In the pre-TV-fifties-the big black headlines and stentorian radio news
of a desperate jungle battle somewhere in "French-Indo-China" at a place
called Dien Bien Phu ignited the imagination of a pubescent not quite
adolescent kid. "Communist insurgents" had surrounded the embattled
and valiant French Foreign Legion in a fight to the finish. Newspapers
trumpeting stories of rescue attempts, airdrops of food and medicine to
the beleaguered French Free Forces chronicled its impending doom, stok-
ing its romance. Even though its defeat and surrender was inevitable, the
new of it came incomprehensibly to me like a thunderbolt from a black
sky. I remember running down the classroom corridors shouting out the
terrible news until my teacher, unable to equate the enormity of this doom
with my hysteria, grabbed me to calm me down. With Dien Bien Phu the
pall of defeat and surrender entered comprehension. 20 years later, was it a
presentiment?

8

DOWN TO THE "BIG MUDDY"

My Tho is a Province town of the same-named province bordered to the south by the My Tho river, the easternmost branch of the Mekong. Since it is the closest urban center to Saigon, it commands a strategic positioning for the flow of the abundant agricultural commerce for which the Delta is so vital. In peace it is the flow point, in war it was the choke point. Thus it became a pivotal axis for military objectives.

We had been stationed at the small Riverine Warfare base at My Tho for the first four months of my first tour in 1967. My time there left me with a bundle of first impressions, fresh in the lens, sharp with the contrast of almost everything we had seen and known of life, before the tilt of Asia's orbit.

As Houng pushes the big car gently along the thoroughfare thronged with people and carts and cyclos and bicycles, I search for something familiar. Gone almost completely is its former shady charm and the quiet bicycles ridden by young girls reminding me of butterflies as their Ao dais fluttered in the catch of a breeze. Today the ragged and extended outskirts have forewarned that urban sprawl has metastasized here in the provinces as well.

Suddenly, and almost too late, I pick up something that hooks my memory. It is a fenced-in schoolyard where brightly uniformed children are playing some organized games and yes, of course, it must be the same school on the very same side of the road where my mind has lodged it from the years before. Directly across is the same three story classroom building that served as our temporary barracks then stacked with steel double-deckers, a few fold out chairs, and some classroom tables heaped high with loose firearms, web belts, weapons, ammo, paperback books, soda cans and, yes, probably a bottle of Johnny Walker. It is the same place.

As we pass, I am of a mind to tell Houng to stop, that I want to get out and go back, and the thought of Moose Boitnott, Jack Rhinebolt, "Pee-Wee" Nealy, "Swede" Tornblum, "Doc" Schwartz, Miller, Muckle, Gosser Two Shoes, the would be ballroom dancer and others come alive in recollection, stripped to the waist and still sweating as the early evening falls like a wet rag, and the guys getting talkative, or quiet, some nervous, some irritable, fumbling with their gear, finicky, trying to get it perfect this time, working through what might go down, getting ready for the night "Op" later on down the river on a hunt to kill people, make no mistake about it.

But before I can make up my mind the old Mercedes has already passed by and I realize that apart from the bare memory of the names and faces of our small platoon, there are few, three of them maybe, that I have seen or even thought about much since I came home and visa versa in return. We were, how should I put it, not unlike an athletic team that, after the games had been played and won or lost with one for all and all for one, had nonetheless drifted apart by the separation of events and the incremental processes of life until not much remained but the details of what memory still held them. How different we are now, I think, from the our official Platoon group photograph on Beach "7" at Little Creek, Virginia, that bright March morning before take off halfway across the world; would be warriors looking hard into the camera lens that froze our youth in the stilted poses that today makes one wonder, Is that really me? I know I have that somewhere.

When Houng pulls into a small riverside park, I get my first glimpse of what I have come to look for. I recognize it as I would a person in my life. I'm excited and like a kid I feel like running off to see it. There is no mistaking the Mekong. Looking east down its broad expanse, I know exactly where I am. It's like finding the blaze of an old trail. I've just arrived from the world and already the trip is worth it.

The Mekong, like the Amazon, Nile, Ganges, Mississippi, and a few others, is the archetype of rivers. Like all the others, it starts from some hidden place, a chance fissure amid the snow and granite, a brow of a hill where rain falls, a rivulet hurrying to mate with another, and then? In the Mekong's case, its origin lies deep in central China. It eventually bundles like a great arm, whose sinews stretch throughout Laos and Cambodia and then lazily into Vietnam, flowing through the broad marshlands of the Plain of Reeds where it opens in the design and function of great hand dividing itself among four major channels reaching eastward toward the South China Sea. The northernmost channel becomes the My Tho and My Tho city is its last by-way before it spills into its own muddy delta joining the ocean some 15 miles away.

The thick green foliage and trees still mound unbroken over the banks, obscuring the land behind. For the next 15 to 20 miles there are few villages for there is no navigable channel for ocean going hulls because of the river's choking alluvial content. Its coastal basin forms a meandering web of tidal fissures, and loose barriers of mangrove mud flats, temporary home only to its isolated fishermen manning tiny thatch huts on stilts, overseeing their fishnets and weirs. I knew that area vividly. I had crawled into them, through them and out of them as if re-enacting amphibian evolution while engaging in our nocturnal game of war. All those nights up and down that dark corridor. How could I ever forget the first one?

We had been in country for about a week, setting up, breaking down and inspecting all the equipment. Everything was new and strange. The days had passed in a blur of logistical set up, multiple orientations, and tactical briefings on top of absorbing the newness of this completely foreign land strangely revealed on the other side of the world. Soon, however, maybe too soon, we were planning for our first "Op". It was the brainchild of a guy named Dick Marcinko, a budding egomaniac who self-styled himself into subsequent notoriety as "Demo Dick" (you can read all about him in his auto-erotic biography "Rogue Warrior").

We were the platoon relieving Marcinko's in rotation (he was a squad leader). It had been the first SEAL Team II detachment sent over to Vietnam. We were the second. He had been there all of 3 months making him the know-all for our "shake-down" initiation. Recent Intelligence had located a VC arms and munitions transport point on one of the nameless mangrove islets at the river's mouth. It was part of the clandestine supply line that snaked up the coast to their Rung Sat zone forces below Saigon.

It began as a major fuck-up, that fortunately ended as a minor one. The plan was to insert with two squads at midnight as near to the islet as possible. Each was to "ingress" separately from insertion points on the north side of the island on both sides of a slight lagoon apparent on the aerial blow-up. We were then to move in a mini pincer fashion southeast where the cache and camp were supposed to be. The plan gave us six hours from insertion to position. The attack was to commence at dawn, blocking VC retreat to the interior and flushing them out to the shore with automatic and M-79 grenade launchers using smoke flares to signal SEAWOLF Huey gunships and the blocking PBRs (Patrol Boat, River) to hit them with rockets and 50 caliber machine guns in the open.

We were excited. It was going to be a classic SEAL Op: clandestine stealth and surprise, awesome small unit fire power packaged with air and sea support, the kind of thing to hone our team-work and talents. At long last it was "Lock and Load" with real "gas" in our "Heaters", going to grease some gooks. Marcinko's briefing concluded with the usual weather and water conditions, 1st quarter moon and high tide at 2300 hours. Insertion NLT 2330, extraction dawn plus one, no problem.

We were armed and outfitted like toy soldiers—dressed in jungle camys, faces painted with nightstick and loaded up with everything, including a lot too much. Boarding the PBR's at 8PM, for four hours under the black night and warm salted winds coming up from the sea, we slept or sat mumbling and smoking in the well with the low throbbing of the PBRs turbo-diesel engines. The air was thick with diesel exhaust, sweat, bug juice and WD-40. Off and on, the squawks and squelches of radio commo broke in the back-up boat units. The infrared dials of the boat's operating systems and surface radar stared and blinked from their hiding places like devils' eyes. Cupped cigarettes flared. The broad river merged in darkness with everything. There was no horizon and few objects for orientation. We were in the deep well of night going to war, each

shrouded in the cocoon of his thoughts about what the first time in combat would be like. This is it. This is what our work is. This is when we see
what we are; going for the "Cherry", the first kill.

By 2300 we were into approach phase by plan but not by sight. In the
broad mouth of the tidal wash, the radar features were confused and broken up by the lack to features to bounce off. Radio commo debated our
positioning as the boat units crowded the airwave. After a confusing huddle in furious whispering trying to reconcile the vague and contour-less
aerial with the correspondingly blurred radar, it was finally decided that
the disputed position blur was what Dick identified as the target. Guns at
the ready, ammo up the ying-yang, we dropped off on our trailing
armored Boston whalers, "Moose's." squad in one, mine in the other.

After about two hundred yards, out of sight of the PBR, we started
dragging. The water was too low. Trying to find a channel we meandered
and separated: First mistake. Pushing on, believing the tide was with us,
we didn't recognize the obvious until it was too late. The tide was ebbing!
Marcinko fucked up big time. The outboard became useless. We cut it off
and tried paddles. No dice, too shallow. Soon it was no use.

"Dead in the Water" and "High and Dry" were usually off-hand expressions; now they weren't. It was coal dust black. We were still about three
hundred yards from the target, a low brow discernible only by its relative
density in the starlight scope. To stern, the deeper draft PBR's were well
out of retrieval range. A squawk on our frequency notified us that the tide
was forcing them to retract up river.

Radio commo was monitoring the mess. We couldn't extract and we
couldn't ingress, just the kind of situation SNAFU was coined for.
Moose's whaler was in the same shit and out of sight. It was about 2:00
a.m., four hours to sunrise, more or less. A lot of back and forth on the
PRCs (Prick—25 combat radios). No recovery for another 6 hours, mini-
mum. The empty whaler was as useless as a bathtub in a flood. Nothing to
do but go for it. Out we went into it the soup, and soup it was, bottomless
silt.

A river delta is a constant sweep of sediment, as it breathes the pairing
of salt and fresh water in and out in its diurnal cycles like a vast water-

logged lung. The washing effect maintains the silt in perpetual suspension creating "quick-sand". Mud flat training is a revered memory for those who have survived BUDs Hell Week, but that was junior varsity to the Mekong. Before we knew it, we were close to chest deep and sinking, no bottom. With all our gear and munitions even with our chest flotation vests, we risked going under if we didn't move forward.

Back to the whalers we flailed. Hanging onto it as a life raft, we shit-canned most of our excess gear back into it: the M-60 machine gun, the two 250 round steel boxes of ammo, personalized weapons such as knives and handguns (one guy was actually going to bring his hand made blow-gun), everything that was superfluous to survival. Even so we still couldn't move forward because our chest flotation kept us vertical like buoys. The only method to get horizontal was to partially deflate the chest pocket, leverage our paddles like outriggers and turtle-crawl with arms and elbows and knees and thighs only, sink or swim. We made maybe five yards a push before a breather, possibly twenty yards every 15 minutes. Within the hour, we were in trouble, and it was serious. Any thought of the operation, or the target, drained away with the slow spread of desperation. The slick of silt covered us like paint. The low brow of the distant mangrove seemed to slide away from us. It was a zero sum game. Helpless, there was no quit to fall back on.

Moose's squad was off somewhere in the same shit. God only knew. In the featureless dark, we could not see each other; we kept track by a grunt and a moan every now an then, that's all. I was in front; behind me, I knew, was Muckle, our radioman, burdened with the extra weight of his radio, trying to keep up. Who was behind him, I couldn't tell. It had broken down to an individual thing. No one could help anyone do anything, no words in any usual form: orders, directions, information, motivation, bitching, nothing to say, nothing else to do but hack it. It was real simple; make it to the mangrove first, do it before sun-up, second. If we didn't have cover by then, a 12 year old with a chicom bolt action could pick us off between sips of his morning tea. We were in "No Man's Land" and before long the sun was going to shine.

Head on to the east, the earth's turn toward the sun made the desire to hide almost compulsive. I could feel the "cover of darkness" being pulled away, a baby being parted from his blanket. Vision came with a minute hand, every nuance of sight ticking as time continued to happen and the night sky dissolved like a black aspirin into the water of dawn. The deep pit of earth fell into a burning rim. A horizon grew wide open before us spreading a glazier's platter on which we were soon to be served up as trivial offerings.

The only comfort was being able to see the rest of the guys, not to be alone anymore. We were a ragged bundle, no more than ten, maybe fifteen yards apart and indistinguishable from turtles. In the dark, we had proceeded as if in lock-down. At least in sight again, though useless to each other, we could reconnect and feed off the group motivator: "If that sonuvabich can do it, I can".

The blood red ball of the sun bulged and shimmered, "Good Morning, Vietnam". Backlit, our islet target hulked in sharp silhouette like the enemy in wait. There was less than a half a "Click" (kilometer, approximately 300 yards) to go. We had to pick it up, had to get there to high ground, form up, set a perimeter, fix the fucking radio, and sort out an extraction plan, for starters. No question about the Op any more. We were in full abort. Linking up with Moose was the first tactical objective. Together we could support ourselves, call the SeaWolf choppers to cover the PBR's in extraction at earliest rising tide, only six hours to go! I had it all figured out. All we had to do was to get to high ground.

In the sharp horizontal light, we could pick out the ragged lumps of Moose's squad about a quarter of a mile away almost in line with us in the same shit that we were. Behind us were the abandoned armored whalers looking like truck tires and beyond them over two kilometers, the squat PBRs useless as junkyard cars. If only we could get to high ground!

But there was no high ground. There was no shore. There was no land. Mangroves don't root in solid soil; for the most part, they are a border fringe between earth and water. There was no elevation at all. In a desperate fantasy I had assumed that we would gain some solid footing where we could reorganize and resume as a stealthy band of efficient commandos instead of ragged save-your-ass blunderers. No such luck.

If we hadn't known each other so well there would have been little to tell us apart. We were totally camouflaged by the same slime of mud except for the whites of our eyes and teeth. We checked our weapons. It didn't take long; they were all jammed. The chambers and barrels were clogged. All equipment with moving parts had a malfunction. The only weapon that had a possibility of operating was the WWII M1A1 grease gun, the kind that John Wayne carried in "Iwo Jima" (a throw-back to the days of simpler mechanisms and more tolerantly machined parts), but we sure as hell weren't going to test fire. Thankfully we had one per squad; everything else was junk. Muckle worked on the radio. Even with the waterproofing the silt had intruded into the washers like oil and fouled the crystal and the contacts. By washing each part in canteen water and blowing on them to dry, he got it going. With radio commo up we called in our dismal sit-rep and learned that our apprehensions were correct—Moose was in the same mess.

Our mud-smeared copy of an aerial photograph without any identifiable landmarks or distinguishable features was useless; neither of us could fix our location. We settled on an intersect direction and course as well as some basic enough signals to avoid blundering into each other along the way. As far as we could see, which was at best 20 feet, there was nothing but mud water and trackless mangrove. The only good news was that no VC squad would be able to paddy through this better than we could, so confrontation seemed the least of our troubles.

But there were many troubles ahead. In the first place trying to operate in mangroves is like trying to break out of jail. The roots and limbs turn, twist and crisscross like a nightmare, forming an unbending and unbreakable maze that catches and snags every static object. For us that was a lot: weapons, slings, antennae's, scarves, "H"-harness with hand grenades, knives, flares, compasses, flotation packs, ammo clips and belts, rope line, strobe lights, first aid packs, and other "what if" contingency gear.

Catching my foot on an unexposed root, I pitched face down into the silt and threw my arm forward to break my fall. A stabbing pain pierced my right hand deep in the mud. The thought flashed that it was a razor, but it couldn't have been. Wrenching it out expecting to see a deep gash and spewing blood, there was nothing, no mark but a little trickle of blood oozing through the silt and an excruciating pain almost taking my breath away. All I could do was hiss and writhe in the mud. The men were staring at me stupefied wondering what the F—could have happened: no shot, no explosion, no booby-trap, nothing to suggest a cause.

That was the ballgame for me. I couldn't think or communicate. A shot of morphine gave me a breather, but not for long. I told the Senior Petty Officer, "Swede" Tornblum, that he was in charge and to figure some way to link up with Moose. My arm was swelling like a balloon. Within minutes it was twice its size, and had no function at all. I dragged myself behind them in a daze completely out of it. At least four hours to go before the tide would allow extraction, not serious enough for a dust-off. I had to gut it out. Christ it hurt!

To make it almost comic, somehow in the stress and disorientation of the situation the Point man, Schultz, one of our steadiest guys, took the wrong compass azimuth and after an hour in the wrong direction we were more separated than before. We never did get to higher ground, and only through blind luck did we stumble on Moose's squad and our corpsman Doc Schwartz. He had the morphine.

Back at base, a doctor analyzed my wound as a sting from a mud skate, which utilizes a wicked spike at the base of its tail to stun and paralyze fish and inflicts what is known as one of the most painful stings in the world. (I was going to experience that as an eyewitness to another's misery many years later in the Amazon). It took about a week to regain full use of the arm, providing a wakeup call that I was going to have to slow down or my tour was going to become a short lived thing.

I don't know how long I have been standing there staring east, but when I turn around large tour buses have arrived. With the tell-tale sound of pneumatic doors opening, they discharge a clutch of tourists, who look around with that characteristic daze of the disoriented and wait passively for their keepers. I wonder how much different we looked circa 1967, getting off the trucks 72 hours from the U S of A; standing around looking at a world of smell and sight and sound on the other side of it.

Returning to hook up with Houng, I notice someone who probably did know and remember what and how we looked. An older man is sitting alone on a bench beneath the shade of a large Banyan watching me. He is in a worn baggy green militia uniform and wearing his soft Mao hat with a red band and gold star in the middle of it. We can see each other clearly. He smiles, I smile, like shaking hands.

He nods hello and on impulse I sit down on his bench. There are few people nearby. The tourists have been herded to the open-air restaurant at the other end of the park before their boat trip. I'm in no hurry. There is nothing we know how to say to each other, so we watch the river instead, as we would the sea, separate thoughts, and visions drifting and wandering from this and that. Small barges and other motorized sampans scurry past doing their business. Fishermen in small dugouts throw their nets along the quay. The mid morning breeze is picking up. The palm trees nod and scrape. The banyan tree we are sitting under has crushed the broken cement buttress to the bank. Its gray roots turn and twist upward into huge arms reaching out like a great umbrella shielding the glistening sunlight that shines white off the water. The air is already heavy from the heat.

With slow but certain ceremony my bench mate pulls out a pack of cigarettes, half turns, leans over and shakes the pack gently at me. I haven't smoked for years, but that doesn't matter. I take one. Then he pulls out an old American Zippo lighter, a relic of the old days still on display in the curio shops of Saigon. The gesture carries a message we both appreciate. His grin shows gold teeth glimmering like old daggers among the fallen timbers of his mouth. It says that he might have wanted to kill me in the war but that didn't mean he doesn't cherish American things (the epitaph for our culture). I take the Zippo. It flicks open like a music box to another age, our age, when we were going to live young forever or just as easily until the end of the next day in the same quick-time in our lives. The chrome is long worn away showing the rubbed veneer of a brass coating, the etching smoothed over except for the faintest outline of its logo. I can just make out the 101st Airborne, the Screaming Eagles, all the way from gliders over Normandy in WWII to the muddy banks of the Mekong. He could have bought it anywhere, but I doubt it; too much JuJu in it for that. It no longer matters how he came by it, though 30 years ago it would have. As for now it serves as our Peace Pipe. The wind whips the flame. The smoke is strong and burning. We watch it drift up and disappear.

Smoking talks for us, asks the questions, maybe even finds an answer or two. Had we been foes, or just two guys sharing a park bench for a smoke? Maybe both. He had a warm face that smiled easily, but don't we all when we aren't doing other things. He may or may not have been a fighter, maybe just a minor functionary in the party, a one time cell leader, or follower. To him, I'm most likely an American who had been here before, probably sometime during the war, maybe even here, or nearby.

We sit with the ease of two men who are prepared to believe anything, as long as we don't care too much about it. Whatever answers might follow our questions, or however our pasts may have intersected, our point of contact is here and now under the shade of a banyan tree looking out at the carpet of brown water soundlessly hurrying to towards its end. If there had been war between us, it is no more. If it had happened it would have been between two who are different than then, so young and far away as to struggle to imagine amid so much to forget. For now, that we watch our smoke drift mingle beneath the shade of the same tree is enough, that we are satisfied to pause together and smoke our cigarettes is peace enough.

Eventually the river reminds us that everything moves on. We have had our smoke and that has been our time. So I get up and hold my arms open to embrace the scene and turn to him to nod goodbye. He responds with another big smile, eyes shining and holds out his cigarettes again, shaking them so I would take one for the road. He waves me goodbye, holding his Zippo aloft shining dully like his capped teeth.

Houng is smiling when I get back to the car. "You talk Vietnamese?" he asks. "No" I shake my head. "Oh" he nods, "I see you talking to man", and points at the bench where he still sits. "Where we go now?"

The Kien Hoa ferry landing is a hodgepodge market of local sundries for the departing or arriving passengers. The ferry is no longer a barge shoved by a little tug lashed alongside. It is now almost modern, or at least self propelled, and three times as large as I remember, about the same as the population growth. I have no need for a reminder; people are everywhere.

Kien Hoa Province, across the river, used to be a Viet Cong controlled area with a rural, out of the way character that was either the cause or the result of its reputation for same. Surrounded by rivers and the sea, it is a natural island densely forested with coconut groves and mangrove estuaries. Like the province, Ben Tre, its Province town, had a quiet and shady atmosphere once dignified by spacious ochre colored French colonial villas and municipal buildings with wide open verandas, dark green shutters, and green tiled roofs regimented around its parade ground square.

The Kien Hoa ferry is crowded with everything that has wheels as well as what could fit in or on every vehicle: bikes, moto-cyclos, wheel barrows, carts, buses, trucks and cars maxed out with multiple occupants including the bicycles. The heat rising off the surface fuels the mid-day rush of wind, stirring the waters into a lively white-laced chop. The tropic air is congested with the thick brew of diesel exhaust, and sweaty humanity and gives me the feeling that I'm back in the Vietnam that I knew so well such a long time ago.

I find a place along the rail to windward to catch some fresh air and watch the river. Its tan surface runs deep and often more than a mile wide in the great arterial flow that pulsates through the anatomy of the Delta, providing the lifeblood of its waterborne world. The spread of its expanse presents a wide-open window into the communal hive of Vietnam's water culture.

Families live entire lifetimes and perhaps generations on its surface. Congregating in clusters that function as communal nests, extended families provide the character and security of small hamlets. Often these groups specialize in particular trades, trades in which communal labor and organization is necessary. Quarry rock and bulk goods require coordinated labor, net fishing, etc., each association wringing out the necessary economic benefits to sustain their riverine life.

The quilt of rice paddies string along the banks as far as the eye can see. They are fringed with coconut groves and other tropic forestation that along with small feeder canals characteristically demarcate property or neighborhood boundaries between one hamlet or village and another. Thatch homes brushed with banana groves sit back under shade trees along the canals in refuge from the unrelenting sun. People dot the fields and banks under the enormous cloud filled sky, their conical hats of woven grass flashing like copper coins. It is a methodically peaceful scene. Even in wartime, it was like this. By day, life maintained its appearances. It was at night that danger and violence erupted in sudden, short and fierce encounters. That was when and where we came in.

I remember how Pee Wee and I used to sit forward in the bow well of the twin 50s of the PBR jawing, unable to sleep while the rest of the squad would catch some zz's in the stern. The boat rode fat and sluggish with the weight of the squad, overloaded, per usual, with enough to start a war and hopefully hold on long enough for help to arrive. The deep-throated throb of the turbo diesels bored through the warm air, its wake whisking by the fiberglass hull with the sound of brooms sweeping.

The night was witch dark, the world as empty as a bare room as we rode along the wide ribbon of the river. Millions of stars streamed above us, circling the universe spun by everyone's God. On the puny globe below, except for the VC and ourselves, the rest of our world was asleep and out of harms way, or according to the laws of curfew, supposed to be.

Even without the moon, the weight of starlight painted a dull pewter shine on Pee Wee's high smooth cheekbones and broken nose, strangely like the features of his half-breed Eskimo wife who was known to cold-cock him when they both got mean drunk. His soft jungle hat shrouded the rest of his face and I couldn't always hear what he was saying over the rush of the wind and the slide and scrape of the boat's wake. It didn't matter. I could tell by the bobbing embers of his Pall Mall always dangling from his mouth in the cadence of whatever he was saying. Pee Wee was my Chief Petty Officer. Aside from that and his related functions, the only particular feature that we shared in common was that neither of us could cat nap on the long boat patrols. Sometimes it took us 4 to 5 hours just to get there and that was a long time to wonder about things out loud. Sometimes we listened to each other and sometimes we didn't. Like I said, it didn't matter at the time. Now that I'll never see him again, I guess it does. Anyway, that's how I got to know him and why I still think about him and miss him, more than most anyone I served with to be honest, except for Rick, but that's another story.

Pee Wee came by his nickname naturally. A runt of the litter guy who probably came out squalling with the clenched fists that he kept swinging for most of his thereafter. It wasn't until the Navy and the "Teams" that he found a rocky home of sorts and scrambled his way up a broken ladder of enlisted advancement. Pee Wee was a SEAL Team plank holder, meaning he was there when it first formed back in 1962 as the Navy's competition for the Army's Special Forces.

On the other hand, I was a newcomer three years later. Out of the 65 enlisted and 15 Officers, the full complement at the time, I was a recent add-on from the Underwater Demolition Teams from which all SEALS were then selected. There were a lot of colorful stories about Pee Wee (and others). One legend of the time was about an incident that took place when his mixed litter of kids wouldn't listen and ignored him while watching the TV. It was confirmed in fact that he then went to his bedroom and returned with his issue .45 Cal. Automatic and shot it dead. There were others, all hearsay, but I was present once at one of our stateside hangouts when he swore to beat the shit out of some great big guy who did nothing more than dare him to make a certain pool shot, and Pee Wee was damn lucky we locked him in the broom closet while his wife was called to come to get him, but she said to leave him there.

But that was a life ago, when all we did was train for everything, everywhere, mostly at the Army's "misery" schools and waited for the Vietnam thing to happen. And then it happened. All of a sudden, it seemed like the rush of orders came from BUPERS to CINCPAC to COMMACV, or simply put, to Vietnam. After that the legends of barroom and training heroics were left behind and the old-timer vs. the new guys leveled out real quick when the first bullets started flying.

The hull speed was making a nice breeze blowing off the bugs. Guys lay around the stern well like gunnysacks, shit was piled up all over the place, everything taped, wrapped and slapped for noise, laminated with WD-40 and drenched in bug juice. We were in our first month of learning via OJT, i.e., how to get there (maps were vague, with few and inaccurate markings including river soundings and navigation hazards), how to find the "there", there (radar didn't work up close and the new magic of star-light scopes couldn't penetrate shadow), how to know the difference between the wrong time and the right place and sorting it out with the right time at the wrong place (the intelligence was third and fourth hand and a day or week too late), how to figure out who was who (good guys bad guys and women and children in between) and finally how not to fuck up (when in doubt, don't shoot).

"Looky here, Mr. Wilbur", or "Tell you what, Sir" were the staple prefaces to most of Pee Wee's comments. "The way I figure it: most of the time we don't know where we are going, how to get there, what we are going to do once we're there, and who to do it to. Have I got it about right, Mr. Wilbur?" Then he would start chuckling and laughing in that throaty whiskey cigarette laugh that ended up doing him in as a truck driver 20 years later. "Looky here, Mr. Wilbur, is that about right? Huh? Now what kind of shit is that?" and he'd start chuckling, coughing and spitting all over again. "Here sir, have one on me" and he'd shake his pack of Pall Mall and conclude "What a fucked up world."

We drift in at slow idle. The PBR crew mans the machine guns in full battle gear: flak jackets, helmets, the whole drill. The din of cicada's rises like a fever, the huge stillness of the riverbank rises up like a head of black surf ready to break fall and tuck us under.

Can't see shit! Nothing! The squad is lined along the gunnel. Point man lying on the bow, one leg slung over ready to go. Everyone is on Auto-Pork. Its hair-trigger time, drop-off or drop-dead, not much choice there. "Just Do It" 30 years before Nike made it a slogan. Night vision tries to bore its way through the wall of darkness throbbing like a headache. "Double squelch the radio key; signal the MIKE boat. We're going in!"

Drifting now, edging in, the throttle shifts to back in a deep moan, the gurgle, and spill of backwash flushes up the stern. The overhanging foliage creates a tunnel swallowing the bow. No depth perception, where are we? Where is the bank? Branches reach out, and drag over the canopy. There is a bending like a bow, then a crack as it snaps and it breaks over the forward fifties, falling and trapping us like a heavy net. Another limb catches the radar guard and whips the Point man off the bow. He hits the water like a stone. Men rush forward wrestling through weapons and gear catching and tearing. Another slips and crashes, more heavy thuds in the water. The rest of us tumble back against the cowling piling into the stern well.

"Back off, back the fucking boat, do it now!" The high revs spit exhaust and the diesel smoke pours over us. The boat is jacking and backing trying to tear loose; the river current shoves the hull against foliage. The stern is caught as we corkscrew into the overhang. More branches and vines crowd us. Desperate yells break out of the dark below us.

"Christ they're under the boat. Get'em out. Get a line out. Put a light on them. Fuck security. We have to keep them out from under this boat. Back full, back full! Get this shit off the boat so we can maneuver. You got'em yet? Where are they? On the Line? On the line? Man the fifties on the bank, open up on anything that spooks you. Keep your stations. Signal the MIKE boat, stand by for flares. No flare yet. Just get us into the bank. Ram the fucking thing. Get these guys out! Ram the fucking bank, get us in there and secure. Are they on the line? You Got'em? Get a light on them!

The light shears the dark bouncing off the shell of the surface. Big sodden lumps with white faces stare out in a dazed surprise bobbing on the water held up by the inflation collars grabbing at vines that drape everything. Where the fuck are they? Wait for signal. Doc, get them the fuck out! Frantic activity in the bow hauling someone on board, and another, "Pee Wee!" Fuck, where are you? OK? Hang on, hang on. "Pee Wee, where the fuck are you"? Pee Wee, in a loud voice: "Get me the fuck out of here before I drown, you Cocksuckers!"

9

FARAWAY IS HOME

The entrance to the river port for Kien Hoa is marked by large billboards featuring an amusement park that has a zoo for monkeys and entertainment for outdoor festive parties. From what I can see of its overgrown and dilapidated facade it's not meeting investment expectations.

The roadside approach to Ben Tre is as ugly and cluttered as My Tho, maybe worse. The town itself is unrecognizable. Nothing remains of the quiet lanes lined with the broad shade of banyan trees and the ochre villas, or the wide veranda of the municipal square with its open market pavilion. In their stead are cramped and crowded streets hastily thrown together, buildings of concrete block often without a coat of whitewash and a treeless skyline sagging with wires.

Memory runs out quickly after driving around. The assumption that after 30 years something would stand out and signify a past that I was part of here doesn't take long to fade in the bright heat of a tropical day.

The local noodle shop on the corner is less than inviting. After a bowl of food shared with the congregation of flies, I am persuaded to abandon my original plan to overnight here. Going over my Lost Planet Guide Book map of Vietnam it leads me to believe we can traverse Kien Hoa and cross the Co Thien River by ferry into Vinh Long Province to the west. This way we wouldn't have to retrace our steps back to My Tho; no such luck. Consulting a truck driver for advice, we're told that the road marked on my map is no good for the car and that the ferry crossing indicated had never functioned. So much for the map.

We pass the park featuring the towering statue we saw on the way in. Positioned to make it impossible to miss, it is the centerpiece of the memorial of the "War of Reunification"; reason enough for me to care less about it. Now with time on our hands and no better plan, why not have a look? The war was especially hard on Ben Tre and Kien Hoa Province. The Viet Cong held on to their turf with the same doggedness of our own civil war annals. So why not have a war memorial? We have ours.

It's a towering 50-foot Iwo Jima knock-off, bigger than anything else in the town. Jack-hammered out of blocks of cast sandstone, featuring a tri-umvirate of peasant comrades advancing forward, mouths open in defi-ance, one arm clenched with raised fists, another brandishing a gun, another, the single star flag. It doesn't take long to absorb the notion that these images are symbolically giving me and ARVN (Army of the Republic of Vietnam) the figurative Bird. So I look at it for awhile trying to think what I feel about that, and how the South Vietnamese might feel about it, those who felt its boot and heel; but then after all, war has always been "winners keepers, losers weepers.

As if blighted by the salt of those wounds, the gardens around the mon-ument show dried up flowerbeds, silent fountains and empty pools. A few people browse around or sit on the benches. They might be wondering what I'm doing having my photograph taken by the monument. Some might be old enough to appreciate its irony one way or another, others would just as soon forget and for good reason.

Forgetfulness allows the Vietnamese not to see things that might drag them back into a confrontation with the ghosts of their past, to avoid all the things and people missing from their lives and to overlook all the unfulfilled expectations that they might have had otherwise. Forgetfulness for the Vietnamese is even useful in ignoring the future that is facing them. Forgetfulness is a tool they use to watch people like me and feel nothing beyond mild curiosity. Forgetfulness is catching and probably good for them. After awhile, I am sure it will come to me.

But I haven't forgotten, probably because I never suffered from "Our" defeat like they did, or felt the totalitarian boot hammering them down into a one Communist size to fit all mold of subservience and monotony: another day of looking down, following with closed eyes, or hearing its incessant cant of dogma without listening, sidestepping their debris of empty promises year after year with no near end. No matter what; no one living in and around Ben Tre on the TET of 1968 (the annual national and cultural holiday of the Vietnamese New Year) when it was almost completely destroyed.

The helicopter, like a frantic hen, finally gave up trying to fly and squatted in a storm of dust. Each time I ran out from beneath the lunge of its huge blades, I was always gripped with the fear that my head would fly off like a chopped melon.

The bright clay earth was oven hard accenting the charred and broken palm trees stubbed black liked half-smoked cigars after the napalm and strafing runs of the day before. Jeeps with high whip antennas flying command signal flags were drawn up in front of a temporary command tent next to the burned out airport hut broken backed and hollow, making me think of horses tied to a hitching post in the "Wild 'West", after an Indian raid.

Parked nearby was an Army Caribou, the largest plane that could land on the strip. American soldiers, many in T-shirts or stripped down to the waist, were unloading supplies from the pallets it brought. There was a lull in the offensive. The big assault to re-take the town had occurred the day before. The 105 and 155 Howitzer batteries in their sandbagged revetments were working over some target called in by the spotter plane, a tiny untouchable god high above in a kingdom much cooler than the oven below.

I had been sent to oversee the Agency compound so Bill Shields, the Provincial Officer in Charge, could fly back to Regional HQ for emergency debriefing. Bill was a retired Special Forces Sergeant Major, one of the originals of that outfit who upon retirement found instead a new war and another career in the gray trade of counter-insurgency warfare/contract intelligence operations (a mouthful in any setting.) He had turned in his starched camys for safari shirts and cowboy boots, which suited him fine, since he was a tall Texan who reveled in acting like one. Hard talking, demanding, but fun to be around, Bill and I got along just fine as long as I played junior and listened admiringly to his tales. After briefing me on the situation and coordinating our radio contacts in expectation of an anticipated night attack, he gave me his "Going Hunting" grin, slapped me on the back side and loped off to the waiting Air America Pilatus Porter aircraft hugging the holstered pearl handled Colt 44 he favored for his wild west image yelling "Don't give away the farm while I'm gone."

I needed to check in with the Senior Military Officer in Charge, provide my radio call sign, and, since we functioned independent of direct military authority, make sure that our defensive patrol movements were well coordinated with the local Command's tactical board. I knew one of the G-2 officers, a MACV (Military Assistance Command Vietnam) Army Captain my age from prior operations. We wandered out together to the dark green Agency Bronco jeep parked in the shade of a large banyan tree where Bill's driver and three Nung guards waited to take me to the compound. (The Nungs are an indigenous tribe renowned for its military prowess and loyalty, a reputation similar to that of the Nepalese Ghurkhas that were contracted by the CIA for its security functions.) Behind the Bronco somewhat obscured in the shade lay large black bags which, at first glimpse from a distance, I had taken for recently delivered cargo from the Caribou, but they weren't. They were too formally assembled, about twenty of them arranged in three neat rows. They were body bags; shiny clean, black rubberized vinyl with heavy reinforced zippers, thick webbed strapping, and built in carrying handles made with precision, with high quality material in accordance with thoughtful, Government Inspected specs. All were occupied: GIs killed in the assault of the day before while trying to re-take Ben Tre after the VC regiment had occupied it.

I had some first hand knowledge of body bags. The week before I had made a lonely trip to pick up one of my advisors encased in one. He hadn't been with me long enough to have known him well, but we had talked by radio the day before while planning the logistics for the Op. The victim of a hand grenade booby trap, by all reports he fell soundlessly, and no one could find a mark on him until they brought him back to camp and the doctor examining him discovered that a shrapnel sliver had pierced his eye and penetrated the brain bringing instant painless death. Anyway, there wasn't enough room to lay him in the small cargo space of the single engine Aero, so we had to sit him up in the seat behind me for the trip and that wasn't easy. He was stiffening.

It was a strange trip flying with a dead man 18 inches behind me and there were times when I felt I should turn around and say something to him as if he was still there, which he was in a strange way. I was grateful and relieved that the bag was there, hiding his gray face, his black curly hair, wet as if he had just taken a shower, and his unshaved beard still growing. Instead it was the black slick bag that took away the burden of seeing him again and feeling what it was like to be dead and dirty with mud and smudges of blood and skin like molten wax, and it was then that I fully appreciated that the bag was more for my good than his. So seeing 20 of them without having to witness their final appearances made them easier to look at, and to forget what or who were inside. Noticing my gaze, Bill said "Graves and Registration are flying them outbound on the Caribou to Saigon or Cam Ranh, then Hawaii where they are addressed. They told us they're busy as all Hell."

"Fucking Gooks", he spat out, "We should never had assaulted entrenched positions. We should have called in the B-52s and buried them. This whole fucking town isn't worth one of them", and he meant it as he said it with the venom and intent that keeps wars going over and over, even until today 30 years later and forever more. So I stood with him for a few moments. He was upset. He probably knew one of them. Me, I didn't. "Fucking war," he repeated.

I looked at him and let him go on, feeling old. Me, at that time, I thought I had it figured out pretty simple. It didn't matter how or where you died, it was just the fact of it that counted. Dying in Vietnam sounded O.K. to me but actual death didn't. Bill kept getting hung up on how shitty it was to be blown away in "Nam", but I couldn't see the difference between that and a car wreck.

I left him to wander over to where a platoon of the South Vietnamese troops were digging a trench, throwing up a shroud of dust at the end of the grass runway a short distance away. They were preparing mass graves. The VC dead had been dumped there in rough heaps of 10 to 15 each, exposed to the sun, maybe forty or fifty of them in all. The ARVN detail had removed their shirts and swathed their faces with them, making make-shift masks to breathe through and cut down on the stench of the bodies.

The afternoon sun was high and the dead had been exposed for at least 24 hours. Above them, the flies were hovering and waving, blurring the air in hazy smudges. Every now and then a gusty breeze lifted and blew putrid vapors across the dry grass, sharp messages from the other side of life.

The VC dead lay entangled like inflated rubberized figurines, their small, fine features bloated and their naturally loose and nimble limbs stiffened losing their original packaging as humans. They were now transiting from the end of existence into the beginning of soil. The diggers looked up, flashed their eyes, hating their chore and probably me, resentful of the intruding "Round Eye" looking down at their debasement and reminding me of my own, an uninvited voyeur at a burial that was none of my business.

I moved off a little ways, embarrassed by the guilty feeling that no matter what I felt for them it was not the same as I felt about our own and how that cut both ways in some deep instinct of primal conditioning. One of the diggers threw down his shovel in disgust and clambered out of the shallow pit to walk away until the supervising officer, standing off to the side smoking constantly to filter the stench, ordered him in the high pitched voice of exasperation to return, hating the assignment as much as they did. Soon it became too much, even for the officer, and before the pit was adequately prepared he shouted out orders and the corpses were thrown down into it, not so much from disdain but from the sickness of everything that hung and filled the air. In their hurry to finish they left it barely covered before they straggled off, dragging their shovels. I could still see a bulge or protrusion of something barely covered by the loose dirt and marked by the frenzy of flies and the stench of death.

Not so far away, another group of ARVNs were gathered, burying their own with more decorum and formality in an area where small headstones or Buddhist testimonials showed a grave area partially obscured by the high grasses nodding in the afternoon wind. More than ours in number but less than the VC, their dead were wrapped in white cloth as tight as mummies and laid beside coffins of plain and coarse planking, of a size suitable for boys. A Catholic priest was in attendance and was apparently providing benediction for the Catholic dead.

The battle to retake the town had been fierce. Looking over to the mounded scar of the burial pit for the VC and then the dark lumps beneath the banyan tree, I had to wonder what, if any, grace would cover this trinity, and how all the prayers and incantations called out in different voices brought no answers to the same endless question.

High above in the incomprehensibly blue sky, the spotter plane circled with the lazy solitary drone of someone bored watching and waiting from a world that was clean and cool. As if unconnected and without presentiment, a distant tremble, and thunder of explosion, followed by the pluming of a black mushroom cloud above the tree line far across the wide apron of rice paddies re-awakened us to work still in progress three to four kilometers away. I scanned the sky, catching a glint of one, then another, and another, three of them, "Fast Movers" (as we called the ground support attack jets, usually F-4 Phantoms or A-4 Sky-Hawks) turning for another run. They were either from Ton Son Nhut or an off-coast carrier on "Yankee Station".

The spotter had found something and, just like a god of old, sent his modernized lightning bolts to punish the guilty. They came on again like incandescent darts in a graceful sweep dropping lower and lower until they leveled off one behind the other, releasing dark pods that turned and toppled lazily end over end (the tell-tale motion of napalm canisters), blooming into violent orange blossoms, that took my breath away leaving a carcass of writhing black smoke staining what had been seconds before immaculate white clouds on a the seamless horizon.

In the overwhelming the silence that followed, it was as if nothing had happened, as if the earth was still the same and the "Fast Movers" had been just a momentary speck in the eye. Once again it seemed as if the war was either never present, or never seemed to leave while I stood in the middle of its hide and seek, trying to find a hold on each end, lost in its crossword puzzle.

The squad leader of the Nungs indicated they needed to get back to the compound for a change of watch. The Graves and Registration detail from Saigon was ready to load their cargo. Bill, the G-2 Captain, must have been detailed for the official transfer, came over and together we watched them at work.

We would have hated their job, but then again, they would have hated ours. The Second Lieutenant was quiet and professional; everything one wanted one to be in handling the dead. I remembered that he carried an aluminum clipboard and, accompanied by his corporal, carefully checked off the particulars of each body bag. Their uniforms were starched and creased, perfect except for the spreading dark crescents of sweat around the armpits and small of their backs, their brightly polished boots carrying a light patina of red dust. They spoke quietly, carefully assuring that the dog tags against the written cards encased in the clear-faced plastic sleeve on the vinyl bag were matching. Then the squad detailed to load their consignment got down to work. The second lieutenant completed the paper work, handed the captain his copy of the manifest, and said politely "It's been a tough week for everybody". He then told us that the bodies would be shipped to CONUS (Continental United States) in 48 hours, but considering TET, maybe in 72. "We weren't prepared for this" he confided.

The Caribou closed its after-bay doors and taxied to the end of the strip. Its twin-engine props whirl up a storm of dust. Shaking as if in anger, the plane lurched forward with a consuming roar. Lumbering by us in what seemed an improbable departure from earth, it miraculously rose ever so slightly still struggling to gain altitude, eventually achieving the spectacle of flight. I watched until it became a dark speck somewhere above the horizon when it disappeared and left the sky and me unbearably empty with all the loneliness of being left behind. "Home" I heard myself say seeing the silent lifeless packages shaking in the cool solitary bay of the plane. At least they were going. Home"—I never knew it was so far away.

10

TWO WOMEN, TWO LIVES

Vinh Long is the Province town of Ving Long Province, separated from Kien Hoa by the Bassac River, one of the fingers of the Mekong that splices off and drains south into the mud shallow South China Sea. In contrast to its near neighbor Ben Tre, Vinh Long used to be perhaps the most prominent and, architecturally, the most sophisticated of all Delta Province towns, thus earning it the appellation "Riviera of the Delta".

The late afternoon drive is more relaxing, as the landscape bends gracefully towards the traditional rice culture. The habitations are handsome and prosperous; instead of the traditional reed thatch and bamboo, many are stuccoed, their gardens full of produce. Cut rice lies in bundles drying before threshing, surrounded all around by their recumbent fields. Smoke from the burning of the husk waves gently against the sky.

Every now and then in the middle of a field or in a small grove set aside from the habitation, the family temple and burial plot reminds that in this peasant society the land is a feature of reverence, its possession and work inseparable from the family and their communal beliefs. Because of this unbroken cultural ethic, communist "Collectivism" was never able to sever these ties between people and land and their stubborn, passive resistance to its methods and policies slowly and inevitably frustrated the new regime's attempt to impose it.

Approaching the ferry crossing to Vinh Long, there is a long detour around a construction project—a bridge spanning the river to link the provinces. When complete in the next year or so it will be the first bridge in history to span any of the Delta rivers. Since the Delta represents at least 30% of the population and accounts for 65% of its agricultural export product and commerce, the absence of such a fundamental infrastructure and the delay in addressing the need dramatically underscores the frailty of the central Government's developmental capacity.

Lack of resources may well be one of the reasons for the government's failures, but there is widespread and justifiable suspicion in the South that the woeful lack of a national transportation system has a political motive. There appears to be no other excuse for it. In the North, for instance, it is a proudly touted fact that the railroad bridge over the Perfume River at Hue was bombed 58 times but was repaired or rebuilt repeatedly throughout the war. In the South, a bridge has not been built in 30 years of alleged peace. This suspicion revives the simmering prejudice that the northern political elements are still punishing the South; motivated by their fear that capital investment in infrastructure would encourage an economic expansion that would disproportionately enhance the South's revanchist tendencies.

On entering the city of Vinh Long, one finds the same overgrown congestion, but when Houng turns off the traffic-choked center and arrives at a small riverside hotel in a quiet and isolated quarter, I am delighted. With these benefits, whatever shortcomings the Cuu Long hotel might have are easily forgiven.

After a cooling shower with a small hand hose, I wait for Houng in the open riverside café of the hotel and order a 33 beer. It's cold and good, the perfect refresher for the tropical day. So far I haven't seen any evidence of other lodgers, which suits me fine. The female vocalist on the CD player has a reedy wavering voice and is singing a romantic love song, or at least I think she is. The sun is almost down and the shadows cast a hint of coolness. Water taxis loaded with workers or marketers criss-cross the river, ferrying them back to their villages or hamlets. The reflection of the yellowing clouds shimmers along its mirrored surface. The backdrop of traffic noise fades. Strollers are coming out of lanes and alleys to promenade along the quay enjoying the same peace and quiet as I, though perhaps with a deeper appreciation. Below me, by the quay wall, three men are sculling their small dugout to the edge of the current. They throw a rope with an iron bar for an anchor over the side and start fussing with their hand lines, smoking and laughing lightly at each other's comments and jokes. A fresh-faced Houng joins me.

The car rental arrangement is to pay a per kilometer rate with the driver included in the charge. Separately I am to pay an overnight "parking" charge and a per diem stipend for the driver. Since it is all quite reasonable, I ask him to join me for the meal. I look forward to the companionship, not to mention his vital assistance.

Houng is an attractive, good-looking, man, with an honest and earnest face. At first glance he could be taken for anything from a doctor to a clerk. Instead, he's been a driver for most of his mature life. At 40, he is married with two boys. He tells me he is very poor, with a shrug that says plainly, "That's life". He had hoped for more, he admits, not so much in complaint, but in the humble candor that is so remarkable and likeable of the Vietnamese.

He is a Northerner who came South after 1975. His father died when he was a child; his mother and two older brothers remained in the North. Apparently, he is the only one of his family to migrate "because no reason to stay", translating to mean that in their stratified structure of family, the third born was not a favored position, a plight made worse by the drastic post-war economy and dreadful state of affairs of post-war Hanoi.

Essentially, the war left the North bankrupt and exhausted. The totalitarianism of the Ho regime was total, but while it was notably efficient, intrepid and indefatigable in war, it was conversely inept at peace. Houng, was part of the northern "carpetbag" migration to the South, one of those who, sensing no future in the North, hoped for at least a little one in the South's "reconstruction"—a situation paralleling in many respects our post civil war "Reconstruction" 100 years before.

The "Cuu Long" riverside restaurant next to the hotel is cantilevered over the quay wall. It reminds me of the one in My Tho many years before and produces the same exotic menu of river species from eels to snails and frogs. We are the first customers, though a large table is crowded with the proprietors' multi-generation family, most of who serve some function over the course of our meal. Houng is very nervous about ordering, fearing that I might not like his selections. To all his questions I shrug just like he does until he catches on to the humor of it and in a stream of Vietnamese makes the choice. We both sit back and smile. We have broken the ice and are now companions.

The meal is perfect: baked eel, charcoaled frogs-legs, fried snails, rice, salad and assorted greens. By the time it arrives I've convinced Houng to have a couple of beers and shortly his wall of diffidence comes tumbling down. His English improves remarkably and he allows himself to be cheery. From now on, I decide to keep him in beer.

As we pass the dishes back and forth, picking and probing with our chopsticks, the afterglow of the sun melts the river into pewter. The last water taxis dissolve into the dark shadows of the distant bank, leaving only the muted put-put coughs of their two-cycle engines in the distance. The activity of the three fishermen below keep us company: the gurgle of a paddle, its scrape along the floorboards, the coughing and muttering back and forth with the tidbits of the day. Their cigarettes flare dully like suspended embers in the descending night.

The two of us watch the scene and drink our tea alone with our thoughts. In the quiet and simplicity of those moments I think how it is all here, what I came to look for. I'm not quite sure what all that is, but it's something like touching the dark.

The motorized sampans wake me at 4:30 the following morning. They are bringing produce to market below my small terrace. It will be dawn at 5 a.m.. A sunrise on the Mekong would make my day. It's still dark when I get down to the quay. The single light bulb dangling from a line on a wooden pole is my only company. There are no sounds from the river or the town. No one is in sight. A light veil of mist hovers. It is cool; I'm glad I brought my nylon pullover. I pull out one of the folding chairs, put my feet up and wait.

Vietnamese are early risers. It may be because pre-dawn is the only cool and private time in their very tropical and communal life. Shielded by the shrubbery of the little park bordering the hotel, a small group of elderly women materialize in silence and without saying a word begin the performance of assortment of morning exercises. It appears to be a form or derivation of Tai Chi. Its solemn pensive movements follow as an elegant, almost ghost-like dance. Others begin to materialize from the folds of dawn: striders swinging their arms with invigoration, exercisers bending and stretching, others just strolling, wordlessly. A penny for their thoughts.

Sunrise occurs with the fine stroke of a calligrapher's blood red brush on a black mirror. Everyone stops to watch as if waiting for a message, unraveling the new hexagram from the *I Ching* declaring the day. On cue the exercisers break up and drift away. The café attendant rolls up his sleeping mat and turns on the loudspeaker. The same music from yesterday starts over, crackling out into the fresh morning air. He hurries to wipe down the terrace tables glazed with dew and disappears to prepare the tea. It comes with tinned sugar biscuits. I settle back to enjoy the growing scene, marvelously alone.

The river current turns and twists with the light flutter of a ceremonial pennant. Sampans begin to spread out on its quiet flow. Pedestrians, mostly women on the way to market, drain from the lanes and alleys behind which they spend their lives. The heat of the day is yet to come. Quiet still lingers; so far just the soft slap of sandaled feet, the tinkle of a bicycle bells, the reedy music, the dull knocking of sampans queuing up to unload at the market landing with last minute produce, and the occasional shout directing its traffic. The rising sun finely etches all the lines and corners, casting shadows in the eaves and touching random windows with fire.

It occurs to me that the same scene has embraced me before. The same is true for the faces with their expressions, people's movements, gestures, voices and sounds. They could be the same cast, with largely the same props, but of course they are not. I start to wonder about them. I want to know what they are thinking and what they see until I realize that I never really thought much about them before. It was all so different then, or rather, I was.

Then I was dazzled by the surface of things, juiced on the intensity of events and my anxious pace within them. I was caught up in the big show: the sounds of choppers and automatic weapons, artillery and explosions, jets and bombs, smoke and fire. I was high on it. For the most part, I saw the Vietnamese as a medium through which I moved, extras without parts, backdrops against which I was acting out the drama of my time and place, propelled along the fast river course of young manhood. Now that is all changed. Now they are the principals—and I am no longer the actor.

The market of Vinh Long is a Garden of Eden, a temple of a fecund world where food is the great offering on the altar. Perhaps because it is still early the people are quiet, all heads bent toward the ancient road leading to the market. After all, it was at the market that culture found its stool to sit on, where ideas and commerce grew from hand to glove, where people found in its congregation the spare time to draw, sculpt, exchange values, hear wisdom, discover politics, and found religion if not belief.

The vegetables and fruits are fresh, ripe, stacked or bunched in neat and symmetrical mounds, forming colorful bandannas of yellow cucumbers and red peppers, dark green and blue lettuce, pearl white onions, deep cream mushrooms, bamboo shoots, banana, papaya, mango, pears and apples, star-fruit, litchi-nuts, etc, etc; all washed bright and dappled by the shear of morning sunrays rushing, spilling and spattering like water through the seams and patches of the awnings.

The flower stalls cluster in bundled bouquets. Spices are wrapped in palm leaves, each carefully tied and parceled with grass or bamboo stripping. The larger fish, silvery and copper, are freshly gutted, cleaned and splayed on beds of washed weed and shaved ice, while the smaller, still alive, herd themselves nervously in the shallow baths of scoured tin tubs. Crabs of deep purple and red are tightly bundled in yarn, indigo snails in bound plastic sacks with water, gold speckled green eels in trays. Geese, ducks, and chickens are tethered in little thatch corrals or deep wicker baskets. White piglets scrubbed pink stand stiff and paralyzed in wooden bins. Goats and even some small calves huddle in stalls spread with fresh hay: all of them scared shitless. Who wouldn't be?

The marketers shuffle in loose columns and form small knots around popular items. It is a gentle crowd, no jostling, pressing, shouting, or straining in competition, but quiet and respectful, each aware of the importance of the business at hand. Nothing remains unsupervised or unattended by the women, who preside with sentry eyes, priestesses of their life's domain.

One woman stands in a shaft of sunlight that makes her glow pale white against the tightly wound black hair bun shining with a jade stickpin. No longer beautiful, her charms have instead softened into grace and calm. She is tall for a Vietnamese, and still slender. She wears a simple high collar sheath dress of silk the color of jade, framed by a fine gold necklace, earrings and matching bracelets. She never looks up but moves slowly with a wry smile. She seems to be looking inward while pausing at an assortment of stalls, occasionally asking a question, before she passes on. She is no doubt assembling the day's menu.

Ladies of the manor, so to speak, are seldom about in the daytime; their lives are spent out of public sight in quiet households behind high garden walls. Most likely the wife of a wealthy local merchant/landowner, she would have grown up with the graces of household artistry: embroidery, calligraphy and music, probably matriculating at a French Catholic school.

The lady approaches a woman sitting on several bags of rice and surrounded by large coarse baskets of chickens and ducks tethered in inert bundles. They greet one another and smile. Both reach out and touch each other. Beneath her conical hat the peasant's broad sun-reddened face beams toothlessly, mouth rotted red by betel nut.

They are a portrait of Vietnam. Two of its daughters framing their world, a dialectic of its yin and yang, old friends whose lives have transected the web of their times. I am invisible to them as they talk, have no place in their lives—or do I? The three of us occupied the same time and space, a momentary conjunction in the far away and long ago.

I would have most likely seen the lady as a young girl with her friends, holding hands beneath their parasols and avoiding the sun's harshness to preserve the rich creaminess of their skin as their white Ao Dais pick up with the street breeze like small sails. I would have seen her long black hair braided in pigtails bounce and swing with laughter as she turned home and disappeared beyond the high garden wall of her life to be.

I saw too the poultry seller in the market, as a peasant girl. She had been sent from her village to become a servant for the landowner's household to learn the skills and arts of town, from which she would return to her ham-let on holidays and ride once again the broad back of the family buffalo along with the white egrets that sought their noon meal among its para-sites, and follow the rhythm of the bowed backs of her family planting or cutting the rice in their world of green and brown, water, earth and sky.

The schoolgirl was to marry another merchant's son and the servant girl to return to the fields when the hard men from the North came and demanded change with all its heedless sacrifices. Then came men like me in jeeps, trucks, and helicopters and with guns. We drove by them, sped through their streets, drank beer in their towns, jumped from helicopters into their villages, crept among canals at night and slogged across their rice paddies, rarely looking back.

But my kind had departed. And the life that the women thought would continue on didn't, leaving them to discover each other again through a different lens, confronting the new rules of a changed life with different hardships. Those that had had much were to have little and those who had little were to have very little more. But the people had nowhere to go and nothing more to provide or do except to return to who they were to begin with and mend what was left. Now the three of us are standing here in this market in a traverse of time none of us could have imagined.

The women end their talking and in saying farewell lightly reach out to touch one another again. In a parting thought, the market woman calls her back and reaching in the wicker basket offers the lady a tethered rooster. The lady demurs, but is nonetheless very pleased, and taking it in two hands she turns and holds it up into the sunlight with her pale slender arms as if making an offering for all of us. The red gold of the rooster's mantle blazes with fire.

11

IN THE BEGINNING THERE WAS TET

The trip across Vinh Long province to the ferry landing for Can Tho is not long and the ferry runs every half hour. While the old Mercedes is approaching the loading ramp, the muffler catches on a flange and falls off, causing a bottleneck and some commotion. With little fuss we are simply pushed over to the side of the wharf and the ferry proceeded to load. We would catch the next one. Fortunately the crew chief of some welders who are working on the wharf comes over and offers to re-weld the exhaust pipe. He is wearing a dirty white T-shirt displaying the flag of Texas. When he hears from Houng that I'm American he gives me a toothless grin and pounds on his chest pointing to the "Lone Star". I tell Houng that it is the symbol of our largest state just like the single star of the Vietnamese flag is the symbol of one nation. Houng's translation makes him happy to tell his crew. Since he has never heard of the State of Texas and doesn't have any idea what it is, I repeat the name a number of times until he can at least mangle the pronunciation. Happy with his new discovery, he energetically gives me the thumbs and yells to his crew to weld the muffler. By the next ferry it's ready to go. When I give the guys a couple packs of cigarettes, they all repeat "Texas" as best they can.

The Bassac is a busy river, wide and deep enough to include small coastal freighters that can work their way up the ever-changing channels from the South China Sea some 20 miles to the South. The crossing to Can Tho is about 2.5 miles. Can Tho is the largest town in the Delta. It is the most centrally located and has long been the capital of the entire region.

The ferry landing on the Can Tho side is adjoined by a central bus station that is the major crossroad for overland transportation servicing all the provinces of the western Delta. The bus terminal area was called Ben Se Moi the northernmost section of the town. The compound where I was barracked was located off one of the back alleys around the corner. As with every other location, the most identifiable features seem to have been submerged, but nothing could have changed the highway along the river except a vastly improved surface.

Ten kilometers north along what is now designated as Highway 91 lay the airport that in 1967 was no more than a well-used landing strip that evolved from grass to asphalt and finally concrete in step with the war build up. I spent more than a year shuttling among the 16 Provinces of IV Corps, so I knew it well, and never more so in memory than in the very beginning of the TET Offensive, January 31st 1968. Of the few signposts left in America's memory of the war, the "TET Offensive" of 1968 is probably the most notable. It was an occurrence that through the medium of television alone became the watershed event for US public opinion, which ultimately and from long distance decided that we would "lose" the war. At the same time, ironically and bitterly for us who were there, TET, far from signaling the defeat of American strategy and tactics, was when we had them by the balls and let'em go.

Just as most people who were alive then can tell you with snapshot accuracy where they were and what they were doing when JFK was shot, for those of us "in country" I'll bet the ranch that the same would be true for the TET Offensive.

It was the early morning of February 1st 1968 and I was riding a beat-up Lambretta Motor-Scooter on my way to an airstrip to start-up the most important operation I had a hand in planning over my year and a half in-country. It was 2 AM (At this time I was Officer in Charge of SEAL Team 2's Detachment "Bravo"—Counter Terror Teams). They were under the control and direction of the Agency through an assortment of mediums too arcane to chronicle.

By the time I hit the starter peddle of the Lambretta it was about 2 a.m. that morning. I was the only one in sight or in hearing—at least on my side—and as I slowly threaded my way up the alley turning right toward the Bus Terminal something wasn't right; something different registered to my senses making me feel a little strange. It wasn't that I had a premonition or presentiment but the first thing that struck me was that the open-air bus terminal was empty, completely deserted. Usually bus riders would camp out on the cement benches overnight to pick up the dawn runs. But then it was into the third day of TET celebration and no one was going anywhere at 2 a.m. even though curfew restrictions were cancelled because of the cease-fire agreement.

And then there weren't any "white mice" at the usual guard posts in the terminal or at the ferry landing ("white mice" was an unfairly derogatory nick-name for the Vietnamese National Police, whose jurisdiction it was to police cities and national arteries among other standard police criminal functions). Even more unusual, there were none at the central checkpoint on the "highway" north. Usually there was a full squad checking all who came in and out of the city—the bus station was one of the five or six permanently manned checkpoints. The black and white cross bar for the barricade was dislodged and askance pointing north almost like an invitation, and beyond it nothing but the weak yellow cone of my dust encrusted headlight staring into the black night like a flashlight into a well. It was very dark and lonely.

If I had paid attention to the signs, I should have known. They all registered, or at least each of them did, but I was in override. I was alone running solo and that was wrong: I could have taken the Bronco and a Nung squad, could have bunked at the Special Forces compound until the helicopter pick up planned for 4 a.m.. My Compound mates; boss Colonel Bill "Bull" Dodds (ret.) yelled at me. Lt. Colonel Leroy Suddath (Lt. General to be) said I was stupid, but I put that down to "old guys". This was my war! And so it turned out to be.

I wasn't afraid, but I should have been. The thought of turning back was as impossible to me as it was unimaginable. I was off to war. I had my saddle bag; a "Swedish K" four clips of 36 rounds of para-bellum each, four grenades, two frags, two white phosphorous, "H" harness, three flares, two knives, a Browning 9mm with two clips of 13 under my armpit, and a

.25 cal. Browning with two six round clips in my chest pocket, and I was headed for the most important operation that I had put together in my 10 months in-country.

For the previous week, I had camped out at MACV IV Corps Headquarters setting up the Operation. Late in December our Choung Thien Province Intelligence Officer had received some information of a big "regional-level" VC cadre summit meeting planned for January around the time of the TET celebrations. It was the highest-level meeting we had heard about with any specificity, the others being at the provincial-district level. We had never come close to getting at key level VC infrastructure except sporadically at the local level and they were all KIA on arrival. The source had contact with one of the VC elements charged with its security. Nothing else was known about its agenda or specifically who was attending, but it was big for us and the strategic operation our units and operations were designed for—on paper. A snatch of some of these guys would make some careers on our side of the fence.

For a while, nothing built on that until we got a follow-up that the meeting would occur in the remote western part of the province (inaccessible by road or navigable canal). But the real bombshell was the item that a "high personage from the North" would be attending. This was even more unusual according to the Saigon analysts, COSVN (Central Office, South Vietnam, the covert VC government) rarely interfaced with their northern counterparts in-country for both jurisdictional as well as security precautions.

Everyone from Saigon down was in a flutter, but so far we had no vitals: time and place—without it we'd be throwing paper balls at wastepaper baskets. Finally, we got the word that the meeting would take place on the last day of the month at a remote Buddhist temple in an area highly secured by the VC. We had five days to get it together.

It was all very hot and very perishable stuff. To make sure it remained airtight we had to plan it in isolation of the CHoung Thien PRU and any ARVN support in case of leakage in our own and South Vietnamese commands. This meant that we could not utilize our local support elements that were often the pivotal factor in our operational successes. Instead we selected a PRU team that had demonstrated an excellent command capability from Moc Hoa, in Kien Thuy, province up in the Plain of Reeds along the Cambodian border. There was a big tall Texan up there, another Six-Gun type like Bill Shields of Kien Hoa, who helped me organize and train a special strike force mostly composed of Hoi Chans (VC deserters who had turned). We had two things going for us: the target area was in marshland environment with which they were intimately familiar, and with the assist of Saigon we obtained blow up aerials (enlarged air recon photos) of the temple area from a special Air Force fly-over. With the latter we could train with reasonably accurate simulations.

The temple complex included a series of adjacent huts built up on an elevated earthen mound about 300 yards from the nearest tree line bordering a small feeder canal. The temple itself was relatively large and enclosed, in contrast to many that are essentially open. This allowed for envelopment of the temple area by the main strike force and a separate blocking element for defense against any security force counter attack. As the saying goes everything looked good at the dress rehearsal. But, the key was air support, and for that we needed to sell MACV on the Op.

Back in Can Tho we had two busy days of briefing. The regional command, Kinloch, my "big" boss, said this was my baby and I relished it. It was fun to be a lowly Navy LTJG. rubbing planning elbows with a bunch of colonels on a first name basis. Just so long as I wore civilian clothes that showed no rank, they didn't care. Stuck in the backwater of advising the slow and cautious ARVN, they became enthusiastic about an aggressive clandestine operation normally out of their scope. Through them, we set up the essential logistics.

The plan required a stick of four Huey troop helicopters or "Slicks" from Vinh Long, to pick me up at 0400 hrs at the Can Tho airstrip. I was to direct them to Moc Hoa, pick up the assault team of 30, then rendezvous with a gun-ship detachment out of Sa Dec and prepare for jump off at dawn minus 10. Ground Support Air was laid down for stand-by, vectored out of a U.S. Navy carrier on "Yankee Station" off the coast or from a USAF squadron out of Ton Son Nhut, Saigon depending. If there was a tactical breakdown we were to have enough air support to extract successfully with a "'Dust Off' asset available for casualties, if any. The CIA Mugwumps were swinging their weight in Saigon. If it all went to plan we wouldn't be on the ground more than 30 minutes. But nothing ever went according to plan.

The first snafu occurred when COMMACV (Westmoreland) announced the cease-fire stand-down for the TET festivities, a sort of truce apparently brokered with the VC/NVA. No "offensive" operations would be sanctioned under its effect and duration. The Chief of Staff looked me in the eye and said this meant us, reminding me that without their logistical support there was no Op.

I was on my way to get drunk when the S-3 "Bird" Colonel sent a Captain over to our compound to inform us that we were to remain on full alert and that we were a Priority One if for any reason the Cease Fire didn't hold. That meant don't get drunk. Within 24 hours of the stand-down the same Captain showed up and took me back to MACV Operations. Multiple "incidents" in violation of the cease-fire were occurring in the north and COMMACV was calling it off. Even though there were no reports of "coordinated" violations in III or IV Corps, orders from COM-MACV were to go Operational—ASAP! I was then informed that as far as IV Corps was concerned, our PRU task force was considered the only "capable" offensive operation on their tactical board, although we weren't under their command structure. Wow! Out of 50,000 or more troops and god knows what other military assets, we were "IT" for IV Corps!

At 0200 a.m. February 1, 1968 I was an operation of one, and getting very lonely. The only thing that kept my mind from thinking just how lonely was the concentration it took to dodge and cut around the potholes and side ditches that appeared like caves and ledges in front of my dim yellow headlight. It was hot and dark, so hot that I was sweating through my camys even on the open scooter, so dark I felt I was the only person in the world, my only company the night moths and crickets that blew past the headlamp and the stuttering cough of the exhaust.

A few kilometers out, I saw some flares blossoming in the direction of the airstrip about five kilometers ahead. At first I took this for the typical random H&I fire (Harassment and Interdiction often set up just to preempt and discourage potential sappers around the airstrip perimeter). Closer still, I could faintly make out the whumpfing of mortar rounds and then the "Kraaack" of 105 howitzers joining in. It seemed like the local VC sapper squad was kicking up their semi weekly rocket attack from the western perimeter, nothing to worry about. Wrong again! It wasn't until I picked up the tell tale spray of tracers that I knew something out of the usual was going on. They were fifties! Heavy stuff for a squad engagement, the perimeter guard posts were really getting into it, but most of it was out west and I was approaching from the southeast. What else could I do but keep on going?

There was total blackout at the strip but I could make out the outbuildings and huts along the road as I drew near the entrance gate. I didn't dare shut off the light in fear my approach would be assumed hostile, and there was no place else to go, so I waited for something to happen. I didn't have to wait long.

"Cut that fucking light you asshole or I'll blow you away!" a tense voice boomed out. "We're under fire here! Shit!"

Normally I would have looked around to see who he was addressing, but I just cut the engine. "Who the fuck are you and what the fuck are you doing out there in this shit?" he bellowed, gaining some courage. A large dark figure held an infrared flashlight on me to check me out. They had a right to be pissed. From a distance, what had seemed to be the bi-monthly night skirmish was quickly looking like a lot more. Tracers were lacing the night and every M-60 at a guard post was pissing away at the dark, but there was nothing like a steady squeeze on an automatic to relieve the jitters when you're under fire, or think you are.

The sentry squad was all buttoned up with flak jackets and steel pots, something you didn't see much of unless out in the boonies and under orders. Soon it was clear that these guys were admin types for the Special Forces C Team and weren't part of the usual ground force. The big guy was the NCO in charge and after he settled down, heard me out.

It was hard to explain who I was or how to identify my operation since it had no official military designation that fit in the ordinary checklist for the average NCO, but it was pretty apparent that I wasn't a VC, so he directed me over to the Special Forces Command Center a few hundred feet up the access road to the south of the air strip. By this time, I learned they had not received any direct fire and there had been no actual assault.

The sergeant walked me part way, complaining how everything was fucked up especially at the Command Center where word was coming in that some of the A Teams were taking fire in other provinces. The CO had gone to full alert and no one really knew what was going on. When we parted he added, "Watch yourself out here. Everyone is spooked and most of these guys haven't had a rifle in their hands since they got here. Me, I'm a short timer, two weeks to go. I've had enough of this shit!"

I wheeled the scooter up to the CC and was practically knocked over by three large guys busting out and running over to a jeep. The sergeant was right—the CC of the Special Forces B Team IV Corps was a Chinese fire drill. Crowded with 20 or 30 men in full battle gear, almost everyone was both wearing radio headsets and talking or yelling information to someone else who was doing the same. The dull infrared half-light threw distorted shadows against the walls bringing to mind a prehistoric cave. Walls were lined with Tac (tatical) boards—maps of vague outline stuck with pins of different colored symbols. Harried PFCs constantly subject to the questions, orders, and directions of everyone else sometimes simultaneously yelled out numbers and coordinates and scribbled on the acetate covers in military pictographic sign language. In the middle of the room the senior officers sat on swivel chairs looking somewhat lugubrious in their steel helmets, trying to figure out what was going on—obviously, the situation was out of control: SNAFU.

I tried to pick out a familiar face or at least someone taking a breather from the confusion. No such luck. All I got for my troubles were cutting glances; the kind that say, "who the hell are you and what the fuck are you doing here?" I understood their problem. In the highly stratified society of the military, who you were and what you were was always identifiable. It was written on the uniform. In high formal military occasions one could literally read a man's career by the markings, designations, medals and campaigns mounted on his dress uniform in strict order and sequence. But here I was wandering around in the middle of a command crisis in "Tiger

Stripes" with no rank or affiliation as if I was sightseeing. To them, I was a "Spook", their label for anyone who was, or might be, affiliated with the CIA. With that ambiguity came the vanity of seeming to be anything with no confirmation of what, if anything, that was. The military abhors ambiguity. This meant that I could amble around in their midst—briefly—but it didn't mean I was welcome.

I left without a word. I had troubles of my own. They were fighting their war and I had nothing to do with it, a peculiar but not glorious status; while we fought together for the greater cause, we were nonetheless and sometimes foremost, competitors. That is, "give me mine before they get theirs". The Guts and Glory of war is or becomes a rare commodity that only the greedy want to earn. I was part of that. They were a part of that. We were after the same scalp and eagle feathers. I had a high priority operational rendezvous with a Huey chopper stick scheduled in 30 minutes, something they didn't care a rat's ass about, and their crises' out there weren't mine.

I shouldered my saddlebag and trudged out to the heliport canopy. Jeeps were crawling about in dull half light cast by their low headlight beams, interspersed with vague shadows of troops milling around trying to locate their collateral defensive assignments. Orders shouted in the dark mixed with the obscenities of frustration that I called "Nam/Speak".

I lit a cigarette, (generally something to do when there's nothing immediate to do), and leaned against the upright of the deserted Heliport canopy, watching the scene swirl around me, an unlikely calm center in an unfolding storm, nowhere to go, and nothing else to do. The night's events orchestrated themselves in the cacophony of light and sound. Out on the perimeter 105 howitzers stalked the far tree line with deep-throated "Harrumphs", out-going mortars coughed and kraaaked and the M-60s and .50 cal. machine guns stitched the darkness with long punctuations of bang bangs. The night sky blinked red with the taillights of Huey gunships swarming above the airstrip like angry hornets rousted from their nests. Their rockets streaked into the far tree lines with white tails, Snoopy's electronic gatling guns whirrred like electric buzz saws loosing streams of tracers that always gave me the impression of some invisible giant pissing green.

Each time a chopper returned for fueling my heart jumped with the delusion that it was finally coming for me. The time for their arrival came and went. Then, from the East over the Bassac, a cluster of red taillights appeared. I told myself it was "stick", my bunch coming from Vinh Long. It was a Go! The Op was still a Go!

I was ready, all suited up, with my Swedish K sub machine gun over my shoulder, H-harness loaded up with grenades, water in my canteen, smokes in my left breast pocket, so I jogged low out to the steel matted helicopter pad. Two to three choppers made their approach. Must be mine! As soon as the lead touched down I ran out and jumped into the deck. "Is this the support for Spec Op "Zulu Charlie". I screamed over the rotor wash. "What?" The crew chief yelled, "What operation?" "The Spec Op Zulu Charlie" I yelled back. The Crew Chief turned toward pilot seats and spoke into his intercom mike and waited. When he turned back, his goggles reflected the infrared light instrument glow of the bay, and with the short radio antennas sticking up behind he looked like a giant ant head in a sci-fi movie. Nodding forward, he yelled, "The Captain said he doesn't know shit about any Op. All he knows is that Vinh Long is under VC control, the airport is overrun with gooks and the order went out to emergency evac here. He said to tell you that the whole fucking Delta is under assault and the radio commo is going crazy." "Shit", the crew chief added, "we were lucky to get out ourselves!"

Getting back to the safety of the Compound was lonely and hairy. I couldn't agree with myself over whether it was more or less folly to use or not use the headlamp making my way. Without having to concentrate staying on the road I would have been scared shitless, which is far easier to be when you're alone than with others. And as I was to find out there were others, lots of them. Captured VC battle order documents later revealed that two VC battle regiments were off-loading from the Bassac, converging along the highway and positioning to attack the Ben Se Moi sector I was headed for, leaving to no doubt that they had to have seen me. But I was too insignificant a target to pluck; otherwise I'd be dead in a ditch in the company of flies. So whenever I ponder fate I can always imagine the hundreds of menacing eyes watching me pass that night unwittingly consigning me to the rest of my life.

12

CAN THO WALK ABOUT

Although I never found it particularly graceful, Can Tho was the only place I was long enough and often enough to develop any personal relationship with Vietnamese. While planning the trip in my mind, I allowed myself to entertain an illusion—the possibility that if I wandered its streets long enough that I might bump into one or two people I could recognize. It took less than the five minutes of driving to the town center to dismiss that fantasy as absurd.

In the first place, any I might have associated with were those targeted for banishment or punishment. The lucky got out, some with official assistance with their families, or as refugees by themselves, the latter leaving behind their families and entire life. Of the rest, with the male life expectancy hanging without much improvement around 65, after 30 years, many are dead.

As Houng navigates the old Mercedes toward the river front I watch the humanity of black hair bobbing along the tree shaded avenue in the blue gray haze of midday exhaust and dust and remind myself of what might have happened to the people that I once knew and realize that I have completely forgotten them, as if I had never known them or had never thought about them, as if I have been pretending to be a tourist who passively looks out the window of his air conditioned car and sees people as scenery like trees or buildings instead of recalling that if one rewound time backwards I would find their fate wrapped around me like skin.

Strains of music from a loudspeaker wander from the corner. Houng and I follow its lead. We come upon a small square overhung by a great banyan. Vendors of cold drinks and snacks of peanuts wrapped in cones of newspaper hover around its massive serpentine trunk. An elementary school is letting out on its noon break and little children in their perfect blue and white school uniforms spill from the doorways, yelling and laughing, to buy drinks and ice cream. Houng and I find a bench and drink our refreshments. In the crowded, impersonal town what better for two aimless adults than sitting in the shade and watching small children play.

It isn't as if I had it in the forefront of my mind. In fact I never gave it any thought until I notice an assortment of buildings that resembles a college and realize that somewhere around here is where it happened. Can Tho University of course has grown considerably from its size and style of 30 years before. Today it appears in the form of an attractive collection of small, well kept one-story bungalows separated by tree lined walkways nicely populated with attractive young people carrying books just as I would expect of a small college campus.

To be honest I can't really remember what it looked like back then. I was there only once, and frankly I had other things on my mind. So when I tell Houng to stop and that I want to wander around for a while, I don't really know what I am doing other than trying to find the place I am looking for. When I come to a small park square at the campus corner, what I see seems to have the same lay-out though I remember some open playing fields no longer there. Now it appears as a small park with a small inert carousel; an array of benches around half-filled cement foot pools featuring inoperable fountains, children's sand boxes and jungle gyms. A weathered animal cage with bars sits abandoned, mercifully empty of flea-ridden occupants. Bunches of small children too young for school crawl and squat examining with myopic wonder whatever is in their hands. Mothers under parasols watch and chatter to their neighbors while the same sort of high-pitched oriental singing penetrates the air from the ubiquitous loudspeakers. It is hot, the sun bleak and uninviting, and, in the absence of any comforting shade from trees, the cyclo traffic on the roundabout reminds me of chain saws.

On the strength of a few fragments of memory, I follow a sense of direction which suggests that up the alleyway between what are now the two pool parlors on the corner is an opening that will lead me eventually to a canal that drains from a small river snaking in from the west. If that turns out to be right then I am where I think.

The alley narrows to a cemented walkway and crowds into a close huddle of small one-story houses of crude cement block on lots of approximately 20 ft. by 40 ft.. Most are stuccoed, each with an open patio in front and a laundry drying and cooking space in the rear. Back here the sound of the cyclo traffic is muted. Shade from sprawling banyans dapple the ground and homes. Although It is a crowded and cramped worker's quarters, they are both both neat, and clean. The front patios are decorated with potted plants. Clumps of banana lean over in the corners, small citrus bushes droop with oranges and lime. The veranda spaces are variously filled with bicycles or (if prosperous) the prized moped, lawn chairs and birdcages. Black electrical cords wind and wander like snakes in and out of doorways, window sills and neighbors' walls feeding the new found appetite for the modern electrical, appliances, the first tendrils of modern prosperity. Work benches, tools, piles of broken parts, evidence the moonlight industry of fix and repair as people try to make old ends meet the new ones. It is all so different that I am hesitant to remember it as an abandoned, blasted and charred mess of destruction. Maybe I am in the wrong place? At least I know I am not in the wrong time.

I come upon a woman squatting in front of me sorting through a basket. She is obscured by a conical hat. Aren't they all? She seems alone, solitary, as if she doesn't belong here, an out-of-pocket vendor trying to ply the home-to-home trade with her little consignments. I have to step around her to get by. Startled, perhaps because of my size, she shrinks back and looks up. Our eyes meet and stay fixed. Time seems to stop.

Her eyes are not quite round, light brown, and flecked with yellow around the iris. They are not Vietnamese. Her pale skin has freckles that are seeds from a distant shore. In the moment she takes to focus, her hand instinctually covers her mouth as if to ward off something, or to hide behind it. In the bleakness of her stare anguish sweeps from her like a searchlight. "Excuse me", I say stepping to the side. She is unmistakably an Amerasian war baby.

War Orphans bear the hidden story of war that over all the centuries has not changed. I doubt that few, if any, Americans know they exist and those who are aware know little about them. We have never seen them, heard or thought about them. She is the first and no one had to tell me. The Vietnamese have an official name for them, "Con Lai", but among themselves there is another, "Bu Doi"—the "Dust of Life". That says it all.

Vietnamese have an acute racist sensitivity. Historically squeezed in between the great Indu and Sino worlds, this society has nurtured its own fiercely independent and distinct sense of self, an ingredient of which is racial homogeneity, if not purity. In their two thousand years of survival, the question of who you are has forever been determined by what (or which) you are. The dismal history of oppression and disdainful segregation of its own indigenous minorities from inclusion in the Vietnamese culture is a clear indication of the bitter distaste and resentment of the Con Lai intrusion in their national life. The Politburo, self righteous and vengeful in victory, saw and treated the Con Lai as a stain on their cultural fabric, the detritus left in our wake, and the boot-mark of our retreat. It was characteristic, therefore, and certainly no surprise, that the government has openly and resolutely sanctioned the ostracism of the Bu Doi by exiling their mothers to re-education camps and quarantining the children in segregated orphanages, calling to mind the treatment of lepers in Vietnam's past. Offended by their presence and insulted by their reminder of the recent past, the Vietnamese have actively sought to make some money from deporting them.

Actually-from a cynical point of view-It worked out rather neatly as a quid pro quo of sorts; an exchange of their shame for our guilt; leaving one to suspect that the result was a secret trafficking of their mongrel children for the rotting bones of US MIA lost among unknown jungle hills. Using various charitable organizations as cover over the years, Vietnam has siphoned Con Lai children out of society, shipped them out in dark consignments of unwanted cargo with a secret bill of lading under a shroud of silence.

Today, approximately 21,000 of them have been re-located variously in the Philippines and elsewhere, and are ultimately destined for the U.S..

But reaching that final destination requires the accompaniment of authenticated family members—which, of course, created new opportunities for fraud, abuse and considerable profit among the Vietnamese.

The ones who have gone, both cleared and waiting, are the lucky ones. The woman before me, who knows? Did she have a choice or, having been born luckless, did she miss the only straw that she could draw in the hope for a life?

How long we stare at each other is a blur, but her eyes seem to grasp at me. Neither of us is prepared and even if we could speak, what words would there be? To her, I might be a reminder of the part of her that will never become accepted, the messenger who brings no dream, from the land she will never know. As for me, maybe she belongs to some forgotten moment, a thrust of an urgent desire, the refuse of casual abandonment—and the boot-mark of our retreat.

I want to hurry away but, as in a bad dream, my legs seem frozen. It is hard to catch my breath. Finally, I am able to move, but a ghost sits waiting in the banyan tree. It pulls at me, urging me to turn around and look back, even go back, but when I do, she is no longer there.

I wander on, trying to put the incident behind me, trying to find some reason to forget. In the warren of pathways, I'm momentarily lost, turning one way then another, trying to move in the direction my internal compass looks for. There is no recollection of war here or anything old enough to show it. The entire neighborhood is new, at least to me. How nice, time heals. I chew on that thought for a while until I come upon a junction of pathways right-angling by a small side canal that seems to fit the picture in my memory. I convince myself I have found the place. With nothing else to do, I sit down to think it over.

13

THE LONGEST DAY

By the time I flew back into Can Tho after a week of covering the hot provinces, I was convinced the VC TET Offensive was finished and done for. I had yet to get into a big fight, though I seemed to be chasing them all over the Delta. My assignment was to be a kind of roving temporary military stand-in while spelling the Province Intelligence Officers who were summoned to Can Tho.

Leaders of government don't like surprises (especially when they are assured that highly educated and well taken care of Intelligence Officers are spanning the globe to uncover them, *a priori*). TET was a great big bad surprise. Hence, the local intelligence types I worked with and lived among were called to the carpet at Region for being know-nothings. Region in turn was receiving its come-uppance from Saigon, who were being chewed out by Washington, two months after assuring the entire House of Representatives, Senate, and nation that they had recently seen a "light at the end of the tunnel".

Back at the Compound in Ben Se Moi, everyone was on the roof, watching an air strike on the western edge of town. Word was that a VC reinforced battalion had counter-attacked to provide a diversion to withdraw the badly bloodied remnants of their main force. It was working.

The ARVN, characteristically, stopped the chase and diverted back to town to deal with the threat. The VC regiment's rear guard was cornered at the University. Black smoke and fireballs from the bombing ordnance and the arty was putting on a show less than two miles away. Everyone around me was just watching. I lost it. I picked up my "saddle bag", got my "K", hopped into the jeep and off I went.

It was to be a long afternoon, or a short afternoon that seemed long. Either way it was very close to a lifetime. When it ended I was hanging outside of a helicopter "Dust Off", strapped to its landing strut, juiced on morphine, and a lot worse for wear.

The ARVN battalion was bunched up behind a string of vehicles and armor. Across the road was an open area that looked like a soccer field. In the middle of it sat a burned out ARVN half-track, still smoking. There must have been about two hundred soldiers with their officers just staring at the wreckage. They were in full battle gear, helmets, flak jackets, M-16s, grenades, the whole American made and outfitted costume. The abandoned half-track was theirs. A single B-40 shoulder held rocket launcher (RPG) fired by the slender finger of a single VC who probably did not come up to my chest had taken it out and with it the starch of a battalion that faced no more than a VC company force of less than 60.

Above in the light blue sky, free of clouds, except the man made black ones, two old propeller type A-6s were circling. The RPG Squad was too small a target for them.

I approached a US Army Captain with an Advisor patch to get the sit-rep skinny. He looked at me funny because of my civvies thinking I was some un-credentialed wire reporter running a story, but when told I was running PRUs he cut me in. The B-40/RPG rocket had taken out the lead Half-track and no units were going in until air and artillery could drop on its location. We agreed that neither air nor "Arty" was going to get a fix on a moving target and in the meantime, the place was being blown apart. Anyway, he shrugged, no one was going in until something got the B-40 squad. He rolled his eyes, lit a cigarette, and bitched about working with the ARVNs.

Before our eyes was the state of the war in a nutshell; a fully armed battalion with artillery and close air support unwilling to go in after an enemy less than one-sixth its size armed with comparative pea-shooters. To us, it was an opportunity to cut off and annihilate the main force possibly winning the damn war in the western Delta right in front of us!

Off to the left, I saw a small squad of maybe six or seven ARVNs holed up forward of the battalion squatting behind a building abutting the field.

They looked lonely. It seemed like a good idea at the time, so I crossed the road and joined them. Once there I realized that there was no going back. Something had to be done and I thought I was going to do it.

I motioned with hand signals for "us" to go out and check out the half-track to see if anything was functioning. We were only about 20 yards from it. I thought if we could recover the half-track, at least enough to use its .50 caliber machine gun or recoilless rifle to set up a field of fire for a lead company, we could get this thing going.

I was loaded up with four grenades, my Swedish K with three extra clips, a Browning 9mm and a little .25 caliber in my breast pocket, so I was pretty well set for courage. What I didn't have was any business being there: no assignment, no orders, no authorization and no excuse.

The recoilless rifle was the only weapon that was going to be successful against a bunkered or defense position with a rocket launcher. That would be the ticket. If I was ever going to get a juicy medal, I would go out there like I was smoking a cigar, fire up that Half-track, man the Recoilless and Audie Murphy that thing up the alley guns blazing. So far, there was no sniper activity. I hand signaled to the squad leader that he and another should follow me over there for a look-see, but every time I did he shook his head repeating the phrase "Number Ten. Number Ten", the phrase for "Very Bad".

I stood up and started, better than watching planes drop bombs, but the effort to remain erect was giving me big trouble. Shortly this posture was not obeying commands. I started to bend over. Soon enough I ended up in a low crouch stumbling forward in a hurry, and wishing I could crawl.

No sniper fire! I reached the half-track grateful for its shield. Surprisingly, two of the squad followed. The half-track was going nowhere. It had taken a direct hit. The recoilless was on a twisted mount that made it inoperable at least to us, a relief because I had very limited experience in firing it and I'm sure the two young ARVNS had none. So what! We did something, hardly a step for mankind but more than the battalion was doing, sitting on its ass along the roadway. So we were a little pumped, adrenaline squeezing our common sense, stretching us out like a drug. Back we went, this time with a little more decorum. At least we impressed the squad leader who, in order to avoid losing face, was more enthusiastic about scouting forward into the next building.

It was a dormitory of some sort with four stories, big for those days in that town, empty, and spooky. To be honest it was the first time in country that I had operated in an urban environment. Gone was the curtain of foliage, the soft ground and the shadows of night. Now it was cement floors, hard walls, confining stairways, empty rooms and naked corridors, where sound bounced off everything coming from everywhere. Hot as hell and scared as shit, we reached the flat roof relieved that it had been abandoned. From it we could see out over the sprawling neighborhood below. Its guts had been torn out; it resembled a broken smoldering carcass open to the vultures ringing the sky. In the distance fire and smoke from napalm plumed along the horizon. Someone was catching big shit over there, wedged tight between the canal and the open plains of rice and marsh to the west. It was the hammer and anvil strategy where "our" battalion was to be the hammer and drive the VC into the heavy bombardment out there in the open, but the hammer was standing behind us on the road smoking cigarettes and shooting the shit.

My little group had its shakedown, no hitches so far. Since we had not received any fire, we were getting braver. I figured that the B-40 squad had pulled back, at least that is what I tried to tell the squad leader. I convinced him that we needed to probe further and then, if any contact, report back to battalion. He looked at me like a man who didn't favor the bet but might go along for the first throw. I figured if we made contact, then at least the lead platoon would come up in support and our job would be done. Wrong!

We were a good 100 yards (who knows?) from the battalion, barely in view. Turning the corner it would be goodbye world. I was locked in on getting that B-40 rocket. Though the guys were not about to get ahead of me, at least they were willing to follow. We leapfrogged across an alley and entered the neighborhood we had glimpsed from the dormitory roof. Less than a week ago it had been neat and orderly. No more.

Off the alleys were the row houses, each opening on to a parallel lane or walkway about ten feet wide. Each house backed up against the other, connected by the drying and cooking yards in the rear bordered by six-foot walls. It was a middle class neighborhood of clerks, shopkeepers, tradesmen and functionaries. In order to avoid the open lanes of fire that the alleys allowed, we cut through the row houses. From a bird's eye view, it was a labyrinth and we were the worms. The game became who was to be lost and who was to be found?

A lot of fighting had taken place. The walls were scarred with automatic rifle fire, roofs were blown out, some gutted by fire, charred and black. The population had fled early. The homes were the mess of panic: mangled bicycle tires, strewn clothing, pots and pans, drooping clothes lines, broken picture frames, children's toys, the incidental things that piece family life together had become the debris of its nightmare.

The mantra of SEAL training was teamwork, and the buddy system its badge of honor; swim buddies, Ranger buddies, jump buddies, you name it. Woe to any buddy team if ever separated in any phase of endeavor. Teamwork was the sine qua non of all-operational planning. Every facet of every operation pivoted around it. Every individual had a backup; every squad had a backup. Leaving someone stranded or out on his own sent you home in disgrace, and if a WIA or KIA resulted, you were likely out of the Teams for good. Now I was a stranger in a strange land among strangers making it up as I went along, not far from make-believe.

Like a shut door, the inside closed off the outside world. Within the confined spaces it was the intimate things of the senses that took over the mind: the dryness of the dust, the deadness of the air, the whine of flies, the rank of sweat bleached clothes, eyes smarting, faces dripping from nose to chin. Each knock of equipment, boot grind on rubble, scrape on the wall was amplified. Straining to listen for others, all we could hear were ourselves.

Outside, the roar of the A-6 Sky-Raiders devouring the sky above the palm trees, the thud of 105 Howitzers puncturing the earth and the Whoosssh of chopper rockets splitting the air were all strangely disconnected and abstract in the background. Somewhere out there were desperate men fighting for their lives. We were close to the real thing, somewhere on its fringe. Everything was condensing.

The remnants of the last main force VC regiment attacking Can Tho were getting hammered. They had held the University area for five days and its rear-guard was covering their withdrawal. They were close up against the canal that ran from the marshes to the west. Its confluence formed a large palm grove by now a warren of mud bunkers and blasted trees. Their retreat lay in the open to the west as long as they could last until nightfall.

We were getting mighty lonely. Nobody from the battalion had come up to fill the gap, but I wasn't much concerned about the VC behind us. Ahead of us was a storm of fire. We had crossed the borderline of our support. The ARVNs were at the end of their tether. I could tell by their eyes and gestures, for on tight patrols the eyes and hands do all of the talking. They looked back and forth at each other, their peepers were big and round as grapes ready to burst, wondering why they were following the big "Round Eye" with the blue tropical shirt into trouble, when they could be back on the road standing down, smoking their Salems in the late afternoon shade, as the air strikes did their work for them. They were about to break on me at any time, and it happened soon enough.

I had just slung myself over a rear wall (about 6 feet high?) separating one backyard from another, and was signaling back to two others to follow when I heard some rustling of stone and scraping of equipment on gravel ahead. I crept forward along the cooking veranda to the side running toward the front. The front casement had a large gap to the right of the doorway of the front patio where it had taken a hit. I had just enough time to get behind it when the AK opened up. The rounds hit high above me showering bits of plaster and kicking up plumes dust filling the room. I threw myself backward and crawled for the drying yard. The ARVNs "Di Di Maued" (bugged out) and I was alone and terrified. I can't remember a worse feeling. At least I didn't vomit.

Fortunately, my first instinct was to face him rather than run. If he, or they, got in the perimeter of the house I would never make it back to the wall or over. It was a lucky choice because I caught him coming on the run. We were both stunned by our apparitions. He threw himself sideways and back out the doorway over the front stoop. I fired a burst and I missed, from no less than ten feet! I raced to the doorway and threw myself behind the rubble of the casement. He was outside. I was inside. I won the higher ground, advantage me.

I was trapped and he knew it, advantage him, but so was he,. He had jumped into a spider hole (a ground hole dug approximately 3ft wide and 4ft deep where a man could crouch almost fully protected from any bombardment save direct hits) dug in the middle of the lane not ten feet from where I was. It was his first chance for cover and I caught him before he could make his next move. The front side of the house was blown out. I was nudged into the corner. If either of us tried to take off neither would have made the distance. He was short and stocky, wide faced, dark skinned and his hair stuck up like a wire brush above a red headband, the squad leader!

With the angles each had, one of us would have to expose himself to nail the other. I had to look around the wall to fix him in his hole. He had to raise up to line his fire. We made damn sure both didn't occur at the same time. In the gamble for existence natural selection worked out a rough rotation; he'd fire and then I would.

The sense of linear time had broken down, collapsing into a confusion of dimensions, where the sequences of time and space became a mess and consciousness a sideshow, sidelined by the five-alarm fires of reaction. Within some desperate minutes, less or more, who knows?, a clip and a half out of the three were gone. Everything was so electrified that I can remember watching bullets buzzing past as slow as bees—wings vaguely registering a gaseous diffusion before the tiny puffs of smoke chipped away at the mud stucco wall behind. The trapped air became thick with dust, dirt and smoke, and dry as cement.

Somewhere, somehow, I heard him barking commands in that piercing staccato of Vietnamese that turns harshly from sing-song into the sound of chopping wood. I didn't catch a word but I understood everything. He was calling out his squad to tell them he needed ammunition, that I was pinned down and how to maneuver to break my line of fire, what else? It made me want to do the same if only to find courage in a voice desperate for company.

I was tumbling around in a sewer of fear. Somewhere in me I knew I was going to have to make a run for it. I had trapped myself in the corner with only one safe angle off to the left looking out and down the lane and across. Everything said "GO", but I simply couldn't do it. My courage bank had sprung a leak. "Clink" I heard something solid and heavy land very close, "incoming". I didn't see it but I knew by instinct what it was, a hand grenade! Right from the movies, "One thousand One, One thousand Two, Three thousand…

Too late to run. I knew by training that only the lowest profile gives a chance at survival as the explosive energy goes up and out, not down. I cringed in the corner in a fetal position of meek surrender. Nothing happened. I waited. How long, I could never know, How many moments can fit in a second?. I couldn't, didn't want to look. Cupping my hands over my face and spreading my fingers like a little boy there it was, five feet away. I hid my head in my arms! Nothing happened, maybe a dud, must be a dud!

Another came in—the same "clink" in the debris. This time I was off and threw my self back towards the back room. The world exploded with a furious sound raining dust and pulverized stucco screening me from the outside just enough to crawl forward again. He was about to make it out of the spider hole. I fired a three round burst that put him aback in. I had 3 grenades of my own in the satchel.

It was not a thing I'd seen in training films. I had never dealt with close-in grenade throwing. It had never been an accuracy thing, just a lob it in the general direction to keep the enemy hunkered down or to clear out a bunker, or hooch.

I am now an expert. In the first place, the cotter pins don't loosen like they do in the movies (any one who has actually pulled a grenade pin with his teeth has lost them in the process.) I'd been flying around in planes so my grenades were doubly secure, making its operation a two-handed thing, that required dropping my weapon. Grenades are timed at 2.5 to three seconds before detonation. How long is that when time is moving at warp speed? Too quick, he could lob it out before detonation. Too long after the spring lever makes it hot and you can become your own casualty. I had a friend dead from that.

The situation required a perfect hook shot and I was as ham-handed a basketball player as they come. Pulling the pin, releasing the spring lever, timing the right interval before throwing so it would detonate at the instant of arrival called for life altering precision.

No dice. I just pushed it out there afraid to expose myself enough to gauge it. The wait seemed forever. It finally blew, shattering the air like a furious steel fist; god help any flesh in its way. It was a miss but kept him down. Frantic, I pulled another, took more care and ducked away again. It looked good. Believe it or not, the fucking thing went in and out. Bamm! The sonavabitch had bagged it. He was too good, too hard. I was over my head.

But it went on, trading bursts. I was getting low, last clip, but he was in the same shape a nightmare we couldn't get out of. All I wanted was for it to disappear. It didn't.

Something moved above me, a scrape of something dragging over the planking. There was a loft with a ladder leading up to it above and behind my shoulder. I hadn't been able to give it any notice. I listened again. Something there, someone crawling. In a reflex before I could think I swung my K up and fired a burst through the floorboards by the hatch. A rifle, a Chicom bolt action, came clattering down.

A man followed. He tumbled and slid down the ladder as in slow motion, limp and easy. There was no time to move and he came to rest slumped against me warm and soft, barely alive. I shook him off afraid of a struggle for his gun and flung it against the wall. He made no sound, no movement. I didn't want to look at him or feel him. I was swarming with revulsion.

In some psychological dissolve, the object became human. He was neither young, nor warlike; an ordinary older man soiled and stained, flung open like a shot bird. His shirt was torn and ripped open showing a smooth hairless chest of coppery skin marred by a dark puckering hole filling with bubbling mercurous blood. I got him high in the gut. His eyes were swollen, grapes about to burst in vague fascination, mouth open with an "Oh" of amazement at a strange dream. No sound came, no movement stirred. Looking down at him less than a foot away, I wanted him to die. Looking up at me, he thought I was going to kill him. He was right. I wanted to. I needed to.

I was getting beyond my resources, a struggling man swimming for a point too far, all his rescues gone. Too much was happening: abandoned and alone, the VC squad leader tougher than me, ammunition almost gone, no more grenades, two clips for my 9MM, this guy staring at me, and God knows who out there. I wanted to scream. Maybe I did.

I had dropped my guard and whirled around to line up the spider hole. No black hair spiked like a wire brush bobbing up and down. No red flash of headband. The guy had made his move, but where? Just as I was clawing some tiny space of sensory reality out of what I could see and hear, the paranoia of the unknown flooded my system. In the crude chemistry of fear, just when one threat receives compensation another creates a new demand, "Better the devil you know than the one you don't". Where did he go, what was he doing, where was his squad? Could I run for it, or were they waiting for me?

The dying man followed me with his eyes, so close that we inhabited the same space hollowed out of the smoke and dust shrouded air, fouled by a fetid soup of blood, urine and released feces that spread out below him in the rubble like a dark snake. I couldn't move without shifting his body around like a loose bag. Every jostle met with a low moan and labored sigh. Not much longer for him. His ghost was gathering up. He was dying, and alone.

Never throughout his entire life, including the day before, could he have seen himself lying in the rubble emptying his life's fluids on the ground next to me. He was too weak to blink and flies settled around his nose and eyes lapping and probing the last moistures of his life. And what about me, would it be the same? Would whoever found me notice the flies getting their licks in? And what would happen then to both of us? He, wrapped in white muslin in a wooden box, me in a slick black body bag ready for air mail, after some confusion of who I was and what was I doing there. Did I have my dog tags on? I reached for my throat to assure they were. "Did you hear about the Wilbur boy?" some would remark. "Wasn't he the kid who ran away from school years ago? Silly war, isn't it" might be the off hand remark and answer in the club locker room. It would go something like that for a few days.

Still alive though, we were the only two people left in the world, each the sole witness to the other. For it was "Us" strangely in the alchemy of mind that serves survival, to leap from foe to friend, companions, if only in despair. And what if he left me, then what? The thought of total isolation withered through me, like a hole in the night.

I caught his eyes shifting away from me for the first time and holding a gaze over my right shoulder then back to me again. He gave no expression. It no longer mattered to him. Something was moving outside and close, sandals ground on the on graveled surface slow and hesitant.

It seemed so long ago, the grenades, the firing, the smoke, the war. I had dropped my guard. It couldn't have been longer than 30 seconds. Still I wasn't ready for it, too busy feeling sorry for myself and now I was slammed back to business, suddenly focused. I flattened my back against the wall. The "K" was out of ammo. All I had left was a Browning 9MM automatic, 13 rounds maybe. When did I last fire it? Was the clip full? I raised the muzzle with both hands in a prayer position and pressed against the wall motionless and still, suffocating with the disbelief of what was about to happen. The only question remaining was from which side. I never had any inkling of what doom actually meant but I'd swear it blew past me.

Our faces appeared no more than a foot away. He was so young, his face so smooth, such big eyes, so surprised, stunned, dazed or drugged. From an unknowable impulse I lunged to grab him. I could have wrestled him to the ground without much effort. I could have captured him, I wouldn't have had to kill him, I wouldn't. He backed up. Slowly, too slowly, he brought up his AK-47, too slowly.

I shot him down dead within five feet, two maybe three rounds. Spinning from the impact, he crumpled like a paper puppet, his life string slackening from the sky. There was no movement. He was without life, twisted, his gun askew and bandoleers splayed out on the dry dirt of the alley and two satchels of B-40 rockets strapped around his chest. It was the B-40 squad after all. The squad leader had sent him in. He thought I'd been hit or Di Di Mau'd out of there. The sonavabitch had ordered him forward, with a gun to his back. They'd dressed him up in a uniform, loaded him with three banana clips, grenades, handed him a new AK, wrapped him up like a bomb, pumped him up with some weed and bullshit and sent him to slaughter. Probably didn't even know how to use it. Fucking shits!

AKs, two or three of them, spit long bursts from across the way. There was some hate and fury in them and I knew why. The killing was ugly. The doorframe was shattered, dry plaster dust kicked up into a fog, then silence. If there was a squad out there they would envelop and find an angle. Either that or they were pulling back. Either way, I'd been too long in the same place. There was no help out there; no evidence that I wasn't fighting my own little war, up shit's creek and no more paddle.

Whatever was going on, I had to get the kid's weapon and ammo. I had no choice. Eight or ten rounds of a handgun left me near to naked. He lay sprawled out, twisted face down, leg bent in half stride as if reaching for his life too far away. I'd have to crawl out and drag him back, a big bullseye at short yardage. It was about six or seven with no cover. No way I was going to run out and strip him. I was choking with the thought of it. I didn't think I had the guts to do it, but I had to. I waited as long as I could. Almost hyperventilating, I crawled out and grabbed his ankle.

To this day I remember the touch, can feel how slender, warm, and smooth it was-like a girl's. The body seemed empty of weight light as a rag-doll. I pulled him half inside the doorframe. Already his bowels had released and their stench lay on him leaving in his path a greasy smear of urine and feces the color of rust. A pool of blood not yet absorbed by the dirt shined like red paint. I ripped off his bandoleers and grabbed the AK leaving the B-40 rockets and potato masher grenades. I was struck by how utterly lifeless he was, how instantly his spirit flew away, leaving only an empty bundle behind.

Exhausted I fell back against the inside wall catching a glance of the wounded man's stare. His eyes had loosened into a dark wonder and I could feel it withdrawing forever from the now meaningless connection with the world we shared. His breathing was only barely perceptible. I loaded up the AK all the while jabbering things like "you'll be all right, I'll get you help, you'll be all right", "I'll get a medic", gibberish to keep me company.

I was getting very crazy. Thoughts were breaking down: hands fumbling with things. Loading the AK with one hand with another on my 9mm Browning, jerking my head about looking for their next move, the dread of unknown and unknowable things happening around me that I couldn't see or react to. My attention was so splintered I couldn't figure out the priorities. Run? Where to? Bring all the weapons? Crazy! Take the guy? Leave the Guy? Which way to go? No one to cover! Where were the VC? No one to cover. Run? When? No one to cover. No teamwork, no team, no Swede, no Pee Wee, Schultz, Miller, Moose, Muckle, Todd, "Fast Eddy", Leasure, Gosser, the ballroom dancer. Jesus! How did I get into this! Lost in this shit hole. You dumb fuck!

Whatever time was, it was flying, I should have been long gone. I looked down at the dying guy. Seconds before I'm babbling like he's my soul mate, but now he's done meat. Like a light switch he was out of my mind, just part of the debris. Everything was back to ME, survival kicked back in. The little boy shit was over. For the moment I had found my armor. Out the corner of my eyes I saw two or three VC break for it up the lane. They were dumping me, pulling back. I went for it.

I hit the back wall with all I had. Coming down on the back side, a strap pulled from its hinged hook and the AK dropped on the wrong side! I was sobbing with exhaustion, my bank of adrenaline emptying, its ragged acids leaching with despair.

"Never get separated from your weapon!" is one of the sternest maxims of the military, all reasons for which become self-evident. Without it, I was simply paralyzed. The difference between fear and cowardice is one of degree. To be separated from your weapon in combat can define this. Fear is a chill that clutches the heart, cowardice freezes it. I could feel it trying to break. I was used up. But it was very clear that I was either going to go back over that wall to get that weapon or sink down into the corner with my head between my knees and cry. I had to get a grip, no choice.

If I was going over, all the terror of my throat was going with it. Together we were going to out-roar the demons. Together we went over. Together we got back. Then we simply ran for it like a jailbreak that it was. I couldn't remember where I had come from but I knew I was getting away from where I'd been. I was in automatic now, feeling fluid, wired and aware. Alive!

Somehow, I found the GVNs who had taken off. It was amazing! They were looting an abandoned house. Some were huddling and smoking in the main room pawing over personal items strewn around, but one that I will never forget was toying with a little girl's doll. I went nuts and fired clip into the walls and ceiling. Inside the semi-closed room the noise and dust was so stunning we were all shocked. Staring wide-eyed at each other, for a few moments it came pretty close to murder. At the height of the standoff the US Army advisor I had first talked to, it seemed like hours before, showed up with his ARVN counterpart officer and took charge. After hearing my firefight, his unit had finally been sent up. When I calmed down a bit I told him that we had found the B-40 rocket squad and that they were withdrawing over the canal.

Breaking out had given me another rush of adrenaline. Having company and some back up made me heroic. I was ready to go back in and convinced the advisor and his squad to follow.

Approaching the canal the firing picked up. There was some serious contact ahead. Some artillery was laying in and a squadron of Huey gunships was making rocket passes. Hurrying forward we passed a dead ARVN. His helmet lay beside him. Some instinct made me put it on. I had never used one the entire year I'd been in country, too hot, too cumbersome, but with all the artillery and gun-ship rockets a lot of things were flying in the air. Nearing the canal, we entered a house whose rear wall had been blown out. The ground fell off down to the canal bank. Everything was a mess back there, broken palms, burnt foliage, mud tossed up with the upheaval of exploded ordnance and over across the canal nimble figures in flight running like hell. A platoon of them. I knelt and started firing, something off to the side appeared. It was all I would ever know.

The explosion was frightening. It had a terrible sound. Smoke, cordite, acrid dust filled the space. I was lying in a pile of rubble surrounded by moaning and coughing. I was dead. I thought I was dead. Everything was sticky and wet. Part of my head had been blown off, my brains were running over my eyes, I didn't want to touch it but what else was there to do? I raised my hand. Why was I thinking this if my head was blown off? I touched my head. It was there. It wasn't brain matter, it was blood, lots of it. I got on my knees. Endless noise, still bodies, smoke, dirt, rubble. I wanted to go home, thoughts of my Mother flashed through me with great yearning. "Medic!" I yelled as if for her. "Medic!" The space began to fill with shapes of people, the Army captain saying something like "You're all right", "You're lucky", he kept reassuring me, "You're lucky".

I *was* lucky: of the guys with me, I think two or three were killed. One took most of the blast. Best guess was that it was a grenade or a B-40 round (they got me at last). The helmet I picked up was perforated and I only received shrapnel splinters in my scalp, neck, left shoulder and back, all of which made a mess of blood but that was the worst. I was lucky for sure. They shot me up with morphine, mostly for a tranquilizer, and carried me out.

After screening at the field station I was tagged some color and sent over by jeep to the airstrip where it all started a lifetime ago. We were Med-Evac'd out on a Chopper late that afternoon. To make space for two criticals they took me off the bay and strapped me to the outside landing strut. With all the sedation of Morphine I was ready for bed. People were yelling at me as if I was far away and I kept nodding because I was. They were worried about the straps holding and I tried to help them until I felt that I was a child in a car seat. Just as they finished, the landing strip was mortared. Swirls of brown dirt and smoke blew up, people started running all over the place. I was slow in figuring it out but the pilots got nervous and the chopper started jumping around. Jim Ward, my boss, tried to run out and see me but he was shouted back. I tried, but couldn't quite wave goodbye.

Dust, smoke and exhaust from the down draft of the rotors billowed into a cloudy haze burnished bronze by the setting sun. The chopper rose, pivoted and hovered waiting for the lead to clear out. Held in by the restraining straps, I hung out over my dangling boots dreamily watching the confusion below. Black smoke from the mortaring drifted through. I wondered vaguely what the problem was.

Spiraling up and twisting to get free we suddenly banked east over the wide brown Bassac River and were gone. The air cooled, and the laminate land of the endless green Delta became aloof and unmoved by the turmoil left behind. Its checkered geometry of fields and dykes became a distant chessboard much too vast for humans trying to mess up the table and ruin the game for the sky gods whose bets were still posted.

At three thousand feet, the chopper blades whirred softly in a poppa poppa poppa. Twilight softened the horizon into an orange and purple divide. The great serpentine rivers splayed out and twisted their slate bodies toward the sea beneath the paling light. I hung over the strut like an ornament on a shade pull peering down in a dazed and lazy peace thinking what a wonderful seat I had of the world and how at some point I would go to sleep. Somewhere behind me, medics were working on the guys on stretchers in the well deck, but I was a universe of one. In this tiny envelope of space gathering into darkness another day was closing with the gentle turn of the earth over a dark and endlessly foreign shore.

We landed at dusk at Dong Tam the US 9th Army Division HQ near My Tho. The ambulatory were put in a truck to await secondary medical vetting and treatment after the criticals. I heard later that the two on our chopper didn't make it. The hospital was a vast inflatable tent of rubberized vinyl wrapped around a prefab structure like a giant jungle gym.

At some point in time I was led to the operating table and the doctor started picking out the shrapnel and stitching me up until I noticed with mild interest that the ceiling was falling down very slowly, or rather, deflating. The doctor asked me if I could get up and the next thing I knew I was carrying out the stretcher cases and loading them back on trucks until I was told to lie down on one. At some point we were hurried with marvelous care to waiting DC3s or Caribous and flown off to Saigon. Our arrival at Ton Son Nhut was coordinated with a med-evac to Japan.

Those who were non-ambulatory were immediately trucked over to big C-130s lined up and waiting for loading from all over the country and immediate evacuation to Japan. I had no desire to go to Japan, and wasn't hurt bad enough to go home. I had some friends who were doctors at 7th Field Hospital at Ton Son Nhut and one of whom by chance was doing the screening. I remember arguing with him about staying. After all it was just some loss of blood, so they told me to sit down. It was a good thing that I did because I think I passed out. It had been a long day.

14

THE FOOL'S GRIN

I am suddenly brought back to the present by little children approaching from various pathways in ones and twos. Who is this tall foreigner back here in our neighborhood they wonder? What is he doing, where is he going; they whisper and giggle among themselves. I am the blissful moment, the stranger, a new and different world to stare at. Joy ripples in the warm pools of their eyes, smiles stretch like balloons, as their young lives spread open as wide as the sky. Too young to know anything but being children, they crowd around, stare and gawk, poke each other giggling in such an open manner as to inspire delight. Their bright light startles me, as if I stepped out of a cave.

Soon their number clogs the small walkway and I become the captive of their attention, the game they want to play. I motion them to pose for a group picture, watching excitement ripple and splash among them. They call out for all to join in and cling to each other like vines. It is a great success that has to be repeated, and then again. I bask in the contentment of being their Pied Piper. As soon as the pictures are taken, wanting nothing but for the fun of it, they run off skipping and whirling around waving goodbyes.

Finding my way back, Houng has his worried look on as if he lost me or the other way around. He had no idea where I wanted to go, and I wasn't much help, so we decided to go west. Finally the outskirts of Can Tho are in our rear view mirror, and we can turn off the laboring AC and roll down the windows. We are heading due west for Vi Thanh, the province town of Choung Thien Province. My recollections of Choung Thien were of it being a wild-west sort of place, overlooked and under-represented in the military-political strategies of the war, but menacing and resisting organized efforts to tame it. It was the outlaw territory of the Delta and Vi Thanh was its "Dodge City". That was why I always liked it. It was a broken swampy region, land-locked between bordering provinces. I had never experienced the luxury of driving to Vi Thanh. In former days it was isolated and cut off by road. In a classic guerrilla warfare stalemate, the VC completely controlled the countryside, while the fortress GVN controlled the city and one or two of its garrisoned towns. Having only one road from Can Tho, blocking it, mining it or ambushing it was a VC operational ritual that led to its eventual disuse and abandonment. When an older colleague reported to me in 1973 that the road was driveable without an escort, I concluded that the militarily war was won, de facto (which of course it was—in the South).

The western half of the Delta had long been the frontier of the country. It had not been fully settled or agriculturally developed until the French arrived in the mid-19th century with the industrial engineering and economic capacity to develop it by draining and canalizing its vast and previously unmanageable wetlands. Before this, it had been variously populated by Cambodian/Khmer elements to the north and Chinese fishing and mercantile interests along the South China Sea coast and the Camau peninsula. In terms of the Vietnamese geography, it was the ass end of the country, and Vi Thanh its least likely attraction.

When the road narrows from two to one lane, I know I'm in Choung Thien. At long last, unbroken countryside appears. Unencumbered by wires, poles, signs, and machines, the Delta regains its utter calmness. Houng slows down, and in silence without the blare and bark of traffic we let the breezes filter our thoughts. One or two times we stop simply to get out to take a piss alongside the road and smoke a cigarette in silence.

The road parallels a long narrow canal, part of the water network that is the traditional and most reliable transportation system for the entire western environment. Along its banks, spread out like a necklace, is a string of hamlets that makes up the village system that, with little exception, forms the essential organizational fabric of Vietnam's agricultural peasant society. The sociology of the village is anciently prescribed and the subject of substantial anthropological study. The mud-thatch family homes and land plots form into the sub-grouping of hamlets, the smallest multi-family communal unit within the village system. Each hamlet generally reflects a certain familial or economic function with its particular nucleus of leadership. The village constitutes the comprehensive version of these communal groupings as the composite mosaic of its environment. In the Delta, this is the "rice", or "water" culture whose matrix is dominated by the maintenance of basic water management systems such as irrigation and dike-building around which collective labor is apportioned. It is this socio-economic foundation that has developed and sustained a self-governance for most of its history What one sees in the Vietnam countryside then is not simply the rustic or pastoral but an anciently interwoven and intricate design whose root-ball comes from the Chinese archetype and Confucian belief system.

Along the canal, the wooden dugouts of hollowed log and molded plank nestle beneath bamboo footbridges spanning over the waterway. Water buffalo are tethered in the thatch-roofed stable. Chickens hunt and peck among the offal. Ducks float on the cloudy caramel surface, swept about as if they were toy boats in a breeze. Small children huddle near doorways in their little groups examining the secrets of ants, crickets and butterflies, poking with sticks or drawing circles or other inventions. Rice bundles dry on mats.

Each home or living area demonstrates a regimented neatness even in the meanest of structures. The "beira", or hearth way, is raked and swept clean, the essential tools precisely hung in their traditional locations, the water jugs by the doorway, the upraised vegetable plot perfectly rowed. Everything is cast in the unadorned earthbound shades of its makeup: husk, thatch, coconut, leather, wood, iron, water creamed by loam and mud transmitting all together the humbleness of necessary things in concert with the endless patience of making do.

A small boy sits upon the thick black neck of the water buffalo. A snow-white egret alights calmly on its broad rump. Together in symbiotic union, they remain motionless as if standing watch over a kingdom suspended in the perfect balance of a deep Buddhist dream. Clouds topple like broken pillars from the blue pavilion of the sky. Spring green fields

spread around them in a vast apron spotted with the bright coins of conical hats that bob and bend over new rice plantings as if in prayer. Not far
from here and maybe over there beyond several tree lines I remember it the
same, even when it was not the same, when the peacefulness of the land
and the quiet rhythms were ripped open and torn apart.

We had worked since dusk to get in position to hit the hamlet where
the VC tax collector lived with his armed enforcement squad. First, we
commandeered a water taxi to go up a canal until it opened upon a broad
and undefined swamp. From there, we poled and paddled in dugouts
along the water's winding course beneath a moonless sky blanketed with
stars. The only sounds were the whine of mosquitoes, the fevered throb of
cicadas, the lacy drip of trailing poles, the gurgle of paddles, soft murmurs,
the slide and scrape of weaponry. Finally, the "Hoi Chan" (Ex VC who
either deserted or were captured and turned to the other side) pointed out
the hamlet. In the dark, it appeared no more than a swollen bruise of
higher ground shouldered by a dense tree line.

Together with my two Vietnamese bodyguards we found a buffalo wad-
dle in a bordering coconut grove to await the dawn flare. The air was
damp and thick, a halo of mosquitoes quivered and circled drawn by the
slick of sweat. Our odor was sweet and pungent. The mud pool was body
temperature. It was hard to tell which part of you was in or out. The waiting seemed to go on forever.

With a pop and cough, the flare burst open like a giant match striking
darkness. The crack of M-79 grenade launchers and the rip of M-16s tore
open what was left of the night. Black smoke with the harsh bite of cordite
plumed up into the trees and hovered over the canal shining dully with the
reflection of the dying flare. More flares, more explosions stitched by knots
of semi and automatic rifle fire. Fierce and fearful shouting, commands
desperate for courage or frantic for escape, were overcome by the screaming of infants and the women trying to gather, and clutch them tight, all
just torn from a dream into a nightmare.

The firing died down, then flared furiously on the far flank. The blocking ambush had snared the fleeing VC. A gulp of silence held, then
another. The strike was over, its shattering violence tailing off into the

sounds of human wailing, crying, and raging. A wounded water buffalo bellowed. Dying flares burned orange and then red reeking a little like smoldering rubber. A distance away, still some shouting and sporadic shots. The wounded had been brought to ground. A short burst of automatic fire seemed to close out it out. Then the telltale single reports of a handgun, probably to the head of the dying or wounded—who could tell which—finished it.

Dawn came as a dirty gray rag. Dogs, dumb with terror crawl low on their haunches, turning in circles tails hugging their bellies, ears flat., Frantic chickens rushed about in the same state, too stupid to fly. Ducks hid under the bushes overgrowing the banks. The weak light revealed a torn scene of sudden disarray and debris that minutes before was an orderly arrangement of careful living. The pop and crackle of a smoldering hootch filled the air and burned our nostrils with acridity.

Using a makeshift megaphone, the Field Commander shouted orders for the inhabitants to come out from their mud bunkers and tunnels inside their hootches and assemble. After the careless prodding of rifle muzzles, the stunned villagers, bent over by the weight of fear, shuffled out into the ruined irreclaimable day.

They were those not quick enough to flee, those who had nothing to flee for, those who were clutching their children or hiding behind them, were too old or too young, too helpless or too hopeless, all caught between the devils of each side; each promising much and delivering little so that when it came time to fill the plate of ordinary fare it was misery all around. In time they were all there, people who lived on a raised mound of earth in a great swamp remote from power but not far away enough from its ability to do harm—and nowhere else to hide.

These were the same who had squatted and had waited in the same spot the week before, or the month before, when the VC came to enforce their tithes: of money for guns and explosives, rice for eating, labor for fabricating ramparts, digging tunnels, setting booby-traps, and for harboring their wounded, and even then and after all this, in the end, to march their sons away, fodder in a dubious cause promising a chimerical end.

And when the righteous VC cadre departed, they left behind the local faithful, the ones who, in practicing their faith, created a target for reprisal. These were the ones that fled or lay dead in the pale morning light, their blood still emptying just over there sprawled in some bush or splayed in a ditch, people who had been too late or too early and not quite far enough away.

Our commander was a tough committed warrior, a veteran of four wars over the last 30 years with multiple scars to show for it. He understood his life, how he survived, and how he became his version of the warlord: how to swear fealty and require it, how to risk all and to gather what he might, how to be fearless and inspire it, and how to be cruel and ask no quarter. He begins his interrogation, strutting like a cock before his chickens. A small wiry man sporting a broad brimmed hat for show, an ugly mouth featuring two shining gold caps, and dwarfing his hand the prize of a chrome .45 cal. Browning automatic half the size of his arm. He makes demands in a high-pitched, slightly feverish voice. It elicits sullen denials, which earn sudden blows, the sound of a boot against flesh and bone, the grunt and sigh of lost unrecoverable breath, a toppled body stilled by assault.

I watched. I was there, but I was not there. This was a presentation for me, but not me, a faulty but willful demonstration of loyalty and fealty that announced "Here we are, we who serve you. We do this to secure our courage and earn our pay." It was not personal, as the assholes of the world are proud of announcing while readying the knife, "Its just business".

I was the counter-insurgency "consultant" sent from headquarters to evaluate production, a phase of our quality-control program so to speak. There was a pricing for the weapons, bonuses for the level of victim, and incentives for "turning" the opposition. They had recovered weapons; two AK-47s, three Chicom rifles of old vintage, and the prize, a Soviet made Beretta belonging to whichever one of the dead was the senior squad leader. The operation was a success and the commander knew it.

The squawk of PRC field radios scratched at the raw morning air. The babble of radio-speak in ratta-tat-tat Vietnamese went on back and forth among the squad units securing the perimeter. We didn't have long before some form of counter-attack. The commander, tired from his physical efforts at brutality, and bent on impressing the villagers that he was a man of power, put on a show of cheap magnanimity. The villagers, trembling in their misery and waiting for their ordeal to come to an end, were toting up their losses and preparing to make the necessary obsequies of submission. With their hands held prayerfully together they cringed and made various required promises to uphold and obey whatever greater power was to claim them at the time, while the commander, knowing full well that the mantle of authority would soon be reclaimed by the VC when we withdrew, puffed and strutted in his momentary ascendancy until he soon lost interest.

In a mordant closing gesture, he raised his huge automatic pistol and fired a hole into the blue sky, releasing the villagers back into their sundered lives and then turned quickly to the more direct practicalities of getting the hell out of there. A VC nest had been kicked. It was their turf, and we were a long way from home.

In assembling to move out, my Vietnamese companions in the mud jabbered at me excitedly, eyes still bulging a little too much with the adrenaline rush of combat and as a gesture of camaraderie stick a cigarette to my lips and light it with the pride of owning a Zippo. "Salem" they confirm the gift. "Yes, it's good", I nod thankful for the cool smoke that curls deep and gratefully into my stomach. "Yes, yes!" he replies, "It is good, Salem No. 1!"

One after another they come up and touch me gently on the shoulder and grin the fool's grin of being alive among others who are dead. "Boucoup, boucoup VC" (sounding "wee see") they say, holding up five fingers as if the KIA were their gift to me. "No. 1" I intone repeatedly as if I am grateful and drag ferociously on my second or fifth Salem grinning with them—the fool's grin.

15

THE LAST ONE HORSE TOWN

Vi Tanh, the province town of Choung Thien, is still a one-horse town, praise be. It used to be a motley and haphazard arrangement of one-story structures grouped around the usual ochre colored prefecture facing a dirt square—and it is little changed. Its location is a crossroads of sorts, or more accurately, a cross-canal juncture, facilitating the waterborne commerce to other parts of the province. While the place reflects the changes between the good times and bad, within the hearths and sleeping spaces, and among their ancestors' shrines and carefully potted plants, the inhabitants seem to expect little more than fate has given them.

The communal center of town is dominated by an iron-trellised bridge. Here the local market comes to life in the cool mornings. It has been raining steadily for last hour; the stalls are closed down temporarily. Business is bustling for the Pho stands hugging the canal bank beneath a multi-colored array of tarps and plastic sheeting strung among limbs of a great banyan tree. We join the huddle of vendors and town's people and find a bench with a makeshift table.

The atmosphere is close and friendly; everyone is taking advantage of the rain delay. Rain mist blows in and mixes with the warm steam and smoke rising from cooking fires and rice pots. Cheap cigarette smoke and damp body odors stir up a swampy brew. The faces of the locals are varnished to a deep sheen, accentuating the varying pigments and shapes that denote an intersection of mixed cultures, the darker Khmer and the Indochine.

Houng orders noodle soup after his assurance that I agree on the choice of ingredients. Being a long-legged foreigner in this group I attract a lot of glances and comment. More than once a man, always older, wanders up stares politely and then retires to engage in discussion with his friends about who, or rather what, I am.

While waiting for the Pho, Houng and I go over the Lonely Planet map. We are planning to go west to Rach Gia on the western coast of the Bay Of Thailand. Houng wears his perpetual frown when he confronts something he is unsure of and turns to the man next to us to ask about the bridge shown on the map. This engages his companions, anxious to get in on the know. Perplexed or unsure of what the map portrays, the man says "yes, the road shown to Rach Gia is the road to Rach Gia, but there is no bridge to cross the river to get there". This news hardly comes as a surprise and forces us to reconsider our route. I decide that instead of Rach Gia to the west we will head due south to Camau at the tip of the peninsula. To this our friend says "Ah yes, there is a road to Camau to the south, but there is no bridge or ferry to cross that canal". In other words, Vi Thanh is still cut off and isolated. 30 years ago that was the case because of war. Today it's because of peace.

It is an emblematic East/West deal where two opposite and elemental perspectives collide. It is also indicative of a peculiar and pervasive disconnect with which the "official" world of Vietnam addresses the real. Other than the map I brought, I never saw a map nor did anyone we talked to have or speak of one. A map is an official presentation of the country, made available at the authorization of the government that is supposed to define the nation's body. That the bridges and ferries do not exist or function where clearly delineated is somehow not as important as the indication that they are actually mapped. Since the purposes of a map relate to foreigners, what does it really matter to the Peoples Republic of Vietnam how accurate it might be? It is all tied up someway in the complex oriental enigma of "face" and the totalitarian government's reflexive, self-protective obscurantism.

Instead of fretting about the lengthy detour, I settle back and enjoy the canal scene and sip my hot tea. Small and large sampans chug up and down the thoroughfare busy bringing bulk goods of stone and sand and other construction materials unavailable in this wetland environment while shipping out the local agricultural produce. Rain slick ponchos and tarps glisten brightly with reds, blues, and yellows against the brown canal and green of the palms and bushes shouldering the far bank.

The foot and cyclo traffic over the trellised bridge is crowded. After all these years, the bridge hasn't been widened to allow four wheeled vehicles. In former days the bridge was the de facto (and tacitly agreed upon) divide between the Government controlled Province town and the VC controlled countryside. This understanding was part of the loose and unofficial modus operandi of live and let live for the non-combatants.

I had been in and out of Vi Thanh often. I liked it because it gave one the feeling of being on the edge of nothing. My mind recalls that image from long before.

The monsoon rain had finally stopped. We were moving out with a force of about 30 PRU. Scotty Lyons was the Team "Advisor". Two machine gun positions guarded the bridge abutment barricaded high with sandbags. We held up at the guard-post to brief the lieutenant in charge of our general operating area for the next 24 hours, avoiding giving any details that might compromise our Op. Beyond the sentry posts, work was to begin; the air was thick, moist and muggy, redolent with the sweet-sour odors of mud and wet tropical foliage mixed with the stale sweat of unwashed men humping the tools and implements of infantryman cinched and harnessed about their bodies. Our boots squished and slopped through the mud and puddles. We passed down the word for the last smoke. In the stand-down each armored his thoughts and tried to answer their questions. We were departing from home and families or girlfriends, leaving and going out into something that was not for sure, where each had his own thing to prepare for.

Off along the western horizon the last gray edge of the thunderstorm trailed off and the last spent thunderhead wrestled its way upward, made golden by the sun. The sight of it, why I didn't know, made me feel the earth was flat and that I was assuredly at some random end of it, where, for some quirk of imagination, the sun was going to lower itself down underneath us, where all would soon disappear except us and the darkening sky. It was then I felt a strange carelessness that I could easily disappear in it all and (like my friend Sean Flynn did later on, though his story left none to tell it) be taken away and that if something happened to me it would be all right and I could face it. After all, who wanted to live forever?

But I am still here, all these years later, and Houng is barreling down the road, honking off the cyclos that dared to impede our course. Flat as a skittle and just as hot under the afternoon sun, the low-lying peninsula forms an extended tidal wash that exerts a slow throb rising and receding from its wetland shores. At low tide, large sampans lie incongruously on their keels like muddy-beached whales calmly waiting to float again and drift their way back to sea. The sun drips down on the western horizon.

It seems as if we are going nowhere, passing the same rice field, the same hamlet, the same people, the same family and the same cluster of children. Nothing has changed although everything is changing. Tired from the long day, Houng leans on the horn. Everyone wants to get to Camau before dark.

Camau is the province town of what used to be named An Xuyen, a stepsister province to the bordering Choung Thien to its north. Like Choung Thien, it had no strategic value politically or economically and therefore little importance or impact on the war. I remembered it from first impression when we landed on its grassy strip trying to navigate around the Brahma cows grazing indifferently in our path declaiming a mild proxy of our mounting war effort.

Camau is another "end of the line" place, especially in its geographic setting. At the southernmost tip of the country on a peninsula that dead-ends into South China, it is as distant as you can get from the Peoples Republic of Vietnam and Hanoi. As its recent history unfolded this feature may be its greatest boon, though at that one time it was its bane.

Today Camau is unrecognizable from the once sleepy open field town wrapped around a serpentine canal. Yet here it is, an apparently thriving boomtown at the end of nowhere in a country that has been stuck in an economic deep-freeze for the past 30 years. Obviously I have little grasp of the commercial dynamic here and what is causing it. That something, I soon find out, is the influence of the "Hoa".

16

THE "HOA"

The ethnic Chinese coastal trading communities that have historically occupied a predominant position in commerce throughout Southeast Asia have been labeled the "Hoa". With the emergence of the Mekong Delta as a principal exporter of agricultural products in the late 19th Century, their mercantile interests sought the same opportunities and influence as the locals and made acquisitive inroads into land ownership, agricultural processing and shipping as well as financing and banking. Over the course of the first half of the 20th Century their cartels, backed by the financial capital of their Southeast Asian and Taiwanese brethren, established an economic hegemony that became a major prop for the South Vietnamese regimes following the 1954 Geneva Accord.

In the Mekong Delta, and among the coastal communities especially, they developed prominent populations. By the mid sixties the Hoa community of Cholon within Saigon exceeded 300,000 and has traditionally functioned in many respects as its own quasi-city.

After the 1975 "Reunification", however, and with the repression of the South's capitalist elements through "re-education" and state abolition/confiscation of private property, the "Hoa's" situation became politically precarious. Nevertheless, Ho Chi Minh's crowd did not target this element initially. This was not due to forgiveness in their Stalin-cold hearts, but because of the disastrous state of a post-war economy that desperately needed all the life support it could get from any source.

This initial restraint lulled most of the Hoa into a false complacency and most (those who had not been able to voluntarily exile themselves with their liquidated wealth) remained in Vietnam. It was, however, not long before this tenuous co-existence collapsed.

The years from the late 1970s into the 1990s were a time of significant Sino-Vietnamese diplomatic tensions, animosities, and even short-lived warfare between the two. While the historic antecedents go back before the rise of Christian civilization in the West, the specific causes arose out of the fractious regional politics of the former French Indo-China (Cambodia, Laos, and Vietnam) festering in the power vacuum left by America's withdrawal and abandonment of interest. The flash point was Vietnam's 1978 invasion and partial occupation of Cambodia.

For ill-considered reasons, exacerbated by Pol Pot's consolidation of political power in Cambodia and the Khmer Rouge's historic animosities involving the Vietnamese ethnic populations along their common border, the Vietnamese Politburo decided it would invade and occupy these contested areas in their defense. Instead of receiving support and encouragement in taking on Pol Pot's infamous regime (a development they had anticipated and relied on), Vietnam stirred up a Southeast Asian regional outcry against what all characterized as Vietnam's "military imperialism".

It was because of just such a threat, and as a counter weight to what it perceived as an emergent and relatively xenophobic Stalinist Vietnam that Mainland China became an indirect sponsor and diplomatic supporter of the Pol Pot regime. In retaliation for Vietnam's aggression, and with remembrance of its Marxist Leninist split towards Russia, China initiated a punitive short lived and limited military incursion into the north of Vietnam in 1978.

The direct consequence of this hostility was the Politburo's reaction against the Chinese, which took the form of persecuting the "Hoa" communities. This occurred on top of, or in the heels of, the persecution already underway in the South of all "bourgeois" elements in its society. The result was that all ethnic Chinese (the Hoa) were stripped of rights and property and directly or indirectly forced to flee. This wave of refugees soon became the flood of the "boat people" that rose to epidemic proportion along the entire Southeast Asian coastline. The Delta was particularly hard hit by this social dislocation and Camau, at its far end, was devastated.

It was a classic totalitarian blunder. The net loss to Vietnam economically and socially was catastrophic. Whatever investment funding that was available to keep the economy's development and growth on track dried up with the flight of Chinese capital. In the one productive area where the exhausted country could least afford it, rice and foodstuffs, the failure of collectivized farming and bureaucratic meddling was becoming disastrous. Resentful and overburdened Southern farmers passively rebelled, resorting to the traditional subversion of black marketeering and production slow-downs.

This combination of socio-economic maladies coincided with the deepest cut of all. After sustaining Vietnam almost single handedly through one decade of war and another of post-war economic restoration, the USSR abandoned its patronage, turned off its aid spigot and went home to confront its own insurmountable problems. Standing at the huge port of Haiphong or the massive American built Cam Ranh Bay where fleets of Soviet ships no longer nested and whose warehouses sat empty of any more relief, the Peoples Republic of Vietnam looked out on a world in which they were all alone. Pragmatic, elusive and inventive at war, the government had allowed the arrogance of victory to make it hidebound, myopic, and obdurate in peace. With the specter of famine and a collapse of production imminent, the Politburo finally recognized that there had to be a better way. For the first time in public memory, factional disagreement inside the government was about to appear for all to see.

Despite these bitter internal divisions, the Politburo broke the monolith of socialism and begrudgingly initiated reforms in 1986, though only in resentful half-measures. It provisionally allowed de-collectivized agricultural land use and a nascent development of proprietary rights and production. The prison doors of price controls and state subsidization creaked open and allowed market conditions to adjust to realistic determinations. In the South this translated into the beginning of a return to normalcy (not so in the North, where rigid adherence to socialist doctrine was slow to yield to economic realism, retarding it and leaving it behind—perhaps for good—in the struggle for economic dominance). A centerpiece of the South's resurgence was the return of the "Hoa" from Taiwan, Hong Kong,

Singapore, Malysia, Indonesia and the Philippines. In the turning of this tide it was somewhat fitting that the Mekong Delta set the pace and the remote southern coastal towns of the Delta would soon regain their former influence.

The political demographics of the South and especially the Delta had always created a certain ambivalence in its attitude toward the North. In some rough parallels to the western states in the US, the Delta had always seen itself as somewhat disconnected from historic northern leadership and cultural supremacy. The Delta had been almost completely liberated of Viet Cong insurgency before the North invaded in 1975. This was achieved not by military means alone. Historically and in general there had always existed an underlying mistrust and resentment between South-erners and Northerners, and the same tensions existed among and between Vietnam's communist cadres in the North and the South. The Delta had never become a particularly successful breeding ground for Ho Chi Minh's brand of totalitarianism, and for that matter it had never been either polit-ically or culturally unified under any government. The "Hoa" had tradi-tionally remained a culturally inassimilable element whose loyalties were unquestionably unto themselves, not the state. Those in the Khmer minority were culturally autonomous and historically resentful of any form of Vietnamese hegemony. The admixture of strange but populist religions of the Cao Dai, and Hoa Hao, as well as aggressive Catholicism, worked against the evolution of any national ideological faith or unity. This all added up to a social climate that was not favorable for any political autocracy.

Not surprisingly, after "Reunification" effective political control throughout the South was beyond the exhausted political and economic logistics of the new Socialist government. Remote from the source of cen-tralized power, and without the resources to enforce control, the assigned political cadre developed more bark than bite and soon relied on a more ad hoc temporization than was sanctioned elsewhere.

By the time the "Hoa" began to trickle back and regain its former prominence the socialist cadre in situ were seasoned enough with corrupt-ibility to understand that the socialist barrel was empty. Those who were greedy saw that the only road to self-improvement lay in collaborating with the "Hoa" who knew how a duplicitous but functional capitalistic world operated. Without each other, there was no profit. Soon the children, grandchildren, cousins, nieces and nephews of former communist cadre found sophisticated positions in widespread enterprises with assets theretofore unattainable in a world where personal capital theoretically did not exist, such as the accumulation of substantial real estate holdings in a country that outlawed private ownership. On and on it went, all the way to Camau.

17

WE ARE HERE

What better place to get away with the high crimes and misdemeanors of capitalism than somewhere like this, at the far end of the short arm of the law. There are more "High Rises" (5–6 stories) here than any town we have passed since Saigon. There are more Mercedes and BMWs, more automobile dealerships, electronic stores and a lot better dressed women with no place exciting to go.

The hotel we stay at has a shiny white facade, half of it of marble. Three young men in slacks, shirts and ties man the lobby. Another couple comes in. I think they are Chinese. All three-manager trainees labor over the same registration form. There is no worker bee to take the guests' luggage. It's a commonplace problem, more staff than service, too many chefs, no kitchen.

The lobby is all marble. The room isn't. The shower works, the toilet doesn't. The window air conditioning unit wheezes with exhaustion, barely stirring the mildewed air. When I ask for the bar, I'm directed to the "hospitality" room. Obviously the architect had planned for a garage. The space is white tiled and furnished with card tables, fold up chairs, and blue plastic coverings with birds and flowers on it. The walls rely on mirrors throwing images like a kaleidoscope. I'm the only customer, and by the looks of things, not that important, although considering all the mirrors there are a lot of me. It's not quite dusk. A group of young women dressed in uniforms of Ao Dais—white silk pantaloons and pink bodices—huddle around a table in the corner talking. They are the "entertainment" girls, part waitresses, part something else and not necessarily prostitutes. Pretty in a uniform way, fastidiously groomed, with tiny narrow bodies, hair the color of a moonlit night, skin as smooth as caramel

milk, their images bounce around the room as one by one they rise to scru-
tinize their features in the mirrors, wearing expressions of bored self-
absorption. They seem to be preparing for work. I wonder if I'm ever
going to be included.

Off to one side are two rectangular "party rooms" that can be glimpsed
through the windows of the connecting doors, with half drawn shades.
They are furnished with longs tables set with ashtrays, water pitchers and a
set-up bar, the workrooms for the girls when the businessmen arrive for
party time.

The gin and tonic come separately. I call to the little waitress about an
opener and a piece of lemon. After consulting with the other girls she
returns and hands me the opener. On her way back, she stops to check out
her hair, then her eyes and ruby red lipstick. So long lemon. Rejoining the
group she kicks off the long 3-inch heels and rubs her feet. The overturned
shoe reveals it has never hit pavement. It is her first pair, first day at work,
next stop, who knows?

When Houng comes down refreshed from a wash, he notes the women,
and looks at me with a smile and winks. We have a drink together discussing a restaurant he knows near the hotel. Talking of it makes us immensely
hungry. While we are paying the bill, a group of businessmen arrive noisily
with much cheer and salutations to the proprietor and his family. The girls
in Ao Dais become animated and scurry about arranging refreshments in
one of party rooms. This is who they were waiting for. The night has just
begun! One of the men makes a toast, everyone laughs and claps. Drinks
are made. The talk is loud. The door is closed. The shade is drawn. We
depart.

A purple dusk hangs down the end of the day. Crossing one of the
many bridges over the main canal that encircles the inner city like a moat,
I see the sweep of the great flatland beyond the low-lying housing heaped
around. The air is thick with burning charcoal fires and cooking oils. The
bark and snarl of cyclos seems to be softened by the descending darkness.
The occasional lights on lampposts over the bridges are dulled brown by
dust and exhaust. Passing figures fade into blurred shadows. Street sellers
are hawking regional knick-knacks. Multi-generational families sit on

curbs, observing passing cars and bikes for end of day amusement. Little children watch over the infants crawling around the sidewalks and heedless of the multitude of passing vehicles, bikes, and mopeds a few feet away.

Stores of electrical appliances featuring TVs and radios draw clusters of pedestrians like moths to the bright New World of electronics just now within their financial reach. Signs with advertised prices are pasted and hung everywhere. Loudspeakers squawk with competing music. Cars glide by with nowhere to go except for show.

The restaurant Houng recommends is half hidden behind a beaded string curtain. It's a Mom and Pop operation like so many, a worn postage stamp of a place but as good as home for the moment to two hungry and thirsty men after a long hot day. Beers first. I order large liter ones of Ba-Ba for old times sake and buy a pack of cigarette's, our Lingua Franca. The restaurant is dim, the single incandescent bulb is varnished with grease. Smoke and steam from the kitchen, partitioned by stained floral sheets, adds a yellow haze to the ceiling until it is washed away by an old rotary fan wheezing and jerking in the corner like a nervous chicken. The smells and sounds of food cooking fire our hunger. We are perspiring from walking and shine like cheap brass. When Houng leans close to speak carefully in his English, his face creases with shadow.

The walls are draped with commercial calendars and other promotional displays, pictorial visits from around the world: Spring in the Rocky Mountains from Heineken beer, Holland, a Nova Scotia fishing village at dawn from Tiger Beer, the Philippines, the Sahara Desert for Camel cigarettes, and the USA. A rusty but well tended aquarium stands to one side, its three or four colored fish steering among wavy green plastic plant vines in a mild stupor. A tiny hard-hat diver leaking air bubbles leans awkwardly over a chest of looted treasure abandoned on the sea bottom. On the surface there is no rescue in sight.

Across from us an older Chinese couple is finishing their meal and sit formal and silent. They are well dressed in sophisticated western clothes. The man has a tie and jacket with pressed slacks and well-shined brogues; the lady, a matching suit and fine jewelry. A youthful man, who appears to be their driver, accompanies them. They do not look at us, or at each other, but seem to focus on something beyond or in between the spaces of their shared years as they carefully sip their tea.

We eat carelessly and wordlessly passing dishes back and forth reaching over with chopsticks and picking from plate to plate. Bones and shells overflow the refuse bowl and table spilling on the floor, a customary means of disposal. More than once the waiter comes with his broom and rag.

Finished, we survey the scene. The old couple has gone. We are the only customers. There are no tasks ahead for us, nothing to conquer, nowhere to go. The passing shadows have thinned, street noises diminish. Sweating from the closed in heat and the flush of hot sauces, loose thoughts rattle around in our heads.

We have arrived from a great distance at a bridge of companionship, struggling over the gulf of language only to encounter in each other just another man. We sit comfortably where we find ourselves, travelers, who care from where.

"You were here before?" Houng suddenly asks, half a statement half a question, while mining his mouth with a toothpick. "Yes" I said. "I was here when it was a small place, green fields all around and not many cars". Houng reaches over and takes a cigarette from our pack lying between us. He holds it up to me. I shake my head, but light his. He's preoccupied with the cigarette for a moment. Turning to square his chair and face me with his elbows on the table he confesses quietly "I could only shoot someone from fear."

Stopping instead of going on, he looks at the floor and inhales his cigarette deeply. For the first time as I watch him I see him as a North Vietnamese, dark featured, slender but wiry, a gentle man, someone who would never become a willing soldier. But I know he would do what he was told to do. He would dig ditches, carry heavy loads, stay at his post, and advance in terror to shoot down those on the other side and lose his life. The face of the boy I killed during the TET Offensive comes back. Houng is the same kind, a simple person who, when young, could not have envisioned a life that included violence and death.

"In war everyone shoots in fear" I say, and believe it is true. "The trick of war is for the generals to get their soldiers close enough to be afraid, then they will kill each other." Houng frowns looking down at the floor still smoking. We are entering a river that can only take us downstream. I look toward a Chinese calendar hanging on a wall showing a distant mountain with clouds ringing its peak and the tiny figure of a man starting to climb from its base. It is a wearisome scene.

"I could not kill anyone," he confesses. "My brothers, yes. My family, some uncles, never come back. My mother say she would hide me before letting me go." "You…" he starts to say and then stops. He reaches for another cigarette and hands me one without asking. The war has intruded, the past has come in, as an uninvited guest.

The two women are cleaning kitchen and closing it down, the whisk of brooms, the slight banging of empty pots and pans, a light murmuring between them and the jittering distress of the creaking fan. The waiter, proprietor, son, husband, who knows, reads the same page of the Chinese newspaper up and down with the same toothpick hanging to one side of his mouth.

Maybe it's the beer, the fullness of the meal, the moist heat, the end of a long day in a far-off place, two people with and without connection. "Here we are," I say to myself over and over as if it means something I can't quite reach, still working on it. Smoke curls and slides up into the cranky fan. The fish in the aquarium stare back and swim away dismissively. The Chinese calendar challenges me, the tiny figure beginning his climb beckons something about the moment. Be here now, the mantra of human life so easily forgotten. Enough of this. I stand up. Houng looks at me questioningly. What am I doing? Am I leaving? Going? Did he offend me?

I open my arms. The world fills it with all it can offer, the air that we breathe and the space to move. "We are here," I tell him, pointing to him and then to me and finally to the floor. At first he thinks that he doesn't understand and then it dawns on him. "Yes" he nods, at first slowly. "Yes", he laughs in relief throwing his arms open to mimic me, "We are here!"

The man looks up in surprise, but then sees our pleasured smiles and goes back to his reading. We continue laughing. In Vietnam, and maybe around the world, laughter is the instinctual antidote to nervous tension. If so, we are the best examples of the hour.

The following morning the plan is to search out the taxi boat that makes daily runs down to the coast to Nam Can. Houng, however, returns to the hotel with the information that the express "tour" boats operate only twice a week and the next one is in two days. The only other recourse is to jump on a local water taxi that is a drop-off and pick-up with an indefinite itinerary and schedule. There is also no assurance that we could get to Nam Can and return before sundown.

Today, the Lonely Planet Guide/Travel book features the Camau peninsula as a great wetland bird sanctuary, and one of the best places for bird watching in Asia. In the blurb about it the name "Nam Can" is mentioned as the destination point for bird watching tours arranged from Camau. What a marvelous change 30 years can come up with! Although the idea of bird watching charms me with its novelty, I confess it was not quite what I had in mind in visiting Nam Can. I wanted to go to Nam Can just so I could tell an old friend that I did.

Kinloch Bull (a nom de guerre), then my Boss of Bosses, the Regional Intelligence Chief for IV corps, sent me there once to see about forming a small PRU team to intercept VC supply routes coming out of the U-Minh Forest and moving up along the eastern coast toward Saigon. It was monsoon season, the time of year when you often felt like you were living in a wet sponge. Nam Can was so small and so wet that there was no airstrip to speak of, so I hopped an Army Huey out of Camau taking in supplies. After forty minutes over a gray and water sodden world we finally circled a clutch of thatch hootches built on stilts. The most memorable thing about landing there were the little boys who ran out and tugged on my pant legs yelling the only English word they knew, "Salem, Salem", the next best thing to chewing gum. Pretty good market penetration, I thought.

The community consisted of up to 20 families and a small platoon of "Ruff-Puffs" (conscriptees to the Regional Provincial militia, sometimes preferred troops because they remained posted near to their home villages and found something to fight for instead of Saigon generals). It was as remote as you could get in IV corps, wedged between the South China Sea and the great U-Minh swamp-forest to the North. The U-Minh, a vast uninhabitable swamp area corresponding to our Okeefenokee in Georgia, was a notorious VC redoubt completely impenetrable during the entire course of the war. From it the VC staged supply caches of arms, ammo and medical supplies smuggled in off the coast to re-supply the VC forces putting pressure on Saigon.

The lieutenant in charge was a highly regarded ARVN officer. The book on him was that he came from a prominent Saigon family and had declined a cushy staff job for his remote assignment that would otherwise bear all the characteristics of an exile. He was gracious to his visitor and prepared a formal tea with an exquisitely lacquered tea set from which we sipped sitting on empty ammo boxes crowded among crates of grenades and mortar rounds looking out at fishermen in dugouts checking and setting their nets in the marsh lagoons that stretched to the horizon. In the fine drizzle the vista made a somber daguerreotype of metallic colorations mirrored by the translucent sky and defined with the darker hues of reed and bush that swept the contour of the widening bayou towards the open sea. In this unusual and fragile moment of repose we listened to the occasional shouts of children playing and the rhythmic sawing of lumber coming from the muddy embankment below where a sampan was being built. In these moments the war felt both distant and near, threatening yet dormant across the bay against the backdrop of the dark brooding U-Minh forest. Here under the gray carpet of the monsoon sky one could feel forgotten or surrounded, lost or at home, where, depending on your disposition, one could either brood apprehensively or be serene.

Lt. Minh inclined to the latter, I to the former. He did not complain or comment on his isolated post in an obscure tail end of the war, but instead talked calmly in educated English of the duty to fly the South Vietnamese flag and protect the community that had no real stake in the matter except escape from harm. Here, quite alone and with that precious combination of the ability to exercise command and a talent for inspiring loyalty, he had cagily kept the VC away and the war on its vague periphery.

Minh had turned his detail into a scouting and reconnaissance force that passed information about smuggling routes and force movements on up the military line, which led to indirect air strikes and avoided direct confrontation while maintaining a relatively bloodless status quo. I asked him what help he needed most and he said to give him a more powerful radio to get his communications through. This way, he explained, he could wage war effectively without destroying the community. To bring in more troops and create a larger build up, he said gently, would only provoke the much stronger VC to take retributive action, and gesturing to include the tiny community, only innocents would suffer. He smiled—and I got the message.

When he walked me out, the chopper was waiting. The medics had performed whatever first aid treatment and medication they could for the people in the hamlet and left the necessary supplies until the return trip the next week or so. As we shook hands a clutch of herons passed overhead heading toward the distant forest. As we watched them in silence Minh put his hand on my shoulder with characteristic affection and looked up at me with a warm ironic smile. "We must even share the birds," he said, "Some day we might share the land". "Wouldn't that be nice" I replied, "I'd like to come back here some day when that is true". "Yes, we will make some more tea, a special kind with rice cakes for your return to our country in peace", and in a slight chuckle he clapped his hands softly and gave a brief Buddhist bow.

When I got back to Can Tho, Kinloch agreed the gain/loss did not justify the build up of an aggressive unit and that the stakes merited a do-nothing approach. It was this reflective balance of reasoning that impressed me with how lucky I was to be away from the knee jerk impulsiveness of military doctrine and how much working for him saved me from my worst. A patrician South Carolinian who chain smoked Lucky Strikes with a studied elegance and the insouciance of calm and patient mortality, Kinloch added that his idea of Heaven would be an assignment to Nam Can as an intelligence officer with only a type-writer as a weapon. The image of him doing so in that thatch hut on stilts intrigued me so much, I told him, that I would volunteer to be his PRU advisor there. (Such a fantasy never came to be, but years later we ended up chuckling about it over drinks in Washington, D.C.) As for Lt. Minh, the best of his kind, I heard he was killed a few months later.

18

CONFESSION

The plan is to drive back to Can Tho, spend the night in Vinh Long at the Cuu Long and return to Saigon by noon the next day. It is a hot and dusty trip. The sky is as bright as a fried egg. We arrive at Can Tho at noon.

We find a place to eat and relax. The little restaurant is busy with people on lunch break. The kitchen is separated from the eating space by a damp flower-patterned bed sheet hanging by clothes' pins to the electrical line running to a grease encrusted standup fan providing the only ventilation (sound familiar?). We wait patiently for the slow sweep of its weak breeze to provide a transient benediction. I look about at the other diners: one is arguing his costs against the other's price; a young woman, tired of her boss's advances, is listening patiently to the older man leering at her over the table; and the proprietor is calculating his take and assessing the market needs for tomorrow.

In the noontime languor I watch the stream of bobbing heads and bicycle and cyclo traffic without any thought until I notice the seedy two-story office building across the tree shaded avenue. It's boarded up and abandoned, splotched with mildew that questions a Rorschach test-looks to me like giant moths. In slow realization I recognize it as the former IV Corps Regional Headquarters for "MACV/RDC/Plans Division-a tortured acronym whose short form translated into CIA. It was where I was assigned to work for much of my time, trying to fight the war and play the "Great Game". Maybe its past history as a CIA field house that is the reason for its mean estate, a sort of haunted house complex, but more probably just the reflection of the dismal real estate market that was yet to draw breath from "Doi Moi. Even in use it was never much to look at. I remember it as being a converted school building (another one!) whose only grace was an

146

open cafeteria with a shady patio out back in the former playground. A sprawling ficus tree now obscures the shuttered balcony of the second floor where I shared a temporary office.

Suddenly a bright recollection appears, the kind that splashes through trees and lands on something that glistens. It was from that balcony that I used to watch her and her older sister sit at the small round tables with parasols and share their lunch; two pretty Vietnamese girls carefully and properly dressed in traditional Ao Dais, long raven hair, sparkling eyes, and smiles that opened like a rising sun. She was a very young female clerk employed as a translator of Viet Cong official documents captured by our units and other sources from the "Plans" end of things. Vietnamese hires for intelligence work were as closely vetted as possible because the educational levels required that most, if not all, were from the educated middle class. The two sisters were very proper and never sought to socialize with Americans outside of the office. When I was there I would take my lunch outside and sit with them, for as sisters they were always together. Sensing her younger sister's attraction to me, the older would rarely leave us alone.

I was large. She was tiny. Once I put my hands around her waist and spanned it between my thumbs and forefingers. She always dressed formally in the traditional long sleeve, ankle length Ao Dais and each day with a Hibiscus flower of different color pinned to her hair with the smile of a wish come true. It was an innocent and platonic thing that grew gently into something more. She undertook trying to teach me some Vietnamese and I to improve her English. So instead of Tea Girls in seedy beer dark rooms hidden behind glass bead curtains, I came to know a Vietnamese woman as a person for the first time, not as an object of desire or a means to an end.

We made a joke about how I pronounced the few Vietnamese words she taught me and I would mimic her English. It was the fun and laughter that led to more. Slowly, and very lightly, it became a romance in the sense that each created an image of the other for safekeeping from reality.

I would be away for days and some times a week or more. Each time I returned I found a note or a flower with a burnt joss stick showing that she had lit one for my safety. She said I was her hero, and of course I wanted to be, who wouldn't? She was a lovely young girl, an innocent in a war torn world (have you ever been in a war torn world?) and I was a lonely, impressionable man who had run out of people to write to.

Eventually, when she learned that I was scheduled to transfer back to the States, she brought me a present wrapped in bamboo strips with the preciseness that marks the Vietnamese care of things. It was a miniature of a pagoda with a figure praying. There were tears in her eyes. She wouldn't say anything and left. The note that came with it said she knew that I must go home to my family and how much of my life I had sacrificed already to save them, but she was very afraid for the future and that things were going to be very bad. She ended by saying that she would say prayers that I would come back and save them. It was heartbreaking—and it was just before TET. No one had ever asked me to save him or her and certainly not a lovely girl-child. I knew she meant what she said. I knew that she believed I could do such a thing, that its pathos was real and that out there in that place in that time such thoughts were not mere sentiments, and I also knew that I had dropped into a deep well where no promises could get me out.

"Of course I would" I said. "Yes" I promised. I would come back for them. To lie was so appealing, so much easier than the truth that would shatter the porcelain of our relationship. She took my promise as if she held it in her hands and carried it away with a look of such trust that I almost believed myself.

Shortly afterward I gave her a ride back to her home in my motor scooter. It was a neat respectable house in a prosperous section overlooking a central canal running through Can Tho to the Bassac. Her father was a professor at the University. She introduced me to her parents and they gave me the very polite and reserved greeting of worried parents uneasy with the blasé round-eye foreigner in the company of their youngest daughter. She said something to them in Vietnamese and they smiled generously and formally bowed. I said goodbye and turned to her and asked what she had said. "Oh", she replied, "I told them that you were going to come and save us if there was any fighting".

A few weeks later the TET offensive broke out. I was sent out to the provinces. The area along the canal where her family lived was the scene of intense fighting and was occupied for two days by a VC battalion. I never went to save her. I was wounded and didn't return. I never saw her again—and now I can't even remember her name.

The fan wheezes and jerks its way back to me and I wait for it to wipe my face cool again. My shirt is wet against the chair. I look down at my food without appetite, so I light a cigarette instead and watch Houng attack with his chopsticks—such a meek man, such an aggressive eater. The lunch crowd has thinned out. The patroness counts her Dong. Her husband sweeps up.

Pedestrians stream by the dirty window bordered with dejected plants. They turn and twist effortlessly through the throngs, busily heading somewhere following or chasing their lives. No, I can't see her features, nor can I tell myself that I would recognize her again if she were to walk in here now and sit down next to me. So I am left to wonder if at any moment since then she has ever looked up from what she was doing or where she was going with the same catch of memory as I have, and what she thinks or remembers just like I am thinking and remembering about a promise never delivered. I can't forget the look she gave me in those last days, her face taut with fear, eyes stretched wide by hope. It was the face of Vietnam then and I've seen it since too often, and then only in facsimile; electronic images flitting around the globe accompanied by somber voiceovers as we sit safely at cocktail hour before dinner.

Today it's Iraq and Afghanistan, yesterday Kossovo, Somalia, Rawanda, (can anyone recall Bangladesh?)—portraits of helplessness, non-partisan civilians, the real victims of war, turned into cattle for each other's slaughter. It is an experience so alien to us as hardly to exist in our nightmares. To see it can never be to know it. To have been a part of it is haunting, best kept carefully for its lesson, private for its feelings.

Finally I get up, pay the bill and we leave as if nothing really happened; as if the converted school building has always been abandoned, as if it never was the CIA headquarters, as if I had never known her, as if I never knew her name.

19

LOST AND FOUND

It is too early to head for Vinh Long, too hot to drive or walk around, yet I'm restless to get away from the cloying memories that have deflated me along with the torpor of the midday with its dust, traffic and crowds. The notion of getting out on the water seizes me with the image of coolness departure and distance.

More than anything I've missed the water, the great brown highways that I always associated with space, safety and escape. Scotty Lyons, one of my PRU advisors, used to joke that the impulse of every SEAL if he got into in trouble was to look for water and follow it where-ever it went (the instinct of every natural amphibian) even if he couldn't swim a lick. Yes, an afternoon on the river would put some wind in my sails. I ask Houng to drive to the riverfront and see if he can arrange to hire a sampan for a few hours. Only a few hours, I promise him.

There are several tourist boats tried along the quay, painted in bright colors, each one with sky blue hulls, white cabins trimmed in red, and all decorated with an exuberant dragon's mouth flaring out of their bows. It is an inviting change from camouflage jungle green. None are in use so the bidding is lively. All want to take me down to the "Floating Market" some ten kilometers away (the biggest tourist attraction of the area) but I opt for going across the river to drift the far bank away from people, something quiet, cool and relaxing. One boatman volunteers. His name is Trung. He has some cloth and linens to take to his sister in the fishing village across the river and the price is right.

Casting off the line, the easy push off the pier, the catch of the first breeze, the balance of drift and movement combine in the kinesthesia of release. The river winds wander and mix, the water wrinkles and shudders.

Buppa buppa buppa, pap pap papp pappp, the old engine pushes us out where the air is free, the breath cool and the weight of cares slip away to stern.

Trung gestures that he needs to pick up something and points to the village on an island across a small inlet that is fed by a large canal not more than a half a mile distant. The lee bank is crowded with sampans pulled up on the tidal muck. As the boat nudges into the nest of river craft that crowd the small pier of sticks, Trung calls out. A small high-pitched yell comes in response. We wait a few minutes until an impish creature of a small boy, obscured by a oversized conical hat, jumps on board with a satchel of goods, jabbering excitedly, then runs back for another. After three trips, he jumps down on the thwart across from me chirping and laughing all the time. In the instant the he looks up, I realize that he is a she, flashing me a smile as quick as mercury. She jumps up again to loose the bowline and we turn out to the river.

Finally settled on the thwart opposite me, she fusses with her bags and, in her first moment of stillness, assesses me, her darting dark eyes fixed on me now as she openly studies this unusual object that has fallen into her life. Taking a deep breath she extends a short brown arm toward me and points, as if to give orders. "You" she announces in English, her face twisting in uncertainty. "You" she accuses, trying hard to remember some words in another language and after a long intake of breath explodes into laughter. She calls out something to Trung. He chuckles from behind, says something back and she doubles over. "I no spik inglish" she squeaks still laughing, her palms covering her face. What a difference a smile makes! Out in the main channel, the clamor of the city disappears. The wind has picked up. The brown water frowns. Ten thousand wavelets glimmer in silver trim. They lap the wood strakes of the boat's hull. Light spray freckles our skin. The heat darkens green banks. The shade of the awning is cool. Clouds are pillars in the sky. We are a tiny boat on a great river flowing to the sea somewhere in the world. In it I feel both lost and found. In the space of a few minutes this little muse has appeared to make a new face of the day.

She is not physically remarkable, yet her personality, her sheer vitality, is compelling. But for that, everything about her would lose her in any crowd among hundreds, if not thousands, more like her. She has a peasant face, wide and somewhat flat, with little of the classically fine Vietnamese features that you see in people from urban areas. She may be Khmer. We are less than 50 miles down river from Cambodia. She has a short, boyish physique though her clothes, tan smock and traditional black, wide-legged pants reveal no distinction. They are earth colors, neat, clean and nicely embroidered, finished without being elegant. She has twined leather wristbands, a necklace with red beads and earrings made from two bronze coins with a dull shine that frame her amber face, still smooth and soft, and eyes set off by swift black eyebrows. Her hair is trimmed short like a boy, arranged into bangs, black as oil, glinting with the sun's paintbrush.

As she talks and jabbers on, I have no idea what she is saying. She tries sign language mixed with every English word she knows. When I get it, she claps her hands and shouts to her uncle. When I don't, she laughs from the inside out, shakes her head, hair bouncing like a ball, and gathers herself up in great concentration to begin again. It doesn't get us very far, but I get that her name is Pham Thy, the boatman, Trung, is her uncle and she lives with her mother across the river. She is bringing some embroidery along with the cloth from her uncle for her mother to finish so they can sell it in the Can Tho market place.

Words, half words, hand signals struggle like hammers and saws to assemble a communication that soon tires us. For the first time her animation slacks. Her face stills. She squints out from under her conical hat, the slightest crows feet has set about her eyes.

Forgetting something, she jumps up and crawls forward to retrieve her satchels and displays some linen. "You buy?" she holds up some napkins. I'm a tourist mark, I'm trapped. So that is it: boatman takes tourist to niece who sells mother's goods, an excellent family deal. Why not? I can't think of anything better to do than watch this happy go lucky girl from a fishing village try to sell me some linens in sign language. I could care less. I'm happy. She's a natural, doing a broad comic routine while keeping her eye on the sale. I buy almost everything she offers. After each triumph she preens in front of us and claps her hands in excitement. Next, she takes on the role of tour guide with equal enthusiasm, pointing out the fishermen stretching their net poles, the herons patiently stalking the bank, the osprey strafing and stabbing at fish, the distant dark of the afternoon monsoon storm. Crossing the broad back of the Bassac, we approach the far bank and quickly slip into a small channel that opens into a lagoon where we enter a new world just as if we pass through a curtain onto another stage. Trung slows to near idle, even Pham Thi becomes still.

Winding along the sweep of its bends a hamlet appears; it is almost hidden behind the coconut palms that drape the banks and dapple the chocolate water with shade. One canal branches off into another and soon another: everything designed by tradition, engineered for utility, built by hand, and landscaped for all the uses of life.

The tour is a meditation for the senses; a "time out" to be a part of the sound and the silence, light and shadow, the still and the moving. People in passing canoes and small dugouts exchange only nods, smiles and casual waves.

The foliage is an exhibition of cultivated nature as well as a garden: banana, citrus, patches of corn, okra and peppers, plots of tomato, beans and scallions. Along the pathways to the canal banks and the rough planked landing/chopping-block/washing boards are bursts of red, blue and yellow flowers, bird of paradise and full-headed iris. Shade and sun stripe and patch the air, earth and water in cubist patterns. Quiet lies upon us. Crickets and bees throb and buzz in orchestra. Parrots caw and shriek from dark holes hiding in light skinned trees. The piping of fisher birds passes the word from one overhanging limb to another. Ducks signal maneuvers in nervous squadrons along the banks and dock, swimming through the border reeds. The thud of chopping and digging adds percussion here and there. Cries and laughter of children skip up the waterway, the mute dance of butterflies flashes through the air. Back-lit through openings and views to the rear of thatch buildings, rice fields shine like pale green mirrors, a reminder of how they dominate the land and all of life here.

Trung eventually steers us to a canal-side "convenience" store. It is a bamboo landing extending over the bank with a "Tiki" thatch roof, selling everything from grain to gum, beer to coconut milk, soap to batteries, in sacks or crates all brought in from the morning market in the city, another world away but just across the river. Stacks of green coconuts and citrus and miscellaneous local produce lie to the side for ready-to-make fresh juices, or a mid-day snack, and of course the news, gossip and practical chatter of the day. While we enjoy the fresh coconut milk, Pham Thi is having fun showing me off and bragging about her sales no doubt. I just sit around and smile. So does Trung and so does everyone else. Maybe four and a half feet tall, conical hat bobbing, she holds her audience with a steady grasp. Against the backdrop of a huge western sky she is both puppet and puppeteer dancing on her life's string.

Though they are so different, it makes me think again about the professor's daughter of so long ago, how she would be a matron by now. While one is the village peasant girl the other the educated bourgeois, each remains a spectral type of the Vietnamese constellation bound nevertheless in the same orbit of their inherited mysteries that are all but opaque to western eyes.

For they live still in the world of gods where the vapors of incense, the low thud of gongs and the sudden outcry of strange horns warn of destiny, where djinns and joss dance among spirits in a preternatural embrace with fate, while Buddha sits in shade dark pagodas dressed in moss and commanding silence and solitude. For them the legends of love and tragedy twist and weave around the ancient vulnerability of their sex, groomed in Confucian bondage to a familial and communal etiquette where women have few choices, their defenses few weapons with fates depending on the caprice of men. In this taut matrix of obedience the wife confronts a life of limited options, bonded more in duty and service than released into free expression of will. No wonder then that to them romance is born of dreams but endures in illusion, where mourning and melancholy become cousins in loss, their music strained to melodies of sorrow borne in the high reedy voice that trills in longing while pitched in the minor chords of lament.

I wonder this about her, how she will fit into a rough-hewn life so busy with labor, so far from the romance destined to become a village woman, knowing and waving to all, shouting news and comment on the daily occurrences such as how much linen she sold to a tall American man today, or whatever daily occurrence is different from another to be worthy of mention. Even so, the sun will dry and crease her face, her feet will splay to the barefoot tread, her teeth go unattended and the grace and litheness of youth to bend to the constant chores and yield to the ague, malaria and tuberculosis that prey on the exposed. Before all of that, one hopes that some honorable son will propose marriage and children will come to bounce and crawl to her tending. Who knows?

The vast open sky, the milling breezes, the glistening of the sun, the lap of water against the hull is so relaxing, so far away from the noise and baking heat of the road, that I think I'll lie back and rest, close my eyes and open the mind to fantasy, rejuvenation, and dreams.

The gentle action of the boat and the shifting shade of the small canopy stir me from my dream. I look up. Trung has re-entered the massive girth of the Bassac. A late afternoon monsoon storm looms, with towering spires and battlements shutting down the horizon of the river like great gray gate. With a sudden ruffle of wind, I am awake again. It looks like we have to run for it.

But the rain stalls and passes behind us and the waves subside. As if released by the passing storm the sky is thrown open with the great arc of a rainbow. Pham Thi cries out something to Trung and then to me, "Good, Good" she yells. "You, Me" she points energetically "Good". She laughs and looks back to her uncle.

Back at the quay the perpetual traffic reclaims its dominion and the heat resurges with its clammy shrouds. Houng, always anxious reclaims his charge and is ready to go. Another thunderstorm is forming and there is nothing left to say or do. Standing on the dockside Pham Thi stands silent and subdued and stiffly erect, so short that she rises only a little above my waist. She looks awkward for the first time, a little out of place, a little peasant girl on the edge of the bustling noises and commotion of a big city, waiting to jump back into the boat and hasten back to her fishing village across the way.

"Hen Gap Lai, Ba Nuoi,"(see you again old friend) she says somberly. "Hen Gap Lai, Pham Thi" I reply and look down at her so small and suddenly so fragile and un-armed against the indifferent world.

At this moment I am acutely aware of who I am as an American: someone who comes into and out of their lives with, is it they who make us inadequate or we who make them tragic?

20

VIET-KIEU MEETS DOI MOI

We make good time to Vinh Long despite a short and violent thunderstorm that finally catches up to us on the ferry. I'm tired, a little wrung out, maybe too much pathos in the past few days. Old energies spent don't recycle well. Perhaps the function of life is not to re-live it. Houng and I find little to say on the way. It is a comfort to know we are going back to the Cuu Long Hotel on the river.

After washing up I go down to the river terrace and treat myself to a café-Vietnamese (expresso over ice with a canned cream sugar syrup) and watch the days end, much revived.

Old men stroll along the river walk's balustrade in loose groupings, some bowed in animated conversation, others greeting and joining for the joke or anecdote of the day. To a person they are slight and loose-jointed with a fluidity characteristic of their slender frames. They are old friends, or at least old. Most, if not all, could trace the crowded mesh of interlocking relationships among them: cousins, neighbors, colleagues, former comrades, perhaps an ex-adversary or two. Whatever their station and circumstance, communist or capitalist, there is no doubt that each in his time had implored his god or gods for the preservation of family, friend, or way of life, and in looking around their hearth found few answers and little comfort for the next morning.

In the near twilight these languid pauses and the apparent enjoyment of the moment seem to be free from the burden of those days. Tonight it is back to prices and costs, the advantages of trade, purchase of goods, the complications of family, the expensive and vexing pleasures of another woman, and lest the most pressing be left to last, that evening's World Cup game, that extraordinary marathon of sport which has allowed the world to speak the same language, vent the same emotions and to think the same thoughts.

Two young Vietnamese men approach and sit at the next table. I over-hear one speaking Americanized English while the other sticks to Viet-namese. They are dressed in a more urban chic way than one expects to see in the provinces. I sense their interest in me from a few inquiring glances so I'm not surprised when one asks if I am American.

The two are brothers and they are "Viet Kieu", refugee sons of Vietnam raised in the United States. I have yet to meet one but know that their ele-ment is becoming a significant sociological feature on the future's horizon. In the course of the next half hour they tell me their story.

Only the older speaks. His speech is a kind of Pidgin English with a garbled accent that I had never heard before. In Vietnam many young peo-ple study and learn English as their second language and their pronuncia-tion and phonetics are surprisingly good. Apparently the young man called Phong missed out on this course. He had learned his English through The State of Nebraska social services.

They are two of a family of eight sons and three daughters born across the river in a riverside village. In the late seventies, during the era of politi-cal "re-education", the oldest son became a refugee and emigrated to the U.S. where he settled in Omaha, Nebraska, of all places, eventually becoming a pharmacist. Following the obligations of familial duty, he arranged for the immigration of his younger siblings when they were at the elementary school level. Both have already graduated from high school and are enrolled in the local community college. Now they are visiting their father for four months and living among the father's second family where they are the only Americanized and English speaking ones while the bal-ance of the family is purely native Vietnamese. This makes them feel, as they explain, like fish out of water.

The irony of their predicament, as they know full well, is that their Vietnamese-ness and lack of specialized talents are not going to carry them far in the States, while their American-ness and disconnection from Viet-namese society leave them hanging in the wind. They try to explain that their extended Vietnamese family is frustratingly parochial and "old fashioned", while they are viewed as strange and uninterested in their native culture. Phong acknowledges his indifference, but finds a lot of barriers to connecting with his Vietnamese heritage. Born as a native in the constricting matrix of Confucian principle and Vietnamese morés, their separation from its developmental design cut them off from the nest of habituated interrelations upon which any Vietnamese success would depend. Divorced from these sustaining assets and excluded by resentment towards them as the prodigal sons, they are discovering that they are strangers in both lands. As a result, they are caught in a vise and lack any demonstrable abilities to escape from it.

They tell that every day, just to get away, they leave the family home and come to town for the evening and sit by themselves. They apparently have not formed any productive associations, nor have they developed any ideas of how to do so. The fact that they are soliciting me for advice is hardly a good sign!

When I mildly suggest that they figure out some market niche or cupboard where their American experience and possible contacts could provide some particular leverage or advantage among the Vietnamese, I find their inventory of confidence and imagination nearly empty. As they respond their pathos becomes more entangled, Phong senses my growing detachment. He mentions that he and his brother need to look out for friends. I wish them luck as they rise and stroll away.

After they are gone, I wonder how these Viet Kieus from Nebraska will fare and which life, if it could be one or the other, would prevail, or whether each would continue to live in a dead zone between two worlds.

Houng comes down after resting and off we go to the waterfront restaurant. As we near its entrance I notice a small café down the quay. My friends Phong and his brother are sitting there, just as they were at the Cuu Long, alone and without a friend in sight.

After the meal, several patrons wander in to watch the World Cup. The large TV mounted on a dais commands the room. It signals prosperity and change, first step of the "arriviste". First, the "News" is on and I am struck how Americanized it is, how the production and direction, tone, dress, gesture, set prompts and other choreographic devices—almost everything but the language spoken—was just the same as it would have been in, say, Omaha, Nebraska.

Even though it is in Vietnamese I can follow the yes, buts and maybes of the broadcast. "News" in Vietnam today is strictly controlled. The fourth estate has no independent voice; there are no freewheeling discussions, much less criticism. As a result, there is no conversation with the citizenry; or rather there is no conversation that is not "official". Talk becomes a speech, speech becomes a lesson, and lessons fall on deaf ears. No one in the restaurant is "watching". They have heard the speeches, listened to the lies, nodded their heads, marched in parades, carried the banners, shouted the slogans and afterwards they turn away, go home and close the door.

In time, the World Cup game comes on. Tonight the match is between Croatia and Serbia, the Yellows against the Blues. The game is spirited, hard and tough; players bound by the rules and their consequences scramble up and down the prescribed field of play. To the best I can determine, the restaurant group is evenly partisan. As I look around, twenty to thirty have assembled to see the game, sucking their toothpicks and drinking their beer. There are no women present.

Perhaps those watching are aware of the parallels between their history and the current strife in the Balkans and the reminder that survivors and perpetrators of one regional catastrophe are unwitting partisans of the victims and participants of another. Or perhaps they are as detached from what is going on in Southeastern Europe as the rest of the world was detached from them in their time of national mutilation.

In the morning, before I finish the first cup of tea, Houng comes out looking nervous and anxious. The health of his aging mother, he says, is failing fast and he is concerned about how long I want to continue touring before we return to Saigon. Given this urgency, there is no reason for us to linger.

The return drive was uneventful and the roadside views only a replay of the week before. We stop at the park where we had paused before. Tour buses are clustered at the quay like elephants. The day-trippers from

Saigon mill around corralled by their various hawkers and guides. I walk out to the most distant pier.

What better lookout point for my goodbye than the place where I first said hello. The river wind flutters down the channel towards the sea, bearing with it the daily scents of water, soil and plant. The vaporous noontime heat hazes the horizon, shimmering and blurring its borders. The palm trees nod and toss. Leaning against a piling, the world to my back, I try to soak it in for one last time. I had come back to this country in larger measure to see it again, but whatever thirst I might have worked up is now slaked. I don't think I will want to come back, at least for some time, and then I might be too old. For it was a young man's place before, and war is a young man's game. I am not that young man again, even though I think I could still die with the best of them. I look around for my friend, the retired militiaman, but he is nowhere to be seen. Somehow I miss him and idly wonder about how nice it would be to share another silence.

PART III
DISCOVERY

21

SAIGON REDUX

Back at the Continental Palace in Saigon by late afternoon, Houng and I say our farewells. He is anxious to go to his dying mother, so our parting is brief. He is a good man who shared with me the comforts of companionship, even while his honest, handsome face remained dogged by the shadow of a fragile life, thinned by poverty and bare of promise. As the old Mercedes turns the corner and Houng disappears into his uncertain world, I stand on the hotel steps steeped in another, emptied by the notion that we are as distant as planets.

The last thing I want to do is sit in an empty hotel room, so I cross Nguyen Hue to the corner where a trendy youth-packed bistro features American sandwiches and rock-hop music. Its décor is bright and colorful Southern California Casual, the entrepreneurial signature of slick, gold-chained Viet Kieus/returnees enjoying the capitalistic lifestyle and savoring the revenge of prosperity. The throb and breeze of powerful air conditioning is a far cry from the hot dusty towns of the Delta. The thought of Houng driving back to his small flat in some backwater project, facing his dying mother and the prospect of an expensive funeral he can't afford, cuts my appetite, though the ice-cold beer goes down nicely. Best have a nap and regroup.

I wake later than I intended. It is already 9 p.m. and a Saturday night. Why not go out? The front desk says there is a bar-restaurant around the corner called "Q". "Very popular", they all smile. "Expensive", they rub their fingers. "You will like!" they insist. I remember Mai and her friends mentioning it as the new "Ex-Pat" hangout. I soon see why.

"Q" is across the square less than 100 yards away on the backside of the old Opera House, tucked into the sub grade loading dock space that used

165

to house the props and the ornate scenes of Verdi etc. circa 1920's–1950's. Now its been converted to a garden veranda featuring backlit bushes, floodlit trees and pillared lampposts. The bar stretches across the dock space and is sealed with smoked glass, that is slightly bowed and sleek like the skin of an airplane fuselage, all set for takeoff, First Class, into the hedonistic future.

Outside, the scene resembles a large cocktail party. Under the chattering of animated voices, the silk shirt, gold Rolex and heavy neck-chain gang clusters around tables spiked with cellular phones in a haze of cigarette smoke. Sleek barmaids in mini-skirts with hibiscus flowers behind their ears and hip waiters with red bandanas wound around their forehead circle them like a dance troupe. They spin and dip with trays of fancy fruit drinks in one hand while the other is decorously splayed with folded dollar bills of twenties, fifties and "C" notes flashing like hand fans.

Inside, the lighting is indirect and dim. The action is less party more drinking and smoking, two's and three's in conversational huddles. A hallway with side tables runs along the glass facing. It is rich and expensive, a L.A. kind of tasteful glitz: polished bronze instead of chrome, high glazed tile flooring, deep wooded paneling, walls lacquered blood red, sunset orange, umber and ocher lined with tasteful inlaid frames, sconces with aged celadon and plum colored vases, jade and lapis lazuli ornaments and caricatures. Off the hallway are three to four separate barroom dens, each with its own decors, and music, coordinated by a customizing live DJ, with funky rock, modern blues, jazz and pop.

The wire-hair lesbians from New York, the gay swishes with greased skin, the fat gold-carded business predators looking for oriental scores, are all younger than I am. It doesn't take me long to figure I'm not only out of my age group, but also that my style has had its day—and nights. Against this backdrop of images and gestures I burrow into a dark corner of one of the small cove bars with a $10 US bottle of Heineken. Something reminiscent grows its shadows. The low yearning of the music and the haze of smoke breeds a complacency in the boozy air, the don't-give-a-shit, do what you want, type is back again. Weren't we like them, somewhere, sometime? Here in this den of store-bought pleasure I want to think it has nothing at all to do with me—if only the "Tea Girl" bars and "massage parlors" of yesteryear would let me.

The fatty acids of capitalism are relentlessly leaching into the sinew and marrow of 30 years of totalitarian prohibition. The people here are getting a little indifferent to the socialist whip and branding iron. This is the place to show off as if the good life had never ended, or to spite it if it ever did. Watch out, I think.

It is enough to make Ho Chi Minh's corpse beat on the eternal roof of his coffin. Getting rich is winning the Peace. Those who had fought and thought they had won the war can't afford to be here, but if they had won enough of it, some of their children probably are. In the miserly garden of planned socialism, "Q" is an exotic and luxuriant weed grabbing its light and water, another version of the opium den of the past that promises sweet dreams before you wake.

22

SINS OF THE FATHER

Such thoughts don't come with much fresh air, so I take a stroll to clear it. There wasn't much else happening, probably because most didn't know about Saturday nights or had nightlife budgets. Not far away was what is now called Me Linh Square, otherwise known as Tran Hung Dao for his statue, a major traffic hub funneling riverside traffic off of Ton Duc Thang (the main boulevard snaking along the Saigon river) into the central part of city. Tonight it's almost sepulchral in comparison to the daily melee of pedestrians, push-carts, pedi-cabs, cars, bicycles, trucks, and of course motorbikes, all trying to sort out of their entanglement under the bilious blue clouds of exhaust, bullied by the complaints of bells, horns, shouts and the piercing whistles of white-gloved traffic cops. In the war days, every time if you tried to finesse a way through its tangle, sooner or later you could run into someone you might know or recognize in Saigon in the same predicament, and so it was that I remembered the last time I ran into Sean Flynn. The recollection is remarkably clear because it was just before I left to go back for good, early September 1968, and it was the last time I ever saw him. He was a sight to see.

Tonight I can recall it as if in a theater, and in a way it was. All the props were there; the swirl and blur of sights and sounds and smells of Southeast Asia in the melting daze of an afternoon and out of it, as if the camera was on "Take", he appeared. Hard to miss, sitting tall and unmistakably American on his motor scooter with hang-dog aviator glasses, golden brown hair waving behind him, bright red neck bandana, and sun bleached safari shirt, slung with a couple of expensive cameras looking like the movie star his famous father used to be. Recognizing me, he peeled off and swerved to a stop with a huge ivory smile that could sell sunshine and used toothpaste.

I always liked Sean. We were friends, sort of. I confess that being the son of Errol Flynn had, and still has, something to do with it, I mean, in those days as young adolescents who wouldn't want to be a friend of the son of one of the most glamorous movie stars of our time. We had known each other off and on since early teenage. It was in the mid-fifties, spring vacations in Palm Beach, Florida, awkwardly trying to break out of adolescence and get beyond just kissing girls at country club and chaperoned beach parties where we would find ourselves and hang out together. Sean earned a lot of points with me for not acting that much taken with himself and working hard at being one of the guys, when really he wasn't. How could he be? For while many of our imaginations might have been fired by the images of his swashbuckling father's escapades both in and out of the silver screen, Sean Flynn was branded by it.

Hollywood got to him before he graduated from Duke University, I think. What else could have happened to him, really, too good looking by half with the inheritance of his father's dashing smile, they must have been lusting after another Errol Flynn and how much better than central casting to come up with the direct bloodline. I heard it was a grade "B" pirate movie, "The Return of The Crimson Pirate" I think it was called; a sequel to what his Dad had made famous, but he was no Errol Flynn, Jr..

Though few fans knew enough about his Errol's real life, and most could have cared less, he was an authentic adventurer. A native New Zealander, before WWII he was a well-known ocean sailor and during it part of the "Shore Watchers" (one of the most highly regarded special war units of the South Pacific, known as the guys who slipped into the Archipelagos of the Solomon's and New Guinea solo to perform reconnaissance and gather intelligence behind Jap lines). It wasn't until afterwards, with the great god of luck and circumstance, that the lure of easy cash presented the movies as a lark of make believe, and famous and beautiful women serial recreation. High living caught up with Father Errol before he knew how to be one, and before Sean could grow up to be his son.

After Sean's awkward debut, Hollywood figured it couldn't afford to invest more into a son who couldn't fill the shoes they wanted; and a disillusioned or perhaps untalented Sean slipped away to Europe for less intensive venues. By this time, he was way out of my radar screen until we chanced together again in Palm Beach visiting our families. It was when I was an Ensign in UDT-22 coming off a Caribbean Task Force and he appeared, working out of France for the Paris Match, slung with Nikons building his photographic portfolios that tended to prefer bikini-babes along the Mediterranean. By then, he was better looking than his father and tacking into the fast living crowd with easy introduction. Little did we know or realize then that soon, one fine morning, we were to wake up and find Vietnam on our doorsteps.

Tonight, close to 31 years later, circling Tran Hung Dao, now like an abandoned stage, I try to sort out who we were then, but maybe that was premature. We were still reaching for ourselves without much thought of the future, assured that we were not mortal; but not much later, one of us was.

Even though we claimed we were in a hurry, we found time for a "33" beer in a "Tea Shop while we took our turns telling our stories. The Teashop was dark and low. As we ordered, the buzzing fans kept up a tremulous wind varying with beer, smoke, cheap perfume and sweat in the leftovers of the ending day. Every now and then the swishing and clicking of glass beaded curtains with someone entering or exiting would splash sunlight and allow a glimpse of the crowded world outside. The wavering songs of oriental sorrow reminded us that we were a long way from home just the way we liked it. It was Saigon, August 1968, a scene I was to remember well especially when I heard what happened.

Sean was a little hopped up on something I didn't ask him about, but he was enjoying his tales eyes gleaming with fulfillment, or something else: how many LRP's (Long Range Patrols) he'd been part of, how many fire fights he lived through and SOG (Special Operations Group) Ops he'd been with. They poured out implausibly but dramatically in the patois of "Nam-Speak": dropping names, places and events in the compressed script of a frenetic war photographer pausing just a precious moment to re-load his Leica before rushing back into hazard for the deathless Time/Life cover shot.

Looking back on it with all the prescience of after thought, I see both Sean and his Father as if they were there together, at least in his imagining; woven in the twists of tales and make believe that, after all, were what movie acting was all about, and that Sean could reach out and touch himself as real. Given this, no wonder he was so excited to see me, so I could see that image, as if he was swinging from the rigging of his Dad's Hollywood pirate ship waving a cutlass for all to see his wish come true.

For all his combat talk, Sean was vague on his credentials and who was sponsoring his assignments. Apparently the Paris Match was a some-time client that lost its interest, which told me he didn't have an official ticket (accreditation with MACV). He was hanging out in a communal pad not far behind the big "Pink" (Caravelle Hotel) with a gypsy crowd of Stringers; the lowest branch on the information food chain who hunted and pecked for assignment work off the UPI/API and International Writers Association's boards at the USIA around the corner. Most photographers were strictly retail, selling their product to whatever market was there: for Europe the shots of maimed civilians, burning hootches and bombing damage; for Home, Dust-Offs (med-evacs) of wounded American boys, strung out patrols bogged in rice paddies, units in rain soaked bivouacs to stoke the media's fire back home. Like moths to the lamp of war, they spread out over the countryside, hanging around airstrips weaseling free chopper rides, and other military transport. None of them had any military training and didn't think they needed it, like casualties waiting to happen and expecting the military types to bail them out like a free lunch.

If Sean was a "Stringer", he was one with an asterisk. With the nod of his Father's ghost, and his flashing smile he could hop a chopper going most anywhere and get more than a handshake at the other end out of star-struck field commands hanging out in the boonies at some fire base with not much more than a latrine for comfort and mail maybe once a week.

What else could he have done? Unlike you and me, he had a destiny, a nail driven in the only direction he could go. Besides what he might have been smoking, or the beer on ice that we were drinking, I recall how careless he was, how happy he seemed to be having discovered what he thought could fill up his shadow, and how I found myself envying his free-wheeling thrill seeking; living in a Hippy pad with drugs and broads and enough dough to bankroll his hirsute gang if need be, and then of course, the grease of access and the seduction of his family likeness. On second thought, I was jealous. Part of me wanted to do that, and always would have, if only.

I don't remember saying goodbye or how we parted. I don't remember when I heard about it, but not long after I got back the papers picked it up, something about "Son of Famous Actor Missing Near Cambodia Border". The articles were sketchy, pieced together with tattered facts, worn thin by conflicting sources, from a place with its heart growing into darkness sealed off by fear and chaos. The facts didn't really matter; but the reality was as ugly as a naked corpse.

I could see it as if I had been there: the sun striped colors of earth and thatch through the shade of palm trees at the raw edge of jungle rot, the rank smells of cooking fires, unwashed bodies in black clothed leggings with splayed flat feet, hunkered down like spindly stumps amid the stains of betel nut spit that always reminded me of blood stains, the black eyes squinting at you from a distance as close as Mars.

By all accounts, Sean was with three or four come-alongs: stringers, un-credentialed, unofficial, unnamed and unarmed rag-tag followers of his self-styled tribe leashed together by the charisma of his smile and name drop wherewithal. They must have driven west down through the Delta to Can Tho, then north on Highway 91 (the only one in the western Delta) through Sa Dec up to Chau Doc, the closest jump off to the border where things were getting more than murky and coming apart in some irreparably dark way. In late 1968, Cambodia was the emerging market for destruction, bloodletting and political gore. For them, instead of pecking, over the dog-eared leavings of the Saigon assignments board and probably running out of contacts and contracts to make ends meet, they must have seen it as the yet un-crowded frontier. There they could get a jump on the competition for the first wave of blood stained news on the door step or the TV cocktail hour.

What chimera blinked at them, bouncing and swerving in a mud spattered rented jeep over an incoherent borderline into harms way? What were they doing there that they thought was not going to happen on those mud hole roads where no one and nothing wanted them to come? Between them and Phnom Penh were only the loose and savage outcroppings of the Khmer Rouge phenomena made up of feral teen and even preteen boys dazed with the primal rhetoric of destruction, given AK-47s half their size and slung with bandoleers half their weight; "Lord of the Flies" Southeast Asian style sliding fatefully toward anarchy.

One of the post-mortem articles mentioned a border stop (or one that pretended to be) when something unexpected but foresee ably consequential occurred, something probably minor; a bribe a rip-off, dollars, possibly dope, or maybe it was the fancy camera with the lens looking like a small bazooka that one of them wanted to play with, or something else small and shiny that caught the eye of robbery. Which way did it go? Was it the tangle of argument or the chasm of misunderstanding that wound them together in some East-West face thing teetering from pissed off into crazy?

They were just photographers, transient writers, and maybe not yet journalists. They had no guns. They were there just to…what? In a world without rules they had lost sight of the obvious: that human life for the opposite race was unimportant, that in a world of guns the holders thought they were to be used and that bullets were for killing. All of a sudden they had crossed the line and all their rescuers were gone. What else could they do but give up and go where they were told, what with the little shits jabbering and poking their AK-47s at them. But where was that? There was no path to follow, no hut or shelter back there off the road, no "headquarters" where some authority, some structure, some "rules" existed where they could explain question entreat, and bribe. As for the Khmer Rouge militia, if that was what they were tagged, they didn't know or cared that the tall one was the son of a famous movie actor or who or what they were, but then they didn't know very much about the next day either except that they were going to have to bury the "Round Eyes" after they were done.

As for Sean, before he was always the photographer. Now he was just the photograph, grainy in black and white herded along with the others. Was it early, or late, was it going to rain, were there great gray tumbling monsoon clouds overhead that caught their last sight seized at awkward angles of bewilderment? There on the packed red mud what had been moving and breathing was now inert spilling and emptying; all those years of child rearing, the seesaw struggle through adolescence, the growth into masculinity, now all over and done with. Dead in a ditch at the bitter end of the world.

23

ONWARD CHRISTIAN SOLDIERS

Sunday morning in Saigon reminds me of the Kris Kristofferson song "Sunday Morning Coming Down", a nowhere to go and no one to see kind of feeling. I'm anxious to get on to a new chapter. My requiems are over, muddy recollections on barren ground finished, and now I'm ready for a new adventure, the "North". North Vietnam, I know, is the heart of the matter. To overlook it would be missing the only real point of the journey; to find out for the first time just what the country is about. Before that, I need something to eat to get beyond my hangover.

With nothing on my plate for the day, I stir my courage to call on Mai and Steve again since they extended me the invitation to do so. Their welcome is comforting and timely since they had planned to have a weekly brunch with friends at a Chinese restaurant nearby about noon or so. Would I like to join them? Why not.

With a few hours to spare, I go for a walk. Leaving the lobby, I hear a call; "Mr. John, Mr. John". It's my old Kim, the cyclo driver, waving his hat and wrestling his cyclo-rig in my direction. "Where we go?" he asks, with his big grin. I wave my arms around and get in. Off we go.

A few blocks behind the Continental is Notre Dame cathedral, the largest Catholic church in the country. Worshippers are entering for a service. In the already broiling heat the attraction of an oasis of Christianity in an oriental sea lures me with a kind of thirst that being so distant from home inspires. The cool dark of its vaulted narthex wipes away the brightness of the mid-morning air. As my eyes adjust to my surroundings, I see there are at least one hundred or so Vietnamese in attendance. Shafts of sun reach through the apse's painted glass oval striking the oil black hair of parishioners, and the white shawls and red robes of the choir singing a Te Deum. The music soothes, swells and lifts into the sparkling silver dust motes suspended high above. The boy sopranos sing with a purity of tone that makes one almost shiver.

It is High Mass. Among the several clergy, a bishop holding the symbolic shepherd's staff, a crozier, rises and ascends to the pulpit. At first it is hard to hear his sermon but gradually, and to my surprise, I recognize that it is in English. I look around. There are few Westerners. He speaks slowly reading from a text, carefully laboring over the phonetics. His message is that to understand Jesus, we must understand how he struggled to conquer his humanity through a series of trials. I have heard it often but not in a place where the message has such stinging relevance.

Outside these walls lies a country that has fought 30 years of war over whose ethos would rule. Every man and woman's life in that time has been dominated and changed by the struggle. From it emerged a victor and the vanquished. Intermeshed within its layers and dimensions were religious conflicts, the most dramatic of which involved the stake of the Christian Catholic Church in Vietnam.

Like the history of western colonialism or imperialism throughout Southeast Asia, Christian proselytism in Vietnam arrived close on the heels of the commercial traders of the 16th and 17th centuries. Its first presence and inroad occurred in the Hanoi, the national center of power, where it achieved hard suffered success over cycles of great repression. The spiritual message of Christianity presented an entirely new vista of faith that questioned and offered a spiritual alternative to the ancient and fossilized strictures of the Confucian/Buddhist model that had reigned throughout the many centuries of Chinese cultural hegemony. Aside from the evangelic, however, it was the introduction of western thinking and education that became truly revolutionary among the then growing Vietnamese middle class that had long chaffed under the stiff Confucian autocracy of thought and the rigidly centralized Mandarinate monopoly of power.

In the course of time, the aggressive zeal of missionaries and converts eventually invited repression and persecution. This was a fatal miscalculation by the Mandarinate, exasperated by its loss of autocracy and baffled by the overwhelming power of western influences. In short order, and in full conspiracy with the Church, France seized the excuse for full-scale military invasion. Following the occupation, which precipitated the demise and abdication of the Nguyen dynasty, the Church moved forward to expand its institutional influence in western education and social reform.

By the early 20th Century Catholicism and its western values seeped deep into Vietnamese internal politics. Vietnamese Catholicism became a derivative of republican thought and experiment that ranged against Bolshevist nationalism. If the Church expressed any one political policy, it was anti-Communism. This admixture was to create a fatal antagonism that played a significant factor in the fomenting of war. By the end of the "French Indo China" war in 1954, the die was cast.

As stated earlier, with the post-war consolidation of Ho Chi Minh's Bolshevik styled "Viet Minh" (to insure distinction and separation from its next door neighbor's Maoism), a significant number of the North's Catholics elected to emigrate to the South following the 1954 Geneva Accords. In the South, the fractious medley of republican groups vying for power but unable to sustain a majority were soon to be overtaken by the cartel of the very Catholic Diem Brothers. The Diem regime was a throwback of the old warlord mentality. It was committed to and aggressive in the proselytism of Catholic Christianity and intent on entrenching western attitudes, at least those which would support the Diem's autocratic power.

Their strident pro-west religious positions, however, antagonized the opposition of Buddhists and other hybrid religious elements. These conflicts hastened incidents of civil, quasi-religious protests leading up to a coup that precipitated their Diems' assassination. (in which the US was allegedly complicit). This created a political power vacuum that anticipated our inevitable involvement—and "the rest is history".

Vietnamese Catholicism played a central part, and had a major stake, in the war's outcome. Its followers were key players and the outcome was for keeps. As a consequence, the military debacle of 1973 was a disaster for the continued viability of the Christian Church as a national entity. Few institutions, if any, were more devastated by the outcome. In wise consideration of the Church's abiding latent influence, and other underlying factors such as the South's historic unreliable allegiances, the communist Politburo did not outlaw the Church. Instead, it was stripped of any public or quasi-official social role other than solely providing worship.

Those worshipping this morning understand how his message is relevant to their struggles in escaping the wreckage of their past. This service in this church reaches a faithful who are not simply mumbling their way through the ritual of mass. The bishop's message speaks to something tenaciously held; it is yet another reminder that life in Vietnam is and has been synonymous with struggle.

24

HISTORY LESSONS

Kim pedaled up as I walked out. "Where to, boss?" he asks as we swing out of the square into the tree lined le-Duan Boulevard. Since the "National Palace of the former Republic of Vietnam" (now "Reunification Palace") stands before us behind iron gates there is no excuse to avoid it. Preserved as a convenient symbol of the conquered enemy it is, accordingly, a public museum. Though hardly in the same status, but not without its own pro-paganda value, the long abandoned shell of the former U.S. Embassy lies within sight, a quarter of a mile down the road.

The "Palace" itself is a 1960's five-story horizontal structure, resembling a squashed birthday cake. Its interior consists of large box-like rooms on the drab side of gaudy. Marble, mirrors, and red carpets with heavy bro-caded curtains adorn the empty reception and assembly spaces, bringing to sight and mind the likeness of a vast funeral parlor. There are only a few tourists and none linger. This is the last fox-hole of the Republic of South Vietnam during the fall of Saigon March, 1975 and for a few dong more, one can have a tour. Fortunately for me, I am the only one interested in taking it. It requires a guide.

Mine speaks halting English and in addition to a demeanor of indiffer-ence, he has neither knowledge about what went on there, nor an interest in its story, which may have been a requirement for getting the job. Unable to conceal his boredom with only me as an audience, he soon retires for a smoke in the entrance well and leaves me more or less alone.

There is no obvious entrance to the complex, merely a nondescript back door with a stairwell leading rather suitably into the lower intestinal tract of the regime's subterranean bunkers. It is here that the final death throes of the ten-year war played out. At the bottom of the landing are corridors, sized for small and nimble men (not American). These lead, via a maze-like series of right angle turns, into a sequence of command and communication centers with rows of cubicles for radio and telephone operators. The atmosphere is dank and claustrophobic. Old rotary phones with coils of wire, cumbersome facsimile machines still stained with the puce colored ink, and ceiling fans with few air conditioning vents, reminds us that this was then and not now, light years behind the computer keyboard and graphic mastery of today's communicative frontiers. There are, of course, no windows and few vents. The ceiling is no more than 8 feet, adding to the premonitory sense that something might be buried here. The gray walls are lined with rusting olive drab file cabinets and crowded with conference tables topped with scarred Formica and iron fold-up chairs stacked in the corners. It is impossible to tell exactly where or which space is, or was, the actual Command Center, but I try to find it walking back and forth in and out of one and another until I find the largest that I decide is ground zero—as if that choice puts me inside the heart of the matter. I then stand in this now empty space feeling a silence that holds its breath, trying to catch the scent and sight of what went on here as South Vietnam's last days ticked down to hours. It is March 30th 1973 and here is the end of the road.

It is enough to imagine the smoke dimmed briefings under harsh florescent lights, crowded with men in green uniforms dark and damp with sweat, their moist, glistening faces, frightened eyes stretched wide, open mouths yammering in the high staccato pitched with fear, the sharp arguments, the panic of indecision, the chaos of see-saw orders, the blaming, the excuses, the failure of resolve, the leaking of courage, the loss of leadership where the gathering shadows of doom became the indescribable shame of surrender.

Here the walls run out of room for lies. Maps with vague topographic contours, aged under moisture stained acetate, confess in different colored markings to the rictus of defeat: final unit dispositions and strengths, faded arrows of last movements, notations blurred by erasure and write-overs barely legible, as if the point of it all was losing its purpose and meaning. The stale smell of sweat finds no neighbor. The furtive eyes of retreat and despair are sightless. Frantic commands are empty of hearing. With their abandonment the only sound left is the sharp scrape of my shoes against the walls as I move and peer at the faint hieroglyphics of a lost cause and the last etchings of a final defeat.

The exit from the command bunker faces the rear of the grounds. Off to the left, beneath a cluster of large banyans, is a line of one story ochre bungalows with red tile roofs. I assume they were once offices or staff residential quarters supporting the Palace compound. They are otherwise nondescript and unattended except for a small white sign with black block letters announcing in English, "War Crimes Museum".

So this is it? I had heard that there was such a thing but had not paused to imagine what it would be like or, for that matter, what it would actually be. I only noted that it should be on my obligatory itinerary, a sort of submission to suck it up and stare it in the eye kind of confrontation. Why not, what could it do to me? I'd gotten this far. I had my two feet, arms, a heart that pumped and so far a brain that didn't ooze, a lot more ahead of the game than the 57,000 other guys, so I'd go in for them armed with a "give a shit" attitude, pumped.

It is a tired place, poorly lit, musty and dark. The ticket taker doesn't seem to give much notice to the only westerner in sight, even one with a large chip on his shoulder. The mildew spotted walls are covered with grainy black and white photographs of all the after-effects of man-made violence, destruction, brutality and gore: a leering GI holding up exploded hunks of dead Vietnamese for "macho" souvenirs back home, a human body thrown out of a looming helicopter unable to fly, posed shots of mutilated civilians and tortured prisoners pointing to their scars, rows of burning homes, streams of refugees, bomb craters in the midst of villages made of mud and sticks, all captioned with repetitive and simplistic Communist slogans of denunciation, pointedly in English. A special exhibition prominently displays large dust coated jars of disfigured and deformed fetuses pickled in preservatives and placed next to photographs of American planes spewing "Agent Orange" over dark swamplands.

The conquered South Vietnamese take a beating as well. There are rows of mug shots of sad-eyed old men in their prison clothes lined up for public humiliation as manikins of treason before they are marched off to disappear and die in jungle "re-education" camps. Next to them are commemorative portraits of martyred Viet Cong and other prosecution exhibits of South Vietnamese treachery and persecution, including a crude mock up of a prison for political prisoners on some isolated offshore island. Everywhere is a jumble of despairing reminders stretching along dim corridors going nowhere, a disorganized maze of the ugly and the old, an attic of human desolation.

It made me recall one night sitting in a shed full of VC bodies stacked for eventual mass burial during the final days of the TET Offensive. Aided by the light of a single oil lantern, I watched, as in a vigil, the light and shadow flicker over the gaping and distended flesh, trying to imagine them as humans but all I could see were soulless eyes and gaping mouths like fish in the market. I believed then that it was necessary to wait for some epiphany to bring me understanding. It never came. In the same stupor, I linger and gaze 30 years later, trying again to come to terms with some echo of "the reason why." But it is the same. Even among these base chords of primal misdeeds the ghosts remain silent, holding a finger to their lips, warning the past to remain silent lest its secrets overwhelm us all.

After the marquee "War Crimes" title there is little in the script or even casting to excite disgust. Poorly presented, cheaply done and endlessly redundant, the entire exhibition gives the impression that it was thrown together as a bureaucratic afterthought.

Predictably, its horizons rise no higher than providing a venue for compulsory political lectures to herded school children. While it may offer a gallery of crimes by man against man, its overall effect reduces it to degradation of the defeated and exaltation of the victors. Whatever the government sought to achieve, this propaganda exercise certainly cannot play well to a South Vietnamese audience.

The most venal of the government's Communist "virtues" is compulsive self-righteousness. Deaf to remorse and blind to self-doubt, the Politburo insists with an atonal condescension that only the "People's" government may speak out loud—believing that when it does, everyone will listen. Thanks to its narcissistic self-regard, it can conveniently overlook, without the requirement of denial or explanation or justification, any culpability or responsibility for what is depicted in these exhibits labeled as war crimes. In doing so it devalues sober recollection, learns nothing from the lessons it is purportedly trying to teach, and consigns these grim artifacts to what is just another warehouse of the forgotten.

A couple enters with a small boy. The parents walk slowly along the corridor, pausing to read the tags on the exhibits while the boy skips ahead and starts examining with bright devouring eyes the oil coated weaponry that is on display on a table in the corner. He calls out to his father and runs up to lead him over to this treasure trove. The principal object of his fascination is an M-60 machine gun sitting black and ugly in the middle of the room as if waiting to be used. Fingering the belt of ammunition like something precious, he looks up at his father with a Christmas gleam in his eye.

Outside the sunlight is blinding; a breeze blows through the trees clearing away the stale deadness of the "Museum". "What you think?" asks Kim. "Not much", I reply. As we pedal away he bends down and whispers low to my ear. "Few people want to come here. It does no good."

25

THE ARRIVAL OF THE FUTURE

The Chinese restaurant is the most formal I have seen in Vietnam. After a busy morning I welcome first class air conditioning. Furnished with formal linen-covered tables and substantial chairs, staffed by white-coated waiters, it's a long way from Camau. Steve and Mai were already there with their friends, plus babies and nannies. Both seem well known to the hovering management. The other couple is also bi-cultural, but a different model from Steve and Mai. Joe is a mid-westerner from Michigan, born, bred and educated there. A graduate of U of M. with a B.A. and a MBA, he is on his second year as General Manager of Procter & Gamble, Vietnam. Thanh is Vietnamese, but born in Portland, Oregon. She is the child of refugee parents, a Viet Kieu, but of a far more sophisticated vintage than my woeful acquaintances of Vinh Long.

Her family was from Dalat, the well-known summer residence/retreat for the wealthy and influential Saigon elite in the alpine—like mountains of South Central Vietnam (and consequently one of the most sought after week-end junkets by the young members of the American diplomatic corps during the war, an invite that far outreached my resources.) It was well known that the Dalat crowd got out safely and early and with most of their personal capital. Thanh later told me that her father was an official with the GVN war office, i.e., either was himself or had friends in high enough places to be U.S. assisted in relocation.

Thanh's type presents the perfect North/South contrast to Mai, both physically and characteristically. She is a willowy southerner with classic Vietnamese southern beauty, fine pale honey colored skin, perfect oval eyes, delicate nose and lustrous straight and long black hair. Though she looks all Vietnamese, she sounds very much part California beach girl, tan, slender, athletically fit, cosmetically well put together and tightly dressed, but she's no bimbo. Tanh's a graduate of UCLA with an MBA, and no slouch. Instead of remaining in the U.S. she elected to take a position with an international finance firm originally located in Hanoi (a cold harbor for a southern refugee) but since relocated to Saigon. A rather brave decision I would have thought, but she shrugs it off with few remarks, one of them indicating that she likes Saigon much better because it isn't as backward. It was in Saigon that she literally ran into Joe at the fitness center in one of the new business-office high rises. Together they make another poster global Yuppie couple.

Joe is a good and major client of Mai's at Saatchi & Saatchi so theirs is a double barreled relationship. Recruited out of business school by P & G he has dutifully, and from all appearances successfully, climbed its ladder. As globalization began to display its career promise, a foreign assignment seemed to be a nice, fast track. When Vietnam began to demonstrate an initial eagerness to open its markets in 1993, the daydream of 70 million Vietnamese washing their clothes and grooming their bodies with P & G products became a dazzling enticement to open up a joint venture project. Joe answered the call.

After a hopeful start, however, a downdraft of reality put a damper on such enthusiasm. The Central Government's chronic ambivalence about foreign intrusion and its compulsive prevarication in decisions required to sustain a commitment in market driven economics down-shifted the eager engines of capitalism just as effectively as monsoon rains bogged down our military machines. Such hurdles as product acceptance, brand recognition, and cultural idiosyncrasies accumulated operational and tactical land mines. "That's why I hired Mai," Steve laughs cutting short his laments, "to help me get out of this mess."

Mai, her eyes glistening with humor, responds, "I've been trying to tell you all along Joe. You're in the wrong market. If you want to be successful in consumer goods there are only two things you can sell to the Vietnamese and make a profit; beer and cigarettes!" Mai is enjoying herself. Looking around, she waits until we stop laughing. "So what do you do? Try and make them wash?" Pausing for effect. "Everyone knows that the Vietnamese don't like to wash!" She claps her hand at her mordant humor and skewering of the westerners' naiveté. Joe shakes his head and responds warmly, "Now you see why we hired her and can't get rid of her. She's right!"

Joe is candid about his stint in Vietnam and whether or not he wants to stay on to wait for a better business environment. He and Thanh have just returned from the States where they showed off the newborn baby to the two sets of grandparents. This provides him pause to reconsider his overseas professional commitment. Like Steve, he feels the growing gap of distance; of being too far away from the safe harbor of Home Office and facing a dry dock in a very peripheral third world market that may not sail well into the future of success.

Thanh pays careful attention to his statements, especially those about their future commitments. For this reason they have recently moved out of their in-town house and taken a short lease in a new and modern townhouse development. Their new digs sound like an oriental version of the "gated" community. Thanh, sounding like the American yuppie housewife that I see she wants to become, joins in saying that there isn't any other place that has the security and conveniences of modern living. It's the first time I've overheard anything about personal or property security. Joe assures me that there is no security issue, but Thanh insists that there is to her.

In the midst of sorting through the dishes and fussing with babies, the issue of child rearing pokes its head up at the table. For both couples it is clearly the Rubicon of their futures in the country. As for Thanh, so Americanized in her tastes and apparent wants, there is little doubt that she is readying to head for the exit. Mai begins by expressing some uncertainty about early education options available but feels she has time to put it off by having her daughter home schooled as long as it is practicable. Thanh looks down at the table while Mai talks. Then, with a sharp glance at her husband, any faint trace of the California beach bimbo façade evaporates and the sharp tough Asian refugee flashes before my eyes like a dagger suddenly unsheathed. "I will never send my child to a Vietnamese school," she breathes in a low and tight voice, full of steely resolution. In her emphasis she darts another sharp look around the table and fixes on Mai. Thanh's tiger is out of the cage.

For a moment, Joe looks at her intently and then there is silence. Beneath this surface there are rocks and shoals that I can't fathom. Somewhere amid the bitter nurture of the exiled Viet Kieu facing the strong willed Northern "invader" there are unspoken feelings in conflict. To erupt in open disagreement would violate the enigmatic elements of oriental "face". Its first principle is that "face" must not be violated—and face is now is stretched taut.

Thanh says nothing more. There is no need. Her throwing down the gauntlet says enough. Vietnam is no longer her country. She has chosen her country, the one with abounding promise, chosen it in preference to one only still bleeding from the wounds of a bitter heritage—exile and ruin, loss and flight, return and retribution, revenge and salvation. She looks down at her little boy in his crib. He is just a year old. He looks up waving his arms and shaking his rattle. Backing off a little she says more softly, "I don't want him to be educated in Vietnam."

Mai's face is still, her usual animation suspended. She weighs the delicacy of their positions and distances. Quietly avoiding the challenge, she responds very calmly and takes a lighter tone, "Oh, some schools are not so bad. But you are right about most of them. At least now there are special schools that are not state run." It sounds apologetic and reassuring, but I can tell by the lack of conviction that even Mai is not sold on the quality of the existing alternatives.

No doubt she is sifting through the contradictions in her own predicament and situation. She is a North Vietnamese born and bred, niece of one of the aging bearers of Ho Chi Minh's semi-sacred flame, a child selected for special schooling among the power elite—and her intelligence and energy has earned her a wide-open future. But what sort of future? In a restricted and frail country shuttered by a dark and brooding past, one still suffering from festering wounds which she and Thanh must feel in their very cores and secret hearts.

This face-off of ties and loyalties brought on by a rational estimation of the destinies of their bi-racial offspring brings into high relief all of the options and uncertainties presented by a world where national boundaries mean less and less—but still count for a great deal. And what of their children, these little over dressed tykes banging their tin cups? In what part of this new world will they find themselves? Where will their loyalties pull them? In which country will they invest their dreams and hopes? Will there be such a thing as a global home that "when you go there, they must take you in" or nothing but a vast criss-cross of different colored threads in a new fabric weaving its way to a design still undefined?

26

SO LONG OLD FRIEND

Before I leave Saigon or Vietnam I know there will remain something left undone unless I visit where I saw my best friend Rick for the last time. With such changes in the city I'm doubtful I will be able to find it. Still, I ask Kim to take a ride down Tan Duc Tranh Avenue along the Saigon River in hopes of recognizing the old French colonial structure that had been annexed by MACV for one of its administration centers, in this case for what was euphemistically known by all as "Bupers (Bureau of Naval Personnel); where we all went to untangle the red tape of our service records and, most important, receive our travel vouchers for going back to the "World").

Rick (Lieutenant F. E. Trani, Jr., United States Naval Academy '62) was an older (but smaller) brother to me in the "Teams". Back in 1966, in a stroke of good luck, I was assigned to be his Assistant Platoon Officer in Underwater Demolition Team 22. After six months of sharing double bunk quarters on an LSD (Landing Ship Dock) in the Caribbean Amphibious Task Force, including long weeks in a beach shack on "Red Beach", Vieques Island, Puerto Rico, there wasn't much we hadn't learned about each other—and after being paired as Ranger Buddies in U.S. Army Ranger School's ten weeks of a seriously miserable lifestyle in January '67, not much we hadn't gone through together.

We were a Mutt and Jeff pair, his five-foot-six, 145 pounds to my six-foot-two and 200. Rick had a Howdy Doody look to him: ears as big as baseball gloves, sky blue eyes and a short haystack of bright blond hair. He was the original towhead, with a lopsided grin that could empty pockets and earn a plate of cookies every time he rang a doorbell. Part choirboy, the other a tough alley cat. Whatever quit one might have had upon entering training "BUDs" (Basic Underwater Demolition Training), it was squeezed, bullied or scared out of you if you stuck it through. Rick was all Grit. Once past the physical and emotional challenges of making it, an officer had to bull-ride a number of pig headed petty-officers, which meant running an eight-mule team on a rocky road. That said, I never knew anyone who didn't say "Yes Sir" to him after he leveled his stare and smiled.

He was the son of schoolteachers to who he was the rising sun, a family guy, married to his high school sweetheart, father of two children under six, an older girl and a boy just like him, if I remember right. Though he was an Annapolis graduate, something that he never wanted to talk about had made him bitter about the arrogance and petty politics he found there. Because of this, he chose what was, career-wise, a back water move by volunteering for the "The Teams" as if to say "Fuck you" to those who's sole ambition was clawing their way up the slippery ladder to Admiral.

As Kim tries to maneuver along the Saigon River in the traffic of Tan Duc Tranh Avenue heading towards the Central district, I spend the time grabbing at too many memories I had left of him. I loved that guy, more than any of them; all of them. I would have done anything for him, or so I thought and believed. That last time was a good-bye of sorts but never the forever it became.

It was the end of August 1968. I had gone to "BuPers" to pick up my travel orders and service records for the trip back to the US and had arranged to meet him at the Vietnamese Naval docks at his quarters in the Vietnamese SEAL Team Compound.

He was enjoying his assignment, proud of his guys having just completed a rigorous training operation with his first class of the newly formed Vietnamese SEAL Team and bragging about their early success on their first "Ops". I was glad for him but worried he was getting "wet" (SEAL jargon for participating in hazardous operations) with them when his assignment didn't call for it. This meant he was pressing the odds pretty tight, but then that was him being Rick. It was one thing with a single guy like me quite another for a husband with two kids. Somewhere in the back of my mind I felt responsible and a little guilty.

Our last meeting back in Little Creek had been some months earlier—neither of us brought it up. For the previous year (1967) we had been separated by different rotations and assignments. After the TET Offensive we found ourselves back in "CONUS" (Continent United States) in far different circumstances. I was hanging around to "DEROS" (date of expiration of service) and planning to go to law school purely out of fear of the future. During that time Rick was pretty tucked away with his family while I had no such closeting, so we didn't have much time together.

He was living in subsidized officer housing, a tidy Norfolk low country type ranch house where the family could look at home with a front and back yard. Rick's wife, Gert, was a nice, pretty woman who was fiercely possessive of him—and why not? She was, understandably, not pleased that her husband's close friend in the Teams was a free-wheeling bachelor junior officer who probably didn't spend much time thinking about the kinds of problems facing a wife at home with two little kids while her husband engaged in hazardous undertakings (not just in Vietnam but at home as well) that, on any given day, could kill him. Norfolk was a long way from Vietnam, and also a long way from their close family lives in Poughkeepsie, New York. Rick admitted that Gert was bent out of shape about him jumping over to SEALs and getting into the Vietnam firing line, which I interpreted as meaning that she saw my influence in it and that I was in her doghouse. If she wasn't entirely right about that, she wasn't entirely wrong either.

Anyway, at one point Rick invited me over for dinner on a Friday night saying he needed to ask me about something, which seemed a little strange and serious, so when I accepted the invitation, I made sure I was on my best behavior. That evening Gert was nice to me because she was a nice person, but friendlier than usual. After putting the kids to bed she stayed inside and Rick and I went outside. He asked me what I was going to do about getting out (of the service) and if I really wanted to go to law school. I confessed that it was just something I thought about to try to make a re-entrance back to life and that the big future out there kind of scared me.

Coming down off a war, no matter how shitty, I felt kind of vacant and didn't want to think much about it—or my future.

That was when he told me he had received orders for another tour, not just the four month TDY assignment that SEAL platoons were rotating on, but a full year PCS (Permanent Change of Station defined by an assignment over six months outside of a home command). His orders transferred him to the MACV naval staff in Saigon where he was to be the senior Advisor developing a South Vietnamese Navy SEAL Team. They had him leaving in 30 days. He had appealed, gone up to the big BuPers in D.C., called in all his Annapolis markers to get out of it, but no deal. It was post TET, discharges were being extended and transfers frozen. Uncle Sam was holding a tight hand. There were a lot of guys without his obligations. A year tour on top of the tour he had just finished wasn't right. He deserved better and he didn't get it. Gert was terribly upset. She wanted him to quit the Navy—but he didn't have the option of resigning. The only thing he could do was get a replacement, pull a switch. But there was no one available he could ask, wanted to ask, or felt he could ask. Gert wanted him to ask me. He didn't want to, but he did.

We had another rum and coke, maybe another after-that's how young we were. Whenever Rick drank too much his blue eyes just got bigger and flatter and his tone of voice more daring, a man wanting to take on the world. Nobody much believed it, but I was the guy who could calm him down only because I was larger. On the other hand, Rick was an excellent officer. He'd taught me a lot about how to conduct myself properly in the military, which was not natural to me, and he would back me up and give me a succinct lecture on appropriate occasions.

We had been physically thrown through the loosely riveted Quonset Hut of Camp Garcia's Marine Officer's Club, high on a hill in Vieques Island, caught in a bad wind drift on a parachute jump in Guantanamo Bay, Cuba, barely avoiding an international pissing contest and court-martials for nearly landing on Fidel's side of the fence. We led Point together for 24 hours on Ranger School's Six Day patrol in a snowstorm in the north Georgia mountains where he had to lead me by my hand off the mountain in a period of night blindness, and now he was asking me to do his full year tour back in "Nam" two weeks after I had just finished one.

He deserved the break and he asked me for it. I don't think we spoke for a while. My memory is that this took place in early spring, because we were outside and something was blooming and smelling new, and there was the promise of summer heat around the corner.

Ten days to go before I was discharged—and I had already been over there 13 months. The war sucked. It wasn't being fought right. Rick's assignment was an open-ended job with a lot of leeway for a free wheeler like me. A year ago, I would have jumped on it, but it was Navy, military, and I was out of that web and somewhat seduced by the clandestine mystique of the para-military world. I was even thinking of going into covert operations in Laos and Cambodia. I told him that if I had any time left I would do it for him, but I didn't. He asked me if I would extend. I told him I couldn't. I didn't have anyone to be responsible for but I did owe something to my parents after over a year in-country. Besides, the military and me didn't add up to a marriage made in heaven—and I had some enemies out there of higher rank. He said he understood, but Gert had really pushed him to ask me and I was the only one he would ask. He didn't have to tell me. I could have recited the chapter and verse of her reasoning, and she was right. I didn't have a family of three to take care of, children who needed their father, a wife who was all alone, had been all alone for most of the past four years while her husband was getting in harms way. We drank some more, with a silence that weighed heavier every minute with nothing left to say. He started to apologize, I started to apologize, until both of us were standing up, two feet apart, not knowing what more to do.

By the time I walked out to the car and drove home, I thought I was clear about what I had done, that I was certain about the things I said. Less than a week later our CO called me in and told me that I was ordered to the Pentagon for a "Debriefing". The term used reminded me of some unfinished business that still wanted to shake its fist and have the last word over a bad argument with some West Coast brass who had long memories.

With my CO's blessing I drove up to D.C. in the dark of early morning, got to the Pentagon and was so lost by the time my last escort led me into the conference room that I couldn't have found my way out with a White House pass. While waiting for the Agency handler to come and protect me, I actually enjoyed engaging in small talk with the folks present, while wearing the beatific smile of one who within 72 hours would be permanently immune from the military hair shirts who wanted to draw my blood for neglecting their orders and calling them assholes a month before. When the handler arrived, he politely cancelled the meeting, instructed me not to answer any questions, and drove me to CIA Headquarters in Langley with a larger than normal swelled head. There I was met by a Bill Redel, my former "In-Country "boss and crafty operator who proceeded to blow enough smoke up a 27-year-old Lt. USNR soon to be (Ret.) to bounce me off the ceiling. I was promised control of special operational PRU unit targeted exclusively on POW recovery Ops in South Vietnam if I went back. The swelling of my head continued while my good judgment kept shrinking. By lunch-time I was committing to going back within ten days on an open tour of 18 months, with two conditions: one, that my transfer be made to an independent command insulating me from the growling dogs I'd heard coming after me that morning; and two, that I could terminate on notice. To seal the deal before I woke up, I was driven to the "Big BuPers" where I was baby-sat by a commander in Navy Security Group—actually an Agency man in uniform. The Commander instructed the Chief Yeoman how to navigate the "Orders" and the Yeoman tried to explain to the Commander that it "couldn't be done." The Commander made it clear that my orders had better be on his desk by the end of the day (it was the time of the *Pueblo* Incident—remember that?)

That particular day was cold and rainy, the kind of day that turned spring back to winter, the kind of weather that any one wanted to flee from—though maybe not as far as Southeast Asia circa 1968. I drove away from the Pentagon in the gloom and icy rain of a dark afternoon strangely relieved to be escaping the insecurity of facing a domestic future that somehow appeared to be as ragged and bleak as the weather outside. I was halfway back to Little Creek before I remembered Rick, my best friend, the guy I would do anything for.

When I told him about my turnabout, he gave me a look I had seen before when I did something that hadn't favorably impressed him. He didn't say anything except that he would have to tell Gert and he'd see me over there when he got settled.

Rick followed me to Vietnam a couple of months later but we were rarely in close enough proximity to allow for a meeting. I felt a sense of guilt—I felt that I was responsible for him being over in Vietnam, in harm's way, but I also tried to tell myself that I was off the hook since we were both in the same fix.

Ultimately, my exclusive assignment was subverted. My good old Boss Bill Redel had sold me down the river. The special POW-PRU team was shelved. In a classic battle of bureaucratic politics, the Agency won a victory by extricating itself from the murky morass of para-military involvement and dumping their programs on the military. This, after the CIA had constructed a complicated and unwieldy structure whose command and control by MACV in conjunction with ARVN was almost certainly doomed, sooner or later, to failure. They called it the Phoenix Program. (It would become a lightening rod of anti-war vitriol and a perpetual target of investigative reporting alleging that Phoenix operations involved torture and assassinations.) So instead of heroic missions to recover POWs I ended up being a transition promoter and part-time briefing lecturer on counter-insurgency tactics. Things looked so bad that I started to think about law school again, or maybe an assignment in Laos "Kicking Bundles" (CIA jargon for flying around and serving as paymaster to indigenous para-military units fighting the clandestine insurgency there).

So when I was getting ready to go home and saw Rick that day in his little compound across from BuPers, a lot of things had happened and we had much to catch up with. Rick told me that Gert and the kids had moved back home to Poughkeepsie, where they would be around their families. He had pretty much decided that he was going to get out even though the Navy was in the process of opening up a career path for "Special Warfare". Like me, he didn't know what he was going to do either.

Maybe we could get into something together? Yeah, maybe we could. We laughed about the stupid things we might get up to, I don't remember what. Time came when one of us had to get back. We started to tell each other to take care, that it would not be long or something like that. I looked down at him. I remember the urgency to say or do something, something to make sure that he would be all right—but all I did was grab him gently by the lapels of his camouflage tunic and bang him lightly against the portico. "Promise me you'll keep your head down." "Yeah, sure, don't worry." "If anything happens to you, Gert will come after me for sure." "Yeah, I know." "I mean it Rick, if anything happens to you I'm going to have to come back and kick your ass, you hear me? I will kick your ASS!" "OK, OK", he said looking up at me with those big blue eyes as I slowly rocked him back and forth in something as close to an embrace as we knew how to manage.

Now, decades later, I am worried that having come this far I might miss the place, pass it by without knowing. When we are across from some docks along the quay I ask Kim to pull over to the side. The docks are built up and servicing larger ships than I remember, small ocean-going cargo ships and tankers. Looking up and down at a corner building, I think there should be a portico, but it's missing, or it never had one, or in all reality this isn't the right place. I find myself willing something to be there, an imaginary memorial plaque or something. How foolish, but then I have never been to Rick's grave either, nor do I know where it is.

When I got back and was discharged, I called an agency guy I worked with about contracting out to Laos and Cambodia but he said forget about it, it's all bullshit, "bag-carrying" paperwork and no fun. But guess what—law school wasn't fun either. Still, I had to do something and force myself to stick with it. Everything that I did those days was like being on a raft that I didn't know how to get off. My self-confidence was going into the tank.

Playing student and living in a third floor walk up, I felt awkward and lonely, half-drowning in the university milieu, see-sawing between the incessant grind of the first year of law and the hysterical anti-war politics of the student population in the Boston area. Rumor had it I was an FBI informant because I wore a coat and tie to class! In October I received an invitation to a friend's wedding in Springfield, Massachusetts, a couple of hours away. It was the first break from school and I looked forward to it. Ted Marks had been in the Teams with me but like so many others who had been tossed around among different assignments, orders and discharges, we had lost touch so I was pleased that I had a chance to attend his wedding and hear some current news about old mates and recent events.

I was late. The church was almost filled. Walking down the aisle, one of the guys approached with the program. We shook hands. He handed me a program and bent forward, "Did you hear about Rick?" "No." "He didn't make it." "What?" "He didn't make it. KIA two months ago. You didn't hear? Where've you been? No one knew where you were."

Rick was already in the ground, buried in Poughkeepsie where he grew up, with full honors and a posthumous Silver Star, and I wasn't there. He had been wounded by a booby-trap but was doing O.K. they told me, until he got a secondary infection and was gone in twenty-four hours—and I wasn't there

A year ago, when driving east and passing Poughkeepsie, I stopped to check out the phone book. Sure enough, there was a Mrs. F. E. Trani, Jr., and there couldn't have been another. I wasn't at all surprised that Gert had not re-married. I wondered what if anything she would say. I finally concluded that it was all so mangled that I should just keep on going. I still want to stop and visit his gravesite one of these days. It's too long overdue. After more than thirty years, the closest I ever got to him was at the "Wall".

27

TOURISM CONSULTANT

When I get back to the hotel the desk gives me an envelope with a note in it. It is both courteous and formal. Would I be able to find time to meet and talk to one of the managers about a professional business matter concerning which the manager was seeking advice? Why not?

I meet him in the bar lounge. He is the same assistant manager I noticed in the office earlier when I was trying figure out my travel plans. He had been painstakingly copying a voluminous book. He is holding it under his arm. Most of the time, I am more observant of the women for obvious reasons while the men are rarely noteworthy. Trung was one of them. About 40 years old, he is handsome and tall for a Vietnamese, around 5'10", and carries himself with an easy elegance. His face is intelligent and gentle. He looks me in the eye and holds my gaze, which is unusual because in some respects, I learned, it is not considered polite to do so. He shakes hands with more comfort than most Vietnamese so I know he is familiar with Americans. He speaks English slowly with a very slight accent, and is extremely polite and appreciative of my courtesy of talking to him (if he only knew how much time I was finding on my hands and my eagerness to fill it up).

He asks me if I would like a drink and we order. He has a glass of water, apologetically telling me he is still on duty. He asks me the usual questions. Why did I come to Vietnam? When was it that I was here before and what did I do. How did I come to stay at the Palace? Do I like it? My approach to meeting someone is to be open and candid, hoping that it will encourage the other person to be the same. Trung listens very carefully and considers. Speaking in a very soft voice and looking down at the cocktail table, he proceeds to tell me his story. Everyone in Vietnam over the age of 30 has a story.

Trung's father worked for the Americans during the war, doing something in "information gathering and analysis" (probably for the C.I.A.). In 1973, when Trung was eight, the North invaded and his parents were relocated to the United States. They now live near Phoenix, Arizona. In the chaos of the emergency, they were unable to get him out so an aunt brought him up. This was during the "very difficult" times. For many years he waited, hoping to be able to leave. But as life would have it, he says and shrugs, he married and soon had three children. Still he waited for the opportunity to get out, but then, when things looked as if they would get better, he decided to stay. His oldest boy is now 15. Three years ago he was allowed to visit the U.S. and spent three months with his parents. At first he thought he would bring his family to the U.S. but then changed his mind. His parents were getting very old. He worried what would happen to his own family in the U.S. when his parents died; then his family would have no roots or direction. Besides, he has lived his whole life in Vietnam and considers it his country even though the communists have made it very "difficult". After his visit, he felt Vietnam was very backward and very slow but he resolved to dedicate his life to make a better place for his family and the whole country, even though it was not as promising as it should be. It is still their birth land, and at least his children face a far better future than he had and he is hopeful they can successfully develop their destiny here maybe as successfully as they could in America. Anyway, he said looking up and shrugging again, now his parents were too old to return as Viet Khieu, and he is too old to go. So he will stay and try to make things better.

He smiles. It is a gentle smile, straightforward, rueful, stoic and, in all respects, disarming. This man has just sat down, asked me some basic questions, listened to me prattle felicitous replies, and then told me the story of his life without the slightest embellishment. In a manner much misunderstood among American men, the Vietnamese are intimate, warm and often openly affectionate among themselves, not that Trung was all of those, for he remained very reserved throughout our conversation. But the notion of not relating his story with me was equally as out of the question as to conceal it.

After a short pause I point at the book and ask him how far he got in copying it. (It is the trade journal of the American Hotel and Lodging Association, listing all travel agencies and tour and cruise enterprises, roughly the size of medium U.S. city phonebook). Not far, he admits and then starts telling me how I might help him. Trung is the Assistant Manager in charge of marketing and some other ancillary functions for the hotel. He was in general management but volunteered to initiate its marketing. The trouble is there is little to no marketing expertise to draw from and the smallest of budgets with which to proceed, hence the book he is trying to copy. He tells me he had ordered it 6 months ago.

He explains that Saigon Tourist is the government's central agency controlling the tourism industry of the South, of which the Continental Palace is a part. It operates as a SOE (State Owned Enterprise). Nevertheless, the Continental Palace has participated in organizing a voluntary group of a number of "historic" boutique hotels numbering no more than a dozen, in locations ranging from Hanoi down to Saigon. This group can function as a loose promotional association only. It has no official authorization and it can't bargain for its members as a group. As a result, each of its hotels remains as its own principal for promotional and marketing funds as well as seeking operating subsidies and capital funding. Trung's purpose in copying the U.S. trade journal is to provide his group with a means to access the US travel agencies directly in order to coordinate group bookings and travel.

What Trung is describing is the most primitive of trade associations and the practical means by which collective memberships may be developed to underwrite the costs and achieve the efficiencies of group organized services. When I ask him whether his "Historic" hotel group has approached Saigon Tourism with a proposal to authorize a semi-autonomous association to finance his approach, Trung shakes his head and gives me a tired look. "No" he says, "Everyone is afraid to sacrifice their special relationships with the bureaucracies so in the end we are competing against the group."

In the end what Trung really wants is to vent his frustration to someone who has lived a different experience. This I am more than happy to do, but although I assure him he is headed in the right direction, his description of the obstacles is depressing. The world of Trung presents a meager landscape limited by ragged horizons while ours, in contrast, is so extravagant with freedom, dazzling in opportunity and blessed by prosperity.

Looking at his watch, he tells me he needs to return to work and says he hopes that when I go back I will say nice things about the country and his hotel and that maybe when I return I will no longer find these problems. As he leaves, he thanks me quietly for my time. Watching him walk away, it strikes me that I am the one who should be thankful.

28

NEW FOUNDLAND?

The North was terra incognita for me. I had never been as far north as Hue, or even close to it. It lies almost mid-point along the coast between Saigon and Hanoi, an epicenter of Vietnam's cultural history when it was established as the dynastic capital in the 18th century. Prior to that Hanoi had long remained the ancestral seat of Vietnamese political power. Hue, since its dynastic ascendancy, has been considered the most beautiful city in Vietnam, particularly because of its palace compounds, its only crown jewels, mostly preserved despite some heavy destruction during the war.

The passenger manifest of our Air Vietnam flight produces a mix of Vietnamese, a few western visiting business types and a few of us plain tourists. I'm seated next to an administrator of a community college in St. John's, Newfoundland, of all places. This trip is his third in as many years and his odyssey exemplifies all the peculiarities of new global bed mating.

His name is Tom and he and I are of approximate age, which is becoming my way of saying that I am only a few years older. His college has been significantly sponsored and subsidized by the Canadian government to specialize in off—shore oil drilling environments and fish farming, among other curricula. In the early 1990's several offshore oil syndicates were undertaking joint venture exploration with the Vietnamese Government. At the time there was both great optimism and yearning over Vietnam's offshore field prospects particularly because Vietnam is perhaps the poorest Southeast Asian country in raw materials and especially in petroleum resources. Since Tom's college had developed an expertise first in the Northern Atlantic and eventually trained people to work in Asia, it was contracted to design and set up the oil rig system for the prospective Vietnamese field.

This initial involvement collapsed after the disappointing exploration results. Nevertheless, with a relationship in the making, Tom's group ended up responding to the new and different proposal for organizing and managing Vietnam's fish farming industry, eventually becoming project managers for some of this effort. In the course of the one-and-a-half hour flight I learn a lot, much of which I have been gathering in bits and pieces along the way.

Much of what he does, Tom explains, is to try to improve the internal dynamics of Vietnamese management. This includes attempting to wean them from their dependency on centralized regulation and to weed the Communist political cant out of their business decision-making. The process is hard and slow because of the fear and insecurity Vietnamese experience when they deviate from party dogma and doctrine. The result is a pervasive disincentive to support taking initiatives and making decisions up and down the line.

When I mention my conversation with Trung of the Continental Palace, he tells me a story about their efforts to expand Vietnamese international thinking by emphasizing the need to network and interface with other regional market systems; those being the other economies in the Southeast Asian axis currently composing ASEAN (Association of Southeast Asian Nations). At first, he said, they were very enthusiastic and anxious to participate. Tom's group set up conferences and workshops, which he felt were successful. They emphasized how productive it would be to establish ongoing relationships among their counterparts in other international entities and the benefits of taking advantage of interacting markets, competitive pricing, crop yield fluctuations etc. Following the conferences, he and his group promoted a follow-up sequence that would build, he thought, a viable network system.

All the key counterparts agreed to this initiative and Tom's group returned to Newfoundland. Six months later, when they arrived for the next stage, they discovered that none of the initiatives had been followed up. The reasons, they found, had nothing to do with the substance of the proposed strategies but rather with the process of the partnering. The Vietnamese didn't want to let their competitors know how inefficient, underfinanced and disorganized they were in comparison. It had come down to a question of "Face"!

29

HUE, THE ROYAL CITY

As the mists withdraw their veils, the morning over Hue sparkles with light. The lacy crescents of coastal beaches hold back a cobalt blue sea. The Perfume River unwinds into the fan of its long fingered delta. Fishing boats on the bay sit like birds on a pond. Nothing motorized, or fast, or intrusive yet mars the still awakening day.

At the Continental Palace, Trung had arranged for a reservation at the hotel Huong Giang. It is one of the "chain" of older traditional "historical" hotels and from all appearances the nicest I have seen. It has an art-deco presentation, a 50's modern style extending in a string of semi-attached bungalows along the high bank of the famous Perfume River. Each bungalow offers a view of the river and the city across with green hills and mountains in the distance beneath a cloudless blue sky.

I feel buoyant to be in a new place and energized by the sense of a new start after a week and a half of mixed feelings. The hotel is surrounded by its gardens, which open to the wide grassy banks of the river. After a relaxed stroll past the huddle of fishing boats I reach a gaudily colored crenellated bridge that marks the entrance to the formerly royal city.

The approach is aesthetically framed by an arbor of large banyans, hovering over a round-about accessed by graveled walkways with fountains and the first well tended garden I have seen so far: rose beds, flowering hibiscus and ornamental palms. The atmosphere is different. Perhaps it is an orderliness or cleanliness that calms the nerves and reduces the tensions of haste. Or maybe it is just me, freer than I have felt before, more optimistic: perhaps "On Vacation" is the phrase.

Hue is a city of bridges, one of which is only for pedestrian and non-motorized traffic. It's bliss to join this flow without the snarl of cyclos and their choking exhaust. I enjoy the unrestricted freedom and the pace of walking when thoughts slow and observation can take its time.

The Citadel of Hue is a vast enclosure, approximately ten kilometers in area, surrounded by great earth and stone barricades faced with brick. It was of 19th century French military design but only the external fortifications yield any hint of foreign influence. The rest is pure Vietnamese. Within its walls lies the Imperial enclosure, at one time a forbidden city to outsiders, perhaps in imitation of the Chinese. Here in the 19th Century the Nyugen dynasty ruled through Vietnam's last Mandarin-ate.

It is hot and getting hotter. The kind of heat that makes me walk slowly and look for shade. The monsoon has yet to arrive here. The dry brown patches of grass, the hard baked uneven pathways, and the spiking tufts of weeds that crowd out of every broken space in the brick walls and facings produce the bleak and unkempt vision of a dishonored cemetery. In fact, under Ho's regime it was allowed to become just that, and remained so until recently.

The battle of Hue City, the agonizing flameout of the TET Offensive of 1968, was one of the most, if not the most, brutal and destructive single engagements of the war. Though most of the considerable damage occurred in the surrounding areas and the Citadel itself escaped most of it, enough was done to leave behind marks of battle that are clear even 30 years later. That these scars should be allowed to remain an eyesore today reveals the official disregard for the integrity of its place in Vietnamese history, notwithstanding its cultural uniqueness. There is nothing comparable to it in the country today. Even so, communist government's ideological dogma called for devaluing the country's historic symbols to mere relics of the country's feudal and imperial ancestry, Hanoi's historic resentment that the Nyugen dynasty removed the royal court from its traditional seat of power in Hanoi may play a part in its official disregard. But unrequited hard times and desperation for hard currency required reconsideration of Hue's revenue as a featured tourist attraction. In typical half-assed fashion, however, not much has been done with the exception of seeking funding from international groups to pay for its reconstruction.

Wandering through the royal living quarters, appearance halls and meeting places, one has to admire the simple grace and open style of their architectural design: the detailed flourishes of their symbolic gargoyles, the deep and resonant colors of their lacquer and gilt. Each tomb, pavilion, temple, or other building stands on its own platform of surrounding steps, leading the eye to look up into the spaciousness that knits the sweep of sky, hills, mountains and river together in a vista of freedom and isolation from of the rest of the world.

Here, one is in the presence of a distinctly "other" world. The lives and functions of the occupants of the royal village were traditionally both screened from the view of those in the "outside" world and confined to these secret spaces. Wandering through and among tumbled walls and bare grounds, imagination can re-create the quiet and private garden it was cultivated to be. Given a few moments of privacy away from tourists one might conjure up a vision of the sedate pomp and ceremony in which the select inhabitants lived their roles as icons behind stiff brocades and painted faces, performing the precise choreography of human sacrifice, staged in an exotic terrarium enclosed by ritual, deceit, and doom.

Noontime finds me seeking the shelter of a tree-shaded concourse along the eastern wall where the awnings of licensed vendors are allowed. While I am bargaining over the price of an "authentic" antique porcelain teapot, I hear a loud and rude American voice. "Make sure they don't cheat you!"

Startled, I look about but see only Vietnamese. "Come on over and join us," the voice insists. It comes from a group of five young Vietnamese seated around a patio table at a refreshment stand. I walk over and look down at the teenage girl doing the talking. She smiles up at me with a cocky grin and says "I thought I was only one from America around here. Where are you from? I'm from Grand Rapids, Michigan. You sound like a Midwesterner." She is showing off. The others, a younger girl and three young men, just look up at me. "Have a seat" she says "and a Pepsi or something, but make sure you don't drink their water. There's nothing worth eating. The food is really weird here." I sit down. The waiter approaches.

"These are my cousins", she explains. "There are a lot more, but they stayed back at home. They don't speak English, but I am helping them. They are trying to teach me Vietnamese like they speak here. We're not getting very far. Do you like it here? It's really backward; I can't wait to get home to normal. The standard of living is really bad. There's no one to talk to and not much to do and the food is yucky."

The girl, Kim, becomes a fountain of unconnected anecdotes in a stream of American accented colloquialisms as she tells me about her two month stay with her mother at her father's family home. It's soon apparent that she enjoys playing the modern girl complaining about Third World inconveniences. The family is from a village "in the boonies" that is about a five hour drive from Hue. "There is nothing to do there: no TV and not even a phone." The family rented a van for the trip and it has broken down. Her mother, uncle, and grandmother are with a mechanic trying to fix it, along with the driver who's a friend of theirs. They've already been waiting for three hours. Her cousins are OK but they don't know much about the world "or things". She "can't wait to get back home."

She is clearly savoring her role—world savvy, hip in modern living and secure in the "made it in America" attitude. Although one might make an allowance for her brashness as a symptom of youth, in showing off to me she seems to display a certain disrespect for her cousins, who, elbows on their knees, continue to look down sullenly in obvious discomfort. There is "face" at stake here so I take it as my cue to get up and move on. I tell her to order another round of drinks, pay the bill, and say good-bye. "See you back in the U.S.A.!" she calls out for all to hear.

On my way back, I cross an open area bordered by a row of large banyan trees and see a van parked in the shade with its hood up. A few people are sitting on a carpet on the ground as if they are having a picnic. There is an older woman dressed formally in a white silk Ao Dais with a sun parasol. Next to her is a plump pleasant faced woman in black tights and a collared blouse with lipstick and rouge. Two men in sleeveless T-shirts have their arms stuck under the hood of the van while another lies underneath. I have clearly encountered Kim's family party.

The women look up, smiling warmly in greeting. "You must be the mother of Kim", I said. "You know Kim? How you know Kim?" "I just met her over there" pointing to where I came from. "She told me you had car problems." "Oh, Yes! Car break down, long trip". She gets up and shakes my hand, still smiling, "This my mother-in-law", she nods to the elderly lady, "and my brothers", pointing. The men had stop working on the van, bow with Vietnamese formality and stand respectfully while the mother explains the situation in Vietnamese. One of the men grins widely and says "Kim, American!" with a big smile and returns to his work. The front axle is on the ground and in pieces. It appears that the van is a long way from being repaired.

The mother speaks clear but truncated English. She stops often and deferentially translates for the grandmother, who is the husband's mother and, in Vietnamese society, the matriarch of the family to whom the daughter-in-law is familially subordinate and owes primary loyalty. The mother has brought Kim to Vietnam to meet her family for the first time. It is difficult for Kim, she explains, because she does not understand Vietnamese life and is not used to its different ways. It is very different here but maybe Kim will get more used to it and better understand how things are she says wistfully. She smiles, but has succeeded in making me understand that it has been difficult for her to balance the situation of being the mother of her American adolescent while also re-assuming the various roles of a Vietnamese woman in her husband's family.

She tells me that they live in Grand Rapids where her husband has a carpet cleaning business. She has not been back to Vietnam since they left at the end of the war. Her husband was a soldier and they had to flee. It took three years before they arrived in the United States and another year before they were accepted for relocation to Grand Rapids. Kim is the oldest of three children, the only one who would be old enough to understand the way things are here. She smiles widely and says something to her mother-in-law, who returns her smile and comes close to laughing for the first time.

"Hey" a shout breaks in from up the pathway. It's Kim, accompanied by her cousins. "You found them. Is it fixed yet? What's going on?" she asks, flopping down on the blanket and talking as if everyone is listening. The rest of them ignore her. The grandmother watches her and blinks frequently. The mother looks over at the men and then back at me and, catching my eye, smiles knowingly.

Vietnamese family life is a tightrope of decorum in which what is said and how it is said is carefully balanced, according to role and position. Kim's remarks and free wheeling behavior clearly upset this delicate balance. For the grandmother, it hitches the weave in the loom. The sheer impulsivity and unpredictability of American behavior make Vietnamese nervous. In Vietnam everyone knows by decorum what should come next—but Americans have no such defined script for behavior so they improvise on the run.

Their etiquette requires them to offer me an invitation to join the family in their noon meal. Kim loudly insists on it, as if I live next door. The grandmother smiles and nods agreeably, but I want to move on. What better signal than setting them up for a group photograph. When I suggest it, everyone runs for a camera.

There, under the shade of the banyan tree, stands a Vietnamese family in its three generations. They pose in all the stiffness of a daguerreotype, calling to mind generations before when a photograph was a formal portrait, an emblem of family solidarity, in an age when all still lived under the same roof in the same town as their forebears buried out back under the paternal shade tree.

What happens to the family of Kim in this sequence of heredity is still an unanswered question; the picture is no longer a portrait, but a snapshot. There, in its first generation Diaspora, they stare out with split visions, disparate opportunities and divided destinies.

Vietnamese history has never recorded an emigration of any substantial significance with the exception of internal peninsular movements like those in 1954. The extraordinary integrity of Vietnamese culture and belief has accounted for this continuity, even in the face of cyclical political and dynastic displacements. Prior to the refugee exodus of 1975 there were no established or permanent Vietnamese colonies anywhere—nothing like those of the Hoa. The involuntary migration to the U.S. was Vietnam's first. Recent statistics indicate that the Viet Khieu population is now 300,000.

Though it is too soon to conclude, the reluctance of the Central Government to commit to a market economy, and its refusal to relax the strictures of totalitarian political power, provides little incentive for the Viet Khieu to return permanently. Moreover, the comparative benefits in material standards of American domesticity and the extraordinary prosperity achieved relative to native Vietnamese conditions seem to have cemented their long term commitment to permanent resident status in the U.S.. In this sense, one can draw a close parallels with the present Cuban situation, including the developing frictions between and among the émigré and native elements as the disparities of economic conditions harden attitudes on both sides. Underlying this issue is the critical dependence of Vietnam as a nation and a people on the money sent back to relatives in Vietnam by the émigré community. How ironic: the "Boat People" of yesterday are floating the nation of today.

30

HEAVEN UNDER ITS OWN ROOF

The Perfume River is another story. It tells me that I am in a different Vietnam quite different than the one I knew and have thought about so much over the years. The Mekong Delta functions as a great sump. From thousands of miles away, from western China, the waters of rivers flow into it, flush out their alluvial sediments and merge into the sea through the delta's tidal sluices. There is something pulmonary about it, though it breathes water rather than air. Everything in its vast kingdom is mud brown and swamp green, flat and swollen. Here, in complete contrast, the Perfume River is like a clear vein; specific in origin, defined in character and simple in quality. One can glimpse its beginnings and ends in one long day's travel.

Looking down into it as the bow of the sampan parts the morning mist and cuts through its mirrored surface, I see its waters are dark and clear. The sun picks up and lights the tops of enveloping hills and distant mountains ranging in the west. The sky begins to clear of clouds and coolness still lingers, though not for long. The panorama of surrounding hills lends the feeling of being inside a bowl in a special world apart and perhaps it was this impression that produced its location for the imperial city and appropriate sites for the landscape of its royal tombs and sacred pagodas that ring the riverbanks facing west.

I found a tour boat operator anxious enough for a fare to take me solo. For the price asked, I enjoy the luxury of having the boatman's small family and a manager/owner at my service. The manager was one of the usual hawkers who hover outside of hotels and follow guests down the streets, pressing their wares, but this one seemed to speak reasonable English and displayed a sense of humor and a little wry wit on the side. His name is Nyugen, a national name that covers the "Johns" of this world.

He points out the series of tombs and shrines that decorate the river-banks west of the city. Graceful stairways flow down to the waters edge. Flaring balustrades are entwined with bougainvillea in coral, yellow and red. Tiered pagodas protected by towering shade trees stare out at us. The river traffic is steady mostly with barges, hulls filled with gravel or rock for construction. They are uniformly 30 to 40 feet with an after cabin for the boatman's family. Clotheslines fly bright garments in the wind, smoke from their braziers and coarse fuel exhaust trail off the sterns.

A few miles up river the crowding of city along the banks lets go. A nest of sampans moor together in a floating commune. The rising sun signals the heat of the day to come. The river bends and weaves around gentile hills prefacing blue green mountains. Riverbanks flatten out into broad field or marsh. Straw hats of workers bob and bend amidst the green fields as the boys and girls tend the water buffalo in the muddy shore pools.

Nyugen offers me a cold drink. He has brought a cooler and food. The service is a la carte. He asks me how far I would like to go. There are several substantial shrines up above, he tells me. We could either see them all or just a few. One, he says is very nice. If we get there early we may see it without a tour group. Much nicer, he smiles.

By noontime, we come to a colossal new electrical power plant project still under construction, surrounded by brightly whitewashed workers quarters so new that they look like presents that have just been unwrapped. Great power lines rise up and out from behind the plant flowing skyward on massive reinforced concrete towers that resemble huge giants marching up and over the distant ridge, hauling power on their shoulders into the promise of the future, lets hope.

In great contrast, The Jade Cup Temple sits up on a bluff half hidden among lofty trees, staring down the river at our approach. This, Nyugen says, is the most sacred but least visited temple among the many for which the river is noted. When I ask why, he shrugs, smiles and says, "It is very small and the climb is steep", as he points up through the overhanging trees and foliage.

An attendant at the landing charges some dockage fee. The boatman, his wife and little child spread out their mat to prepare the afternoon meal. Nyugen offers to accompany me up the steep path but I see he would rather take a nap. He is relieved, and I am left alone.

The path is made of hewn stone and winds up along the granite face of the bluff. At the top is a garden entrance and a sign and booth indicating payment of an admission fee is required, but there is no attendant to take it. Off to the side of the balustrade overlooking the bluff I see a hammock pitched on the steep slope and some feet sticking out. The attendant is napping as well. The afternoon sun is now in its western quadrant and burns through my shirt.

The temple is not large. Carved stone icons of dragons and wild dogs guard its approach through an archway that presents a small courtyard. The pagoda's peaked roof swings gracefully out into a pavilion, shading the entrance steps. Tall carved wooden columns gilded in gold and draped in heavy brocade announce its opening above. I climb to the threshold.

I hear footsteps behind me. It is the attendant. He has put on his shoes. I think he's coming to admonish me for entering without a ticket. Instead, he holds out his arm politely beckoning me to enter, and indicates that I am free to wander. With a small bow he turns to leave but points out the tray presenting bowls of flower petals, incense, and candles for offerings, with a plate set aside for contributions.

With the sun at my back it takes a while to adjust my vision. Left alone, I stare into the dark interior as if it is a well. Stillness and shadow are wed here. Only the quiver of flame from candles and the spiral of smoke from incense allow motion. A universe of materials, forms and objects lie, sit, stand and hang somnolent as if in a trance, awaiting. On tables, shelves and hooks, prayer flags, wheels, beads, scrolls and banners offer, proclaim, recite, chant and intone a soundless dominion. Swords, scepters, staffs, spears, gauntlets, robes, cloaks, helmets, caps, crowns and masks wait like props waiting for use in some drama. Cups, goblets, pipes, plates, bowls and utensils are on hand for a feast. Everything is in sleep—or is it?

I pass by the large tapestry that shrouds the rear of the sanctum. A great purple candle sits in an ornate bronze bowl on a crowded altar. Buddhas in all embodiments watch with inner peace while large porcelain jars and vases portray demons and warriors wrestling with eternity. To the side, a ladder leads above. I climb up.

Splinters of light pierce through tiles glistening with sliver motes. A shaft of it splashes on the foot of a throne of carved wood embossed in jade and semi precious stones sitting vacant, its scepter and staff athwart. Lead-heavy drapery, silk banners brocaded in gold and silver hang in the breathless air. Here it must be that holy men perform their rites, move with unearthly mien, isolate in their dream of the sacred. There in the farthest recess in deep gloom sits a smaller altar presenting a series of jade and glass bowls filled with sand and unlit candles. Beside it, in bronze trays, incense sticks are set out to be purchased and burned as offerings. The table is prepared.

Shrouded in quiet the rasp of my match tears off a patch of it. The candle's flame trembles and stretches into the gloom. Shadows grow and quiver behind the peaks and edges of innumerable objects. Flecks of silver and gold sparkle in the threading of robes and curtains on the hilts of swords, an eyebrow of a Buddha. Oiled bamboo, varnished tables and polished teak glisten and smile from the dark.

What is this place? A useless attic littered with the discards of soulless treasure waiting only for its theatre? Where is the design of hierarchy, the trinity, the circle, the slow revolutions of the Yin and the Yang, the thousand heads of Shiva, the left or right side of the "Father"? Who is addressed in prayer? It doesn't matter.

There is something sacred here. Worship is going on. I am not alone, but in the company of an essence of things, an assemblage of beliefs inhabited with spirit, enveloped in completeness. Out of bountiful disarray a way emerges, blazes a trail of emblems signaling attainment. What is more, it is for me, as well as for anyone, a passer-by who stumbles in from the road.

I light incense sticks in each bowl and then all the candles. Light spreads out like freedom. Everything glows. Solitude inhabits. The moment empties. Incense becomes prayer. I can see it and feel it, rising, wavering into its slow dance, uplifted to a heaven under its own roof.

On the trip back, the motorized sampans passing by are almost all family affairs clustered with children grouped around the stern, playing interminable games or scuttling about busy with deck chores. As always, each minds the younger, down to the still suckling infant tucked on the hip. As if in a chorus they never fail to wave, point and call at any unusual sight such as a tall tourist stranger gazing over at them

I am always returning to scenes of children, always present, always open, cared for or minded, always touching and being touched. In cities and villages, fields and boats, everywhere, caring is prevalent, togetherness palpable, cheer and laughter everywhere. Are they always happy? Probably not. Do they have dysfunctional families? Of course, but I've never heard tell of it. In this age of intensifying examination of the learning characteristics and capacities of infants and very young children, the development of emotional health and a sense of well-being may be found to depend on the ready expression of joy and the gentle laughter of loving kindness. Who can resist being inflated by these buoys marking the channels for the arrival of their future?

That evening a tall young waitress is elegant in her sweeping white Ao Dais uniform as she leads me to my table at the hotel's sky-top restaurant. On the fifth floor, it overlooks the Perfume River with softly illuminated bridges leading into the city. It's a pretty sight in the dark of the evening. As she seats me, I say "Cam Anh Co" (thank you, young lady) in my best Vietnamese. She lights up with a smile of surprise and says in a soft lilting English "Oh, you speak Vietnamese?" (It is one of the country's charms that while many of the young adults not only speak English well but also correctly, they are delighted when there is some responsive effort to attempt Vietnamese). She follows up with the question "You have been in Vietnam before?" "Yes", I tell her, "A long time ago". "Oh, you are American?" she asks, pouring my water. "Yes, I was here during the war" I tell her. She pauses looking at me wide eyed and then down, embarrassed at being so inquisitive and withdraws. I wonder whether I should tell people right off, but then what else would I say?

When I've finished with the meal, a man in a white dinner jacket and black bow-tie approaches with the check. I assume he is the maitre d' and reckon he is about 40. In a soft voice, he asks me about the meal, but then inquires how long I have been in Vietnam and where. Word has gotten around. "Vietnam much better than before", he says, "People happier now. We now have a future. What do you think? May I ask?"

He looks at me closely. His expression is penetrating and he is hoping that I respond. I wanted to assure him, yes of course everything will be better, just wait, but I don't. Instead I say simply, "Anything is better than the war".

His eyes turn down. He drops his head and lowers his voice almost to a whisper. "Yes", he urges, "anything is better than war. We cannot forget! War is terrible thing! Terrible!" he repeats. "Such misery!" He rushes forward now, "We must never let it happen again! We must put it away!" he repeats and then catches himself, suddenly uncertain, and steps back changing his tone "I am sorry to speak so about this, I should not say more. I am sorry." He then bows from the waist, his face looking down, and withdraws.

His words still me. A stranger has approached me to unburden his deepest feeling as if it were a confession and then disappeared, like a shuttered window flung open and then suddenly closed. The movements and noises of the dining room return to the background of my consciousness. The lights of the Trang Tien and Phu Xuan bridges off to the west resemble shining bracelets on the black satin of the river. The headlights of cyclos trickle like small streams along the boulevard, which scene is the dream now or then.

The Communist occupation of Hue at the initiation of the 1968 TET Offensive became the greatest single atrocity of the war. Taken completely by surprise, the GVN forces abandoned the defense of the town and left the citizenry at the mercy of the insurgents. By carefully preplanned design and direction almost the entire class of bourgeoisie living in the city was rounded up and imprisoned. Over the following two weeks more than 3,000 people, many women, Buddhist monks, schoolteachers, clerics and those considered bourgeois, were systematically murdered. The extent and number of the victims remained sketchy and little known until numerous mass graves were gradually uncovered, some of them years later. This short lived reign of terror was largely prepared for and carried out by local indigenous Viet Cong cadre under the authority of North Vietnamese regular forces commanders.

Although they were long inured to the cruelty and destruction of war, the Hue massacre shocked its citizenry and still haunts them with the depth of savagery it unleashed among and within themselves. It is especially humiliating, considering the cultural superiority with which Vietnam has historically viewed its baser neighbors, Cambodia, and Laos. For a people who both honor and fear ghosts as powerful influences in their cultural credos, the ghosts of Hue's dead lurk still as dispossessed souls in a state of unrest and suspended retribution.

31

HANOI

Hanoi. A name for a hard place, ruled without remorse, dooming an entire generation for their obdurate and now corroded ideals. The East Berlin of the East. I have imagined it all these years in barrack gray, a sunless citadel bare of color and a place naked of laughter. Now I will see it for myself.

When we depart Hue, it is a sunny morning with blue skies, but overcast gray by the time we make our approach. Rain clouds lie upon the dark line of western hills like dirty towels. The countryside is flat, a dull plate stained with the lazy stroke of a great winding river that spills in huge meanders around and through a patchwork of rice fields intersected by canals. Along their banks, thin tree lines offer scant shelter to dreary dark roofed hamlets. From the airplane, it is a bleak, depressing monochrome—and I think that it serves them right.

Hanoi sits in the middle of the Red River Delta, ringed with highlands and mountains to the north and 60 miles from the sea. Throughout history it has been a bull's eye for devastating floods. What keeps it dry, if not high, is a complex and historic man-made system of levees and dikes that diverts and canalizes the river around it. The topography is so flat and the city so low that it is only from the height of the great Choung Duong bridge spanning the main channel that the city can be glimpsed as an entity: a dark moated amoeba squatting along the western bank featureless, plain and smog smothered.

Ever since I thought of returning to Vietnam, Hanoi, the going to it, the being in it, has stirred a resentful pissy streak of ambivalence. For a while I considered passing it up altogether—better than picking at the scabs of defeat. Anyway, it could have been a long story, but I decided to make it short. So, here I am, after 30 years. I'm about to enter a place I would never have wanted to go unless I was riding on top of my own tank—and "poof" all of a sudden in a strange epiphany I find I'm going to like it.

I like the layout, the wide streets, the uniformity of style, the organized way their traffic seems to flow, and the neat aspect of the people. Astounding to me, the broad sidewalks are piled high with electronic appliances as if there is a citywide fire sale on consumer electronics. In short, it gives a first impression of a busy, workable place. The ambience is bustling but subdued, organized and clean and I remember reading somewhere that Hanoi claimed at one time to be the Paris of the East but I can't tell how much Paris there is. Maybe the rest has yet to come? So wouldn't you know it, by the time we arrive at the center of town the chip rolls off my shoulder and I'm hooked on the place like a secret agent.

It is an adventure to secure a cyclo and get to the hotel that Mai had reserved for me. Loading up a 200 lb. Yankee with a large duffle, valise, and day-pack on a 2 liter moto seems to be no problem for the pith helmeted driver with big wraparound Ray-Bans who almost grabs me off the airport van. I show him the hotel card and the helmet just nods, loads the duffle over my shoulders, drapes the day-pack over the handlebars, and heaps the valise on the gas tank. We follow and weave among the tight knots of cyclos that stream down wide straight streets. Although the cyclo's springs bottom at every bump and a few of our turns threaten to lay us down, with the duffle hanging out like a huge pair of shoulder pads providing the downfield blocking we make the goal line for about a buck fifty.

The Thuy Nga is a small boutique hotel, a renovated townhouse of 4 floors and 12–15 rooms catering mostly to Vietnamese business types like Mai for their Hanoi layovers. It's around the corner of the historic Hoa Kiem Lake, considered as the most attractive district of the city. As soon as I check in I'm out on the street to case the place.

For something to do, and to provide some focus to a completely undefined venture, I'm in search of Vietnamese art work in lacquer. The only place I found in Saigon that showed some contemporary impressionistic work had nothing suitable on display small enough to transport and I didn't want to test the perils of shipping. They told me back in Saigon that most of the lacquer work originated from Hanoi. With time and a poorly printed business card of an artist given to me I thought I would wander through some local art shops in search of more information.

My taste and interest in decorative lacquer-ware I owe to a Major Thanh of 30 years ago, one of those quirks of circumstances that fill the small spaces of our lives. Thanh was a handsome, un-ambitious but well placed officer on the South Vietnamese general staff. I was assigned to brief and train him for the liaison role with our special operations force. In the organizational upheaval of post TET counter-insurgency war strategy, a major decision was made to rapidly expand and transfer the Agency's management and direction of its PRU operational program by turning it over to the MACV/GVN military authorities. This, as I noted earlier, led ultimately to the "Phoenix Program".

I was to baby-sit the good Major Thanh and encourage him to sign on to our policy objectives. He was a pleasant though somewhat formal man who felt ill at ease among rougher sorts, but following our return to Saigon from the northern provinces of I Corps. he became more cheerful and out-wardly friendly. I was invited to dine at his family home. It was a set-up.

Arriving at their handsome townhouse, I was generously received by the parents, sisters, brothers, and uncles and entertained at perhaps the most sumptuous oriental meal I will ever attend. The family turned out to be merchants of fine arts and valuable goods, including exquisite lacquer work: trays, plates, bowls and panels from which I was to make a selection. These would be gifts given for my worthy friendship and protection of their son, the Major. I was suitably impressed and enjoying the profuse offerings of vintage rice wine when the issue of the good Major's son's sen-sitive draft status came delicately to the fore. They were worried that he would be drafted, which to them meant front line duty, and assumed that our new friendship and camaraderie might secure some consideration in arranging his enrollment among our units; perhaps a rear echelon slot on the order of truck-driving, or even better, driving a jeep, which would assure a higher ranking accompaniment. I expressed my sympathy. After the scare of TET and its twisted fortunes it was hardly unnatural to seek a safe refuge for their flesh and blood.

But first, before we "talked", as they summoned their retainers, they wanted to tell me about how they made their lacquer-ware and ushered me into the part of the house where they had their artwork on display. Entering a high lofted hallway lit with large candles on recessed sconces, an array of mirroring objects seemed to shine and flicker against the backdrop of dark polished mahogany and carved cabinetry. Trays, vases, boxes and chests, many inlaid with several colored mosaics in classic design, lined the recessed walls, each space presenting slightly different textures and intricacies of style. It was the grandmother who took over and slowly, in somewhat stilted English, began to explain the several stages and laminates that gave the finished product its luster and design. She would occasionally stop and watch me, following my eyes, so that when my gaze fixed on something one of the retainers would bring it to me so that she could point out its artistry. She smiled constantly, but her small squinting eyes gleamed like a snake and I was in her den.

It was a marvelous set piece—her oriental delicacy against my midwestern obtuseness. Had we been left alone, who knows what the outcome would have been. I was taken by the beauty and subtlety of the lacquerware and eager to take advantage of their generosity—right up to the moment when they brought in the major's son and lost their game.

He should have been warned not to wear his gold chains, not to talk with a cigarette in his mouth and insolent look me in the eye. I bet his family lacquer inventory that he was a "Saigon Cowboy", a genus of wartime; well—off Saigon adolescents who developed a treacherous combination of black market smarts, feline viciousness and capitalistic pimp skills.

Why, yes, I thought it could be arranged, but there might be a slight problem with the very arduous combat training required by the entire complement of our special force, and if he could graduate from that, such an assignment could very well become available, and yes, I would be happy to take some lacquer back to the U.S. to demonstrate the artistry and loyalty of the Vietnamese.

Laden with gifts, avowals of lasting friendship, and the soupy cement of promises, I departed with not the least intention of lifting a finger for the snot-nosed, draft dodging little shit. Neither did I feel any remorse for the taking of the "very old and rare" objects that I carried with me, and still possess, as good and valid consideration for an agreement I had no intention of keeping. I never saw or heard from Major Thanh again. It was just before I resigned from my contract and returned home for good. I still enjoy the few pieces of lacquer-ware that have survived the years despite the knowledge that none of it was either "very old" or "very rare".

With this almost forgotten incident coming to the fore, I wonder what I'll find this time. Two blocks down the street I find a small store of objects of art and decide to make some inquires. Three or four Vietnamese men are lingering in the rear discussing some small objects taken from a bag. They look up when I come in but continue their transaction. The narrow space is lined with glass cabinets of jade and semi-precious stones, ceramic ceremonial figurines as well as traditional drawings of Vietnamese scenes, but no lacquer hand-paintings. As I turn to leave, one of the men calls out in English, asking what I'm looking for. He is a very slight, pale, almost frail man with a crooked face and a lopsided toothy grin who could be anywhere from 20 to 50 but his brown tobacco stained teeth put him at the far end.

I tell him about my interest in lacquer work. He asks me why. He then tells me I am an American and that it is strange for Americans to ask about Vietnamese art because they don't know anything about it. As he goes on, it is obvious that he wants to talk English and has lost interest in the others who are watching and waiting to find out what we are talking about. He says that lacquer work used to be very popular but there is little of it these days and that he has never heard of the artist whose name I show him. It is unusual, he insists, that he would not know about this artist because he is a writer for one of the Hanoi newspapers and covers the arts in a weekly column, but that he knows of one who has done some lacquer painting. Would I like to meet him? He lives not to far away and I am lucky that he has the time to take me if I want.

I have been in Hanoi less than an hour and this string bean of a man with a lopsided face and toothy smile wants to take me somewhere to meet someone to engage in possible transactions involving something I know very little about. I start checking out whether this is a good idea and then conclude that I am completely on my own in a strange, but suddenly compelling place, and that I should go with this guy because I have absolutely nothing else to do.

I follow my new friend, Nguyen, out to the sidewalk. He starts his cyclo, kicks the stand, gets on, instructs me on where to hang my legs and how to put my arms around him and off we go conjuring a scene of a monkey driving a gorilla that introduces a slightly homophobic anxiety. He, however, doesn't seem the least fazed by the cumbersome predicament, nor does he bother to exert much caution as we weave and nudge through the melee unhindered. I wish I had a picture.

I might as well have been kidnapped with a hood on my head for all I know of where we are or going. We have left the city and trail through some ragged suburbs into the scattered outskirts of Hanoi, pockmarked with semi-industrial fabrication sites, warehouses and haphazard apartment buildings resembling of army barracks, long low things, squatting on barren ground often littered with left over construction debris and the odd field of random cultivation. The only thing missing in being ugly is graffiti and there is absolutely none of that anywhere if you leave out billboards. We stop on a paved levee bordering a small canal whose refuse-ridden surface seems to render it nothing more than a ditch.

Nguyen gets off and shouts to an open window on the second floor of a corner building. A youngish woman with an armful of laundry peers out and replies. "He's here," Nguyen announces and steers us down to a side alley threading through the mud puddles and among the chickens and ducks that litter our path. The woman motions us to enter a low door that leads us to an iron circular staircase. Everywhere, a jumble of odd lots of frames and rolled canvas lies about in the darkened corners amidst paint cans and brushes. A man's low voice cuts in from above. Kim talks to him, gestures that we will wait while trying to clear some space for us to sit down and arranges the teacups. The woman goes to make tea. I peer around among the frames at his paintings, but no lacquer work. It is damp and without light except from the window and it has started to drizzle again.

He enters the room with a sturdy barefoot stride and wide-eyed energy. He is dark, short, square shaped and commanding. Black cropped hair sticks out like wire in all directions framing deeply set eyes under thick eyebrows. He looks for Nguyen for an introduction as he calls instructions to the woman. We are introduced. His name is Pham Loc. We shake hands. His grip is firm; the handshakes of most Vietnamese are limp and non-expressive. Watching both of them together, he is the yang of Nguyen's yin. Two young boys come into the room shy and hesitant. Pham Loc reaches out as they go to him. I may very well be the first westerner they have ever seen. The woman brings the tea. Now we have something to do besides stand round. Chairs are cleared. We sit down and wait for Nguyen to get things going. It is his show.

Pham Loc asks about me and Nguyen asks me where I have been in Vietnam. I tell him in the South. He then asks me if I was in the war and I say yes and Nguyen tells me the artist is a former Lieutenant Colonel in the North Vietnamese Army and then translates. Pham Loc nods and asks if I want to see his lacquer work. He has very few things he did a long time before but does not do it anymore. He leaves the room returning with three small plaques and hands them to me. One portrays the hand of a small girl holding out a little chicken. It was the first he ever tried. He then shows me a framed brochure of his art recently reviewed in a Hanoi newspaper in both English and Vietnamese. The article discusses Pham Loc's army career as an infantry battalion commander in the Cambodian war and the development of his painting. Nguyen wrote it.

As I might have suspected, his style seems to resemble his own aspect. It features bold short strokes in dark strong colors, blacks, browns, reds and cobalt blues. He brings out some of the oil paintings featured in the article. I see city and suburban scenes with people in columns and clusters melted into a dark earth reaching out like plants, or leaning, sometimes falling, out of bent buildings, lining muddy roads under low clouds that could be smoke. They are all strong statements of the march and struggle of a herded people. I don't like them and wonder what I do now except hold onto the little lacquer piece with the girl and chicken.

He looks up at me and smiles with warmth that glows like the little boys he holds to his side. I like this man. He has a strong honesty about him. He says something to Nguyen, who tells me that he wants to sketch me, he has never sketched an American, do I mind? No, I don't. A gust of wind blows into the room. Outside, a light rain sweeps over a field across the canal. The room is bare of comfort, the furniture worn and old; it is the home of a North Vietnamese Colonel. I am in Hanoi, North Vietnam.

I'm positioned where he can use the available light, he to the side with his sketchpad, staring as he begins to draw. I stare back to fix him in sight. My heart starts to bang, I feel tingle in the temples. It could be now or then. Infantry, after all, is about ground and maneuver: getting it, getting out of it, wheeling, flanking, withdrawing, assaulting; a fatality of choice fired by fear, the lust for the kill crowded with doubt. We both know each other is there, out there, as if peering from or into the tree line, forming to cross the canal or lying in wait.

Pham Loc's hand stops. His eyes leave mine for the first time and we relax. He mumbles something to Nguyen who responds. Pham Loc rips the sheet from the pad and gets up, first showing it to Nguyen and saying something. Nguyen says that Pham Loc has told him that I looked like someone he had seen before many years ago and that he thought for a long time that all Americans looked that way. Pham Loc smiles boyishly, slightly embarrassed, and asks in broken English "Do you like?"

I buy the lacquer painting of the little girl and everyone is pleased that I like it. The meeting becomes merry and he brings out a bottle of old rice wine to share. Nguyen explains that he must go back to work. He has a deadline for his newspaper article in the weekend magazine of his paper. Pham Loc, with his two sons still hanging on to him and the young mother at his side, graciously accompanies us to the mud puddle road. Erect and proud, against the backdrop of his mean estate, he grabs my hand and I his, both of us smiling like sudden friends sharing a secret we both enjoy. The rain has stopped; the sky lightens slightly with the promise of sun later on.

Nguyen brings me back to the hotel. He is getting better at his English now and tells me how he had spent several months in Texas on an exchange program for Vietnamese journalists three years before but it has been a long time since he has practiced. He likes Americans and thinks it important we are well treated and take a good impression back with us because there is so much misunderstanding between our two countries. He says he will stop back at the hotel the next day to show me some more things if I would be interested and makes a point of giving the desk manager his card.

32

THE GOLDEN COCK

The restaurant recommended by the entire lobby staff is a converted colonial residence with elegant French windows bordered with green shutters and barrel tiled roofing well guarded by up-lit palms, ginger plants, rubber trees and Bird of Paradise. Four or five large black sedans with waiting chauffeurs line the street around the portico. A doorman in a dark western suit and bowtie ushers me to a smiling young lady in orange silk Ao Dais with skin as smooth as caramel and a gardenia as white as vanilla ice cream against her ink black hair. After checking her list, she escorts me down the sunken veranda surrounded by hidden fountains past the tuxedoed duo of cello and guitar playing classical duets for strings. I am seated nearby in the corner of an arabesque terrace alongside a remarkable exotic fish tank. It bubbles "Welcome to Hanoi" and the fish coming over to see me seem friendly.

Its only 8:30 p.m., early for dining, and it is a Saturday night, a worldwide excuse for the next day off. From my corner I can case the joint and the clientele, noting the protocol of the management's welcome and seating. It is an "in" place for sure, mostly clumps of business men greasing the skids of deals and kickbacks, occasionally decorated with the good-looking bimbo on the side; matronly wives are universally uninvited. The only exception appears to be large family parties gaily assembling behind me in private alcoves where large trays of seafood appetizers zoom past under the watchful eye of a maitre d'hotel.

Yes, peace seems to be winning all over: in the motorized streams of the streets, the busy huddles on the street corners, the crunch of adding machines hidden in the backrooms of shops, in front of flashing TV screens in the living rooms of the recovering bourgeois. But there is no better indication that the good times have returned than the five-star restaurant. The Golden Cock could be in any capital city where political power always goes to bed with wealth. The egg of socialism has broken, Humpty Dumpty is all over the floor, and all of Ho's tanks and all of Giap's men will never put Marxist/Leninism together again.

Recessed lights spill shadows off Buddhist sculptures smiling in deep grace from wall sconces. They brighten the gilt-edged paintings of colorful pastels with sun and flowers, blue skies and white clouds, and I think of Pham Loc's works stacked in the landing of his barren pensioner's apartment; his proletariat straining with outstretched arms and stuck in their mud lives, open mouths calling out for something still withheld, bent behind beasts yoked to the murk of dark fields under slate skies with an indistinct sun sometimes appearing on the horizon, or is it a distant fire burning?

The retired colonel's short darting strokes punching the canvas with the worn out scenery of yesterday's struggle is but a puny challenge to the expensive bright beauty around me. I imagine him walking in with sturdy step, wary of foreign terrain, awkward among the trappings of luxury, his eyes confused. Perhaps he feels betrayed by the uselessness of his life, saddened by forgotten, irretrievable losses, and he wonders about the price he and his men paid to buy a future like this.

If we were to meet here in this restaurant what would we talk about over the food and wine? If Kim arrived to interpret we could still laugh just as we would shake our heads in both forgetting and remembering our younger lives, so obscure and even unrecognizable today. So, warmed with wine and falling momentarily silent, we would toast each other and the spirits of those who have not been so fortunate. The hell with anyone else.

Over an extravagant meal of lobster tail with some French white wine, I enjoy the human scenery and the impeccable service, watching my fish tank friends flamboyant in their gold and silver stripes and plumed fins spinning and wheeling, wide eyed with the same bored grace of dance girls in a strip joint.

But then something memorable occurs. An exotic couple followed by an eager captain enter, stage left. They are seated at a reserved table next to the musicians' dais. They are oriental for sure but costumed like a rich Cowboy with a ten-gallon hat and bushy mustache riding into town on a Saturday night with his Senora. He is wearing pressed blue jeans, sporting a Texas size belt buckle, and a florid western shirt showing off a large and elaborate silver and turquoise string tie. All this is a set up for the pair of cowboy boots that has all the endangered species of exotic lizards on the run. Not to be undone, his wife wears a loud low-cut matching floral silk dress with high heel pumps, fire-engine red lipstick and silver jewelry to drown with. A bottle of Champagne is brought out and opened ceremoniously as the man sits his cowboy hat on an empty chair and lights up an expensive Cuban cigar.

As soon as the musicians finish their last classical selection, the man calls out his request and after a short exchange the melodies of old American stand bys flow from their strings: "Moon River", "New York" and "San Francisco" "Chicago" a geographic side trip that the musicians seem to have enthusiastically tucked into their repertoire. After each favorite the man beams and claps, calling out another and shoving some USA greenbacks at them. When the musicians take a break, the Hanoi cowboy summons the captain, orders more champagne and insists that the musicians join them. It's a great show whose story line shouts "Viet Khieu's Final Revenge" and from where I sit they deserve every bit of it.

When I pay my bill, I ask the waiter about the couple. He smiles and says they came in every night this week and did the same thing. "He big shot now!" the waiter nods with a big grin of approval, "Make big money in America come spend it Vietnam, Good!", he says. "We like!" he adds enthusiastically. "Some day we do same too!" He laughs as he takes my money and walks away.

It is only 10 p.m.. The traffic at the busy intersection outside has died down. Without the commuting hordes of cyclos, the scarcity of car traffic reveals its minority role in the current scheme of things. A shorter row of black cars shine under the streetlight. Beyond it is dark and quiet as if the city is under curfew. A single taxi slows and stops, but I wave him on. Walking down the deserted side street I see there are few lights, just small hooded door lanterns. High walls line the sidewalk cobbled with worn tiles glistening in the light mist. Behind the walls darkened buildings loom, giving no hint of habitation or activity. It is here, or not far from here, on such a street undistinguishable from many others in the central district, and in the same worn obscured buildings undifferentiated from their neighbor, that the likes of our now U.S. Senator John McCain and current Ambassador "Pete" Peterson endured the "Hanoi Hilton" for more days and nights than most of us can count, much less recall, while the populace walked past, as I am walking past, but slowing my pace in the quiet wondering about the checkerboard of ironies and vagaries in the days and years of black and white.

By the time I come down for breakfast Nguyen has already left a message. He wants to talk to me about a "project" and will be by around four in the afternoon. I take coffee in the small dining room. Nhia, the tiny desk clerk, asks me what I would like to see. When I tell her I want to buy some pearls for our grandchildren she smiles as brightly as the sun coming up and writes out directions.

It has rained during the night and the streets are wet and black. Turning the corner from the hotel, I come to the park of the Hoan Kiem Lake, considered by many to be the traditional center of Hanoi and made famous by a national myth. Legend has it that in the 15th century Emperor Le Loi was given a magical sword by Heaven to drive the Chinese out of Vietnam. Afterwards he went boating on the lake whereupon a magical turtle arose from the depths, grabbed the sword from the startled hero, and disappeared into the lake to restore it to the gods from whom it came. Thereafter, it was named the Lake of the Restored Sword, an interesting converse of England's Arthurian legend of the Lady of the Lake and the sword Excalibur.

Great sycamore and oak trees shadow the water's edge, filtering out the din of traffic and shrouding the lake in quiet. A rough sand and gravel walkway circles the lake. I find a bench almost hidden in shrubs where I can watch the parade of city dwellers pass and pause: a child with a stick and a ball running ahead of the mother and grandmother, a handful of elderly men, one with a beret and scarf another in a battered campaign hat and yet another stooped over a cane. They greet and stop to pull deeply on their unfiltered cigarettes and mildly wave away their smoke clouds while watching with knife eyes the ankles, hips and breasts of the young women jogging by in tights and headbands listening to their portable CD players.

Hobbyists arrange their easels, play their clarinets, assemble their kites and ready the sails of toy boats to set out gently aweigh on their sea. Among the tables beneath the trees and obscured by shrubbery, several championships are being contested in chess, checkers and mahjong, attracting small bands of enthusiasts around their favorites who lay side bets and argue over tactics. Tai Chi players solemnly wave and undulate through the dream sleep of its origin while little children run and kick the ball inspired by the World Cup ablaze in every TV and their imagination. An early badminton player sets up a net and carefully extracts his precious bird from its housing in a worn coca cola can. Urban theatre.

I like Hanoi, being in it, walking around in it, discovering that it is somehow nicer, easier and more interesting than most cities. Maybe it is that even though I am often the only westerner visible on the street or in the shop or passing through the park, I don't attract particular attention and am not subject to any nuisance. While I don't feel alone or alienated, I don't feel crowded or ignored. The citizenry, while taciturn, are pleasant and polite. When a street hawker presses me to buy his sunglasses or cigarette lighter he keeps his distance and stays within his space. When I am unsure where I am going I can stop and someone will try to help me or point and sometimes take me to someone they think might. When I am trying to buy pearls for our granddaughters, one merchant who doesn't seem to have just what I am looking for passes me on to another. I mean where else does the slightly anxious traveler have someone of a different race and nationality approach him/her and say "Are you American, I speak English, can I help you?" This in the land where we have been branded outlaws for most of their lives.

I like the feel of the place. Its is built low and sturdy, organized and laid out to work as if regiments could form there quickly and rush off like arrows to put out fires, stem floods, and, of course, march to war. There is little to show off, nothing intimidating, a horizontal building line of low, even proportions, not pretty but handsome, with several tree lined avenues bordering carefully tended parks, elaborate roundabouts with fountains, columns and pedestals awaiting statues to replace the ones that have been tumbled by the past.

The French provenance is clear and it fits. Not for the first time has Hanoi both rejected yet accepted the mantle of another culture. The Vietnamese have exercised their capacity for pragmatic selection, both taking and assuming the benefits of what France provided. Despite official resentment and rancor toward the French imperial century, its imprimatur of western liberal thought has left its dye deep in the sense of Vietnamese bicultural sophistication and achievements. After all, it was France and the exposure of its 20th Century politics that provided the young bourgeois Vietnamese intellectuals like Ho and Giap-to name the most identifiable-with liberal principles that leavened their communist religion.

The most prominent and lasting influence of the French is demonstrated in Hanoi's urban architecture. Today most of the official buildings that house of the Communist regime are the very same that the French erected to bring Vietnam to its knees. They are now aging heavy mansions along quiet streets, all ochre in color, with wide verandas, tall windows with dark green shutters, unchanged (save the excrescencies of cables, air conditioners and antennas), behind the shady parasols of arched sycamore trees with trunks painted white like sentries. The French colonial style's preservation, notwithstanding a certain indifference or lack of maintenance, sets the tone and ambience for much of the city's center.

There is more necessity to this than design, for Hanoi is and has been effectively bankrupt since the French left in the mid fifties (and lest we forget, the gratuity of the US's policy of not bombing it during the war thus allowing its preservation to this day, not to fail to mention its complementation by the U.S. orchestrated international economic embargo over the past 30 years that has effectively crippled Vietnam's ability to attract and utilize international lending for significant redevelopment).

Although many of financial restrictions have been removed and large projects are commencing, the coming developmental changes of skyscrapers and "Planned Community" westernized projects may eventually degrade Hanoi's "preserved" tourist attraction. Given the sputtering rate of indicated growth and apprehensions arising among foreign investors about allocating capital for Southeast Asian investments, however, this will take some time, and a lot more of everything else.

33

IT'S A LONG WAY TO HALONG BAY AND BACK

The driver arranged by the hotel knew no English. He had instructions to deliver me to the hotel in Ha Long Bay 180 kilometers away. The trip on a decent highway would take two and a half hours. It became more than twice that.

The early morning hangs down in a drizzle that reminds me of old gray hair. We pass out of town across the Red River and the embankment as if we had turned a corner in time. The country immediately reclaims its monotony of drowned brown fields. Black figures like sticks in conical hats struggle with water buffalo or crouch low planting new rice. An old lady with a basket on her head pauses for a moment and finding no reasonable alternative awkwardly rolls a pant leg to urinate by the side of the road. In the unbroken expanse a few tractors can be seen laboring almost axle deep in the mud. We come to a railroad crossing barred by a bamboo pole with a crossing guard sitting on a stool with an umbrella. I wonder if he is getting a union wage. A train appears from the misty distance as if from another country slicing across the drab fields like a shuddering snake in a helluva hurry. The train is made up of five cars, vintage Soviet Army green worn pale. It hurtles by conveying, if only by speed alone, an importance unsupported by the empty seats and vacant windows.

At intervals of several kilometers, platoons of construction workers with picks and shovels, along with old earth movers and battered dump trucks, attempt to widen and resurface the highway from one lane to three lanes and span the ditches and dikes along the way. Instead of providing a route by-passing the towns and villages, exasperating temporary detours through, in, and around their narrow lanes and squares create knots of entanglement and disruption. The local gendarmerie busies itself mostly in watching, or at times engaging in, arguments with drivers amidst a cacophony of competing horns and whistles.

The five-hour drive exposes the ongoing collisions and conflicts that highlight Vietnam's fitful struggle to modernize; urban/rural, tractor/ water buffalo, mud/pavement, cars/bikes, lantern/electricity, hotel/hospi- tal are just some of the developmental dialectics that befuddle the planned departure from the old and frustrate the half-hearted movement toward the new.

So far as I can tell, the driver has a back to his neck, a battered hat, two hands on the wheel—and knows no English at all. After two hours, with no explanation, he turns off the main road and detours to the east. A blan- ket of clouds lies over the flat fields. A steady light rain continues to fall. Small hamlets of mud and straw huts huddle in broken mounds along the side of the road. Children and women stare bleakly out of the entrances to their dwellings as if a mud-spattered car is a matter of solemn interest. A few wayfarers on bikes weave among the mud puddles as the car twists, turns, and slows to avoid the potholes, missing one out of three. For all the eye can see we are in a bare and dun-colored world. Maybe it's the day, the weather, the feeling of being driven off into the very ends of a weary world, but it's depressing.

This is not South Vietnam, where the fecund soil of the Mekong has nurtured a mixture of socio-economic elements. Distant from the more disciplined and regimented fist of central power, the South was freer to practice the pragmatism of accommodation while understanding how to use foreign technology and methods to ensure survival.

Here in the hinterland of the North, poverty, regimentation, and denial have been the staples of the adult population. Famine has visited here more than once, unchecked by the prevailing dynasty, royal or ideological. Today, and for more years than the majority of the population has known, public thought has been confined to the narrow bandwidth of dogmatic communist placards, crowd-speak through megaphones and raised fists under hard watchful eyes. Here the only green light is "Follow-The-

Leader", that seems to provide enhanced value to the virtue of never being wrong if you do.

The driver stops before a featureless hut. Holding up a package wrapped with the ubiquitous rough brown paper, he gestures me to follow. We enter the dwelling that at one time was covered with a rough cement stucco skin and white washed. Now the stucco is faded and worn through, revealing rough mud and straw. The roof was a combination thatch with broken tile. The entrance opens into and provides the ambient light for a main room minimally partitioned by a bamboo reed enclosure for the hearth and cooking area. A woman with infant on her hip comes forward at his greeting and goes to get the man. Her three other children appear from the rear and stare; no smiles here. When the man arrives he greets the driver and nods his head at me in welcome.

I am invited to sit down on the stool as we wait for the woman to heat water for tea. The driver offers me a cigarette. The smoking ignites an exchange of news and the driver passes the package to the man, who disappears into the back room and returns with payment. The driver asks him for something and the man goes and gets a smoking pipe that resembles a bong. Extracting some dark tobacco, the driver presses it into the small well and lighting the pipe inhales the smoke as if he is trying to become a balloon. When he releases it in a slow practiced way, the long funnel of smoke that spreads out into the dusky light of the bare room tells me it is just tobacco after all. Calmly, he repeats the process three times. The technique follows the slightly more sophisticated water pipe in achieving a dubious and momentary "high" of mild self-asphyxiation, a habit that demonstrates that even in self-destruction the Vietnamese are poor, so what kind of fun is that?

The tea comes. It is pale and weak, not even hot, as if to say this is all we have, this is the cupboard of our lives and the bareness of our ken. See the faded newspaper picture that is our wall's only decoration, the tattered chicken that wanders in to hunt and peck the hard dirt floor, the snot running down the nose of an infant who needs medicine, the low roof that keeps us in the dark, the open hearth that can't keep out the damp, the look that every day brings the same dead weight of hard times, that like

Pham Loc's paintings await either a light at the end of the tunnel, or perhaps just another fire.

Word is out among this huddle of somber huts that a "Round Eye" is visiting. Six or seven men and a couple of women with the usual attachments of infant and child appear and I watch them gather silently.

Sitting there I am wordlessly shown what it is like to be so foreign, so un-belonging, and unreachable. I try to sense what they are thinking—how alien I am, or where do I come from, or when was the last time that they had seen an American in the flesh. It could very well have been before some of them were born, or back in the "American War" when others were old enough to recall, or maybe heard about, or even made up the legend of that one day. It had started out just like all the other days until an American pilot in the hated silver fighter jet so untouchable high above exploded into a petro-storm of instant junk by a Soviet missile in these same gray skies and I wonder now what they first imagined when they saw the tiny dark object sprawling and falling into the sky until suddenly, as if caught on a hook, a parachute blossomed like a flower and a body swung miraculously beneath and dropped into these fields, like Brueghel's Icarus. Only then could it have dawned in their minds that this was indeed a mortal arriving in deliverance as he tried to rise but stumbled and fell, and how a cry had burst from their throats as they gathered to run out and exact their revenge on the first and maybe the last American they ever saw.

With such sour thoughts brought on by the relentless view of the flat earth outside, I look to the driver to get me out of here. Understanding it is past time, the driver gets up and shrugs. Nodding his head he leads me out to the back by the garden plot and wood and charcoal bin where, arranging ourselves, we piss against a broken brick wall. I look up to the slate sky and thank my lucky stars.

The driver winds up a steep, exotically landscaped drive and deposits me in front of the high marbled pavilion of a 12-story high-rise hotel, brand new. I am greeted by a score of attendants eager to handle my two pieces of luggage. The doors are opened by two more who assume possession of the bags and place them on glistening brass cart where, embarrassingly enough, they look as forlorn as worn shopping bags. I'm escorted through a vast empty lobby of stuffed leather sofas, past huge paintings of tropical foliage 20 feet high, to a marble front desk that shines with my reflection. Here I am, the enviable recipient of inquiries from no less than three uniformed young ladies and discover that I am, for the present, the only guest registered.

It is a stunning example of the cart arriving before the horse. An opulent hotel built before the highway to get there is completed, a showcase of bad planning and poor execution. As I am led to my room the half lit hallways and rows of empty rooms seem to mock the hopeful faces and eager gestures of the young employees to whom this palace of leisure is the meal ticket of their new future.

The view from my 10th story room is magnificent and the scene of Ha Long Bay's approximately 3,000 islets among the most dramatic in the world. From the distance of five to six miles, the dense cluster of jagged rock formations seem ominous, like an ancient flotilla or armada standing off at sea, anchored forever in position staring at the coast as if waiting to take life and gain the beachhead of conquest at last.

This is not a Mediterranean archipelago in Ionian waters where an Odysseus escaped Hellenic sorcerers and slayed their demons. It is another world from that, a swords thrust through its center and out the other side from anything told to a kid from Cleveland, Ohio. I had never heard of the Inner Empire or the established fact that in someone else's eyes it was "The Center of the World".

At the desk I'm informed that the restaurant is temporarily closed for "renovations" but the bar is open. No lights shine through the ornately etched frosted glass doors. I walk into a cavernous dining area, glistening with oiled mahogany shining brass. There are no customers. At a far end, a cluster of uniformed waiters and waitresses are gathered around a large dinner table. They look like they are playing cards. When they see me they all jump up and approach with embarrassment. "May I help you?" the tallest girl asks precisely with an excellent accent. Others following her hesitantly bow to my service. "May I have a drink?" I ask. "Yes, please; you want?"

As she meticulously prepares my gin and tonic, the others hurry around turning on the lights and taking their work positions. They smile and whisper to each other, which means they are embarrassed at being caught unprepared. The woman tending bar explains that they were practicing their English lessons and as proof pulls out a pamphlet which presents lessons for daily dialogues. She tells me that they were pretending to go the airport and buy their tickets. I play along and ask her where they were all going. "Oh, the United States of course. Everybody wants to go there!"

She is 24, skinny, bony, and with her boyish gestures and close-cropped hair could almost pass as one. Quick to smile and animated, forthright and confidant, she reminds me of Mai. She is treated as the natural spokesperson and leader. To her, the job of waitress, and even bartender, which she has studied to master is a giant step up from being the third daughter of a family of eight children to a couple who work at menial municipal jobs. Though she speaks as fluent English as most, including Nguyen who as a journalist worked in the States, she has never been as far as Hanoi, a half-day bus trip, where someday she hopes to go to find another job. As if she's afraid I might let the cat out of the bag, she rushes to assure me that she likes present job "Very, very much!"

The dining room doors are opened and a cheerful portly man in a western suit with tie marches up and greets me. He is the manager, just four months in place. A Filipino by birth he has lived and worked all over. Two years before he ran a Holiday Inn in Indianapolis until he joined a Thai-Singapore consortium to start up a hotel in Indonesia and now this one. He is a lively talker and anxious to overcome the embarrassment of the fact that I am currently the only paying guest. He regrets that I arrived in the off-season when things are not "lively" because the weather is not so good. He recites the occupancies at "high" season and becomes enthusiastic about their international variety. Though he doesn't name Americans, he does mention Canadians, Australians and Europeans. When I complain to him about the transportation and ask him about air and rail service, his expression becomes somber. This, he acknowledges, is out of his hands. The government promised the developers that a new fast highway would be finished by hotel completion, but…he shrugs and lets the explanation trail off into silence. He soon finds something else that requires his attention and gets up. He insists that he buy me another drink and that the dinner be on the house. Looking around at the partially lit chandeliers and the empty tables waiting like a cancelled party, I thank him and say I would like to get out and see the town. He looks at me apologetically and departs.

The dock for tourist boats is as busy as a market, which in its way it is. There are more hawkers than boats and, unfortunately for them on this day, more boats than tourists. After waiting for an hour to hook another customer without luck, my crew reluctantly takes to sea with only one.

Halong Bay is a true labyrinth of volcanic outcroppings that harbor innumerable bays, coves, caverns and passageways. Their shape and size conjure a marvel of every form and shape on the mirror of a limpid green sea. Here, in accordance with legend and lore, its perils have doomed the once dominant mercantile empire of Champa, who preyed on the coastal Chinese trade, and pillaged the unwary. One could lose both one's bearings and way forever among its twists and turns. On the other hand, one who is both native and knowledgeable could hide a lifetime and hoard a treasure forever unknown.

Indigenous fisher folk maintain floating villages and spend their lives meandering through their various fishing grounds. Tourism is a great boon to them; the tourist boats that purchase their catch for noontime meals have inflated their currency and their earnings supplemented by side trips for tourists through caverns and secret pools. These intrepid travelers are packed into boats rowed by guileful children who in a half an hour garner more than they could earn in a week on the mainland.

Today the air is still and the water a sheet of glass. Every scene reflects itself, twinning perfectly the darks and hollows in the rock, green vines dripping off the ledges and bushes sprouting from the crags. The boat chugs along in the quiet. Kites and swallows dive and swirl like darts among their lairs. No birds sing and a lifelessness envelops us.

Houng, the young man who, with his sister as first mate, manages the boat, tries in weak English to engage me in conversation. We are both lonely. He is the second son of a poor working class couple. The father is disabled from a construction accident and the mother is a part time laundress. He has worked his way up from a dockworker at Hai Phong to a tourist boat operator. His agreement with the Chinese owner of the boat includes a percentage of the take from each trip, but the net leaves him little after he pays off the pilot and his sister. The empty benches on the after deck of this 30-foot converted fishing trawler tell his story better than he. They are from Hai Phong, which in addition to being the North's major port, though diminished since the disappearance of Soviet support, remains a significant semi-industrialized city. His tale is another in the sad flow of worry and want that characterize life among the urbanized poor. When the walls and gates of the state economy fell in 1993, a life culture of communist dictates and obedience became bankrupt. Many North Vietnamese like Houng found themselves, with some bewilderment, tumbling through the promised socialist safety nets of support, which had been rendered meaningless by the government's threadbare capabilities. Without the lifeboats of education or the backstops of the traditional village communal integration, Houng and his colleagues find themselves on their own with unreliable lifelines and not much hope of rescue. Like their parents' generation, those who grew up within the totalitarian monologue have neither the skills nor the means to navigate the confusing currents of market capitalism. In this regard they are way behind the open-market acculturation of the South, a disparity that is already exacerbating national divisions.

As he struggles with his sad eyes and broken words to give me a sense of his life, I can almost see the bare walls of their home, the few possessions other than bedding, the naked wires and dim light bulbs and can watch them squatting around the baked clay hearth digging at their rice bowls, see their tangle of sleeping forms on the crowded communal bed, smell the charcoal fires and the steam of weak tea, their only greeting on the cold damp dawns of tomorrow.

He gets up and wanders off to take a turn at the wheel, passing by his sister who, though knowing more English than he, ignores her brother's concerns and for the most part, everything else too. She is lying on one of the benches propped up by pillows, reading a beat up, much dog-eared woman's magazine filled with pictures of lingerie models offering the pleasures of luxury. The magazine is a glossy pirated knock-off of a Hong Kong publication that, being too expensive to buy, is passed around among the circle of lethargic dreamers like her. She is a long and lanky 20-something who, provided the right paraphernalia, could pass as a slick city girl for whom she would gladly become an understudy should the right wrong guy come along. For the present, she stares at makeup ads and see-through lingerie wishing for almost anything better than reality.

34

"CHEERS"

Arriving back from the countryside, Hanoi, unheralded by towers or spires, assumes the shape and function of a huge sponge. Through the potholes of town streets, along the halting pathways of roads, under the drizzle of rain falling on the fields, the heels of a shoeless people wear a trail here as if it is the only higher ground to the approaching flood of change. In this process of displacement they mimic the urban migration of the entire Third World. For a nation whose great epic has been the integrity of a peasant world rooted in soil and obedient to its ancient traditions there is, and has been, little middle ground between city and field. Today with the incipience of a market economy and the potential capacities of the "technological" workplace, the forces of modernity are awakening. At the same time, having been weighed down by the yoke of someone else telling them what to do over the last four decades, along with the banishment of any thought of how they could do for themselves, the great cloud of passivity is stirring the break up. In the dangers of the meantime, the urban epidemic grows as the country is increasingly like an over laden ship setting an uncertain course on hazardous seas.

As so many other aspects of Vietnamese life, the future will become another endurance contest. Some will both make their way and find it; the waitress and some of her colleagues at the Ha Long hotel will do so; Pham Loc or "Lucky Girl" probably not. Nevertheless, and regardless of the assortment of urban blights that affect them, the groping cities of Saigon and Hanoi stir with the energy of expectation even if it may be short on reality and long on hope.

Happy to be "back" at the Thuy Nga, I find a message from Nyugen. He wants to meet with me after work around 5 p.m. and discuss a business proposition. How nice to come into a city as a foreigner amidst three million people and receive a welcome note from someone you've known for maybe four hours. Whatever his proposition, it is more interesting than another day all by myself.

At 5 p.m. he arrives with his same lopsided grin and pleased with his patronage. He is taking me somewhere "special". I hop on and off we go, rush hour in downtown Hanoi. I marvel at the method of unmarked intersections, the balance of giving and getting around, when to yield at the last second and when to dart forward, the docile quickness of minnows swerving and parting currents. We go down Quan Boulevard and enter the Quan Thanh parkway around West End Lake. Nyugen pulls over into the lakeside parking and tells me with a big smile that the timing is perfect.

It is nearing sunset on West End Lake, the largest and most public body of water in Hanoi. A short pier off the bulwark offers access to two ornate floating restaurants fluttering with large blue and yellow fish shaped kites and red banners accompanied by the soft and tonal clacking of carved wooden wind chimes. Nyugen is greeted as a good customer. Indeed, we are directed to an end table waiting for us at the barge's railing where a paling sky and its perfect reflection twain in the mirror of the undulating surface. Nyugen orders beers and appetizers of fish, shrimp and octopus. He lights up his non-filter cigarette, snapping his Zippo proudly, and sucks deep, holding it upright with his forefinger and thumb. "You like?" he waves his cigarette around in a circle, indicating the lake that spreads off to the west. It is approaching dusk. The waiters are lighting the candles in the decorative paper storm lanterns.

We are an odd couple, a fortuitous connection offering small windows to each other's world. To him, I am a welcome diversion, an opportunity to patronize, and perhaps a moment of chance to his interests. To me, he is a key to some unopened door, the view of something otherwise unseen. Over the beer and prawns, he says that he wants to write an article that includes me. As he speaks, his pallid face glistens and black eyes shine earnestly. He couldn't weigh more than a hundred pounds. If he was told to stand quietly in a field with a hat he could pass for a scarecrow, a slight tassel of sticks surrounded by ill-fitting clothes flapping in any wind.

Leaning over the table and speaking low, he explains that he wears a number of hats at his paper. In addition to the Arts/Culture beat he does features on human events. His current topic is the World Cup soccer championship that has tapped great enthusiasm throughout the country (according to a recent story in the Chamber of Commerce Newsletter of Saigon, which is printed in English, more Vietnamese workers were utilizing their vacation time during the series than during any other national of cultural holiday!). Nguyen has been interviewing foreign diplomats in Hanoi about their views on the sport's global participation and its influence on improving international relations. The last two weeks featured Sweden and Denmark. This week it's America. He has tried to line up an American but isn't familiar with their availability or the composition of its Consulate staff. The combination of a fast approaching deadline and the news hole for this week's interview piece pushes the priorities down to me, an unaccredited American tourist who he met in an art shop three days ago. This is not, I think, a strong endorsement of either his journalistic clout or the gravitas of his newspaper.

I look at him, trying to see behind his game, if any, while holding a weak hand with few reasons not to say "Yes" on the one hand and essentially none to say "No" on the other. After all is considered, I mean, why not?

As we talk, young couples, many arm-in-arm, stroll along the lake through the thinning light and darkening shade. Older couples occupy the benches surrounded by infants stumbling and crawling among their legs, seeking something to grasp in the dirt, aimless as chickens. The closure of day, a coming together of parts, a quieting of sound all seem so serene and normal.

Nyugen suggests our script should emphasize that the World Cup is an event where every team must play by the same rules, a common ground kind of thing that brings strangers together, an event that favors better understanding and acceptance, etc.. We agree that the war and who fought it serves no present purpose and that maybe some conclusion that American "soccer" might some day attend a Vietnamese tournament could be a feature of getting to know each other, this time in peace.

Dusk is falling. The first evening breeze flutters across the tables. The strings of paper lanterns sway gently in a loose necklace around the barge that is becoming more and more like a boat and we a part of its journey into night. Nguyen lights another cigarette and watches the smoke drift away. Two beers, maybe three, have coursed through his slight frame. He leans forward across the table eyes glazed to the color of syrup, his crooked smile wide as a split melon and says loudly, "John"—his pronunciation makes it sound like "Joan"—"We must drink to this and our efforts!"

"Yes", I tell him half in jest. "How about Peace on Earth and Good Will Towards Men." Repeating it slowly in English, "Yes, Yes!" he says, illuminated by it all. We hold up our glasses into the blue purple sky to propitiate the spirits. Nyugen repeats it loudly then turns to a group of men behind us. Emboldened, he rises and makes a speech. I have no idea what he says, except nodding at me as an American and using "Peace on Earth" as his motif. The party being addressed has been polite and is smiling at me so I smile back, trying to figure how I feel about this.

The sun has set. The translucence of the sky melts into the dark. The barge is a lighted stage on which we become a momentary drama. The moon, whose reflection is so famous on "West End Lake", has yet to climb out of the earth. Inspired by his own Bacchus, one in the surrounding groups rises to lend his speech with another promise for mankind. Another man follows him—and then it is my turn.

So I stand up and look around at their moist, shiny faces, notice how their olive dark eyes glisten in the warm air, and how their black hair shines. The beer has warmed me and spreads out like arms that open and find me here in Hanoi standing among North Vietnamese and how strange that is, but I don't feel strange, don't feel I am any less the soldier that I was, don't feel that they are any less the enemy that they were, but I do know that the war is over, buried somewhere underneath a forgotten moon, and that we are forgetting it as we look each other in the eye, just as sure as I stand to drink to them and as they are when they raise their glasses to me.

So it is with pride and no regrets that I raise my glass as high as I can and bow to Nyugen and drink to him. When I do the same for them, we all rise.

It was what they wanted, what was expected. By recognizing them, they could then recognize me. In the rough calculus of "face" we gave permission to ourselves to be one for the moment, nothing more or less. Then it's over. Nyugen becomes business again. He calls for the bill, which I pay, and we leave without more ceremony. The surrounding tables barely look up. Everything has moved on.

Nyugen tells me he will do the interview the next day with a tape recorder and might bring a photographer if one is available. He also says he would bring copies of other interviews so I can see the proofs.

35

EXCUSE ME, PLEASE

I have the whole day to wander about the enemy's city. Ever since I arrived, now more than two and a half weeks ago, I have carefully observed the world of the cyclo drivers and traffic. I have this crazy idea of trying it on my own. The hotel has two cyclos for rent. It is now or never. By this time, I'm on friendly terms with the entire staff since the little lobby is almost like a kitchen table for both guests and workers. Half say go for it the other say don't dare, which touched me somehow.

Making sure that I choose the right time in the mid-morning when the traffic is lighter, I climb on the little 75cc Honda and bump off the curbside into the street, knees up to my armpits and head hanging over the handlebars, an awkward fit. Worst of all, I realize that for all my observation and experience riding on the back of them, I don't know what I am doing. It's as if I have to learn how to swim, nobody is holding on and I can't touch bottom. I believe "hoisted on my own petard" puts it about right.

I have in mind an easy turn around the block, but before I can get over to right lane, I'm swept into the mainstream just like a novice canoeist in the midst of class three white water, no way to go but down. By the time I give up trying to maneuver lanes I'm jammed into a pack of them behind a red-light intersection. I try to appear cool and unconcerned, but already I don't know where I'm headed and a little desperate about not stalling out while I am knee to knee with several youngsters hooded like Darth Vader giving me sideway glances and probably smirking. Off we go again.

Essentially, I'm trying get to West End Lake where Nyugen took me last night to the floating barge. From there, I think I can simply drive around the lake. It's 11:00 a.m. and I have five hours to get lost and found.

Though I'm never comfortable with the whole thing and suffer a number of embarrassments with one or two humiliations, I get around West End Lake and find the occasion to visit some odd places. The east side of the lake has become "developed" with the emergence of soon to be completed high-rise "Gated Communities", new icons of modern prosperity advertising exclusivity. Take that "Comrade"! At one, I pose as an American businessman scouting a suite of rooms for my various import/export enterprises. This gets me a guided tour with a man in a suit and his high-heeled assistant from "marketing". The features and accessories are knock offs of North Miami Beach overlooking the tennis courts and kidney shaped swimming pool, hot tubs and "massage" room.

From West End Lake I can guide on the signal tower of the new and imposing Ritz Hotel, a foremost feature of approaching modernity in Hanoi, putting the city on the overnight map for S.E. Asia. I follow the levee road into the dense and precarious traffic of the Hanoi "Old Quarter". By this time my bank of self-confidence has dwindled to near empty, confirming the admonition that he who hesitates gets lost.

"36" Streets is the Vietnamese version of the Istanbul bazaar's where whole streets and sections in the "Old Quarter" are devoted to particular trades and goods. The human traffic is constant and every corner knotted with activity, so dense that a tourist after wandering through the bends and currents of congestion looks longingly for some space of repose where he or she can become out of the way.

By luck I find a short lane, a cul-de-sac that dead-ends around a great twisting trunk of a Banyan whose spiraling arms lean over and give shade to a terraced tea and coffee shop with an overhanging balcony, away from the turbulence of sight and sound. I push my cyclo into the nest of others in front and wander in. The décor is modern and spare with the charm of oriental understatement. Light tones of melon and peach blend into the palm fronds and Bird of Paradise plants sprawl out of large ceramic urns in the corners, partially obscuring the live songbirds in filigreed cages, a wonderful touch! The walls are decorated with contemporary drawings of symbolic figures interspersed with abstract designs. The moldings and framing are polished bamboo. It is tasteful and the proprietor blends it tastefully with lighter music of Vietnamese/European rock and pop which sets it off nicely from the more Americanized style of Saigon.

Compared to the mainstream avenues, it is an oasis of quiet. The chirp of the songbirds keeps me company as I wait for a table to be open on the balcony that overlooks the cul-de-sac. A vagrant songbird arrives on the balcony and trills to its captured brethren in their bamboo cages, then impudently dips down among the limbs, hides behind the green leaves and perchs there, waiting for the answer. I have two hours to contemplate the relative state of the birds' affairs; whether to be free and hungry or in bondage and fed, or else ponder my "interview" with Nyugen and go public with our "Peace-through-the-Word-Cup" format.

I am seated between two young girls on the balcony. The one to the left, leaning against the railing, is sultry and self-possessed. She reads a book, glances at her watch and continues reading. The other is anxious and frets, reading and re-reading what appears to be a letter while she watches for someone below. I order tea and scrawl entries in my journal. Three more girls come up and join the anxious one and politely ask for my extra chair. It is a study group and they go to work right away as I return to my journal, or pretend to.

"Excuse me, please." I look up. One of the girls from the table is smiling down at me and blushing. "Are you American"? I nod. "Excuse me, please" she repeats. "We want to know if you will come and speak English with us."

They are students at the nearby institute which provides degrees in business subjects, though it is unclear whether it is the State University itself or a state sponsored and accredited school. Each speaks with varying proficiency. The taller, prettier girl at the table is the more fluent and assists in translating for the others when necessary. They tell me they are all majoring in Tourism, which requires speaking English. They have a presentation coming up and are meeting to divide the work and want to hear about how tourism works in America. They have never talked to an American before. Would I talk to them about it? Why not?

What better way for someone from the past to spend a final afternoon than to talk to those who want to express the future! Their enthusiasm can only match my gratitude. As I signal to the waiter to bring a round of tea, the songbirds in their cages trill in the corners and a slight breeze invades the balcony under the shade of the Banyan. I try to answer their questions and tell them about my experiences in Vietnamese hotels and villages, what tourists look for and what they don't. They have never been to Saigon, but want to go. They have never been anywhere, but want to go. They see tourism as some flight that will lift them out of their closed world—and are eager to escape.

They ask me where I've been, why I'm here. When I mention the war, their faces become closed and still for the first time, and then one, and soon all, looking among each other as they silently agree to confess they know nothing about it, that no one talks about it so how can they? But that is not it. I know by now that this is their way of cutting out the Past, or the State, or Politics, as one would step over an obstacle in the road that simply impedes the journey. They know because in every family there is some ghost to whose spirit they have dutifully knelt and whose loss, while not spoken of, is always honored in the curl and rise of an incense stick on certain days.

So it is fitting that we talk about other things and of course they ask about America, where they all want to go. The woman who is their leader vows that someday she is going to live there—and they all insist that they will live there some day, so would I give them my name and address and they will write me.

They laugh when I ask them why they want to get away, and then look at each other nervously. In each answer the short story of a life unwraps: family, upbringing, the vagaries of fortune that have led all of them to want to escape to a far different future than the ones their parents and grandparents hoped for. For now they are dazzled by the modern world's Technicolor images of opportunity and unfettered freedoms. At the same time they fear restrictions of the past, the chain of arranged marriages, the obligations of tradition, the prison of status that consigns them to the bottom of the pecking order.

Their politics, the only kind that they can speak of, or overtly rebel from, is the sexual inequality so embedded in their culture. What they want is a level playing field with men: to choose whom they want to live with, to go where they want, to be what they want. They want to feel what they *could* be.

Before I know it, we have exhausted our time together. I have to go and meet with Nyugen and they have to go to a class. With great enthusiasm we exchange names and addresses and even phone numbers as if we will see each other next week, and I contribute to this illusion by taking their pictures. When I leave, they call down from the balcony and I see them again, one more time, arms around each other, cheerful and robust, waving at their future. If only there could be blue skies.

36

ROLL-EM!

Nyugen arrives with his photographer right on time and proudly shows me some proofs of pictures taken during other interviews. He is all business. Sure enough everything appears on the up and up. It becomes a mini event for the little hotel—the set up takes up half the small lobby. The hotel staff busies itself assisting with extension cords and some extra lighting. The photographer darts around at different angles and people passing by the front window begin to stop and watch. Show Biz in Hanoi about nothing. I'm both amused and a little bit nervous that I say something relatively appropriate about something I know nothing about, but it's not the first time.

When all is ready and the photographer has shot his stills, Nguyen sits me down, goes over the points we discussed and turns on the recorder. All of a sudden, I am live from Hanoi!

We are suddenly strangers and questions come to me from a distance. Nguyen's lopsided face suspends itself. I am described as an American businessman who, in visiting Vietnam, has become a friend of the Vietnamese people and who shares their enthusiasm for the World Cup games. The Vietnamese people want to know what the Americans think of the World Cup and I find myself telling them that we love sports and are learning that "soccer" is the greatest international game in the world and that America is just beginning to develop teams to participate in it.

So far, so good. Nguyen says that Vietnam is such a small and poor country compared to the United States that maybe United States teams might not want to come and play football here? I want to remind him that didn't seem to be much of a problem 30 years ago, but shy away from opening that door! Oh yes, I tell him, Americans would be honored to participate and the more games we played together the more we would enjoy it. Flags are now waving gladly in our minds. A fat oriental with a much more attractive girlfriend comes in with their bags to register at the desk. He's wearing a Cleveland Indians (!) Tee Shirt picturing a happy big nosed Indian gladly brandishing a Tomahawk in one hand and a waving a scalp in the other, not exactly the scene we are looking for though its my Home Town! Nguyen is angling for the World Peace theme and I am just warming up. The question of what I am doing drips in my mind. The hotel staff is standing around watching in that way in which they always appear to be spellbound and aren't. Outside on the street the city people of Hanoi move about the corner tangling and untangling from the lights and the traffic that throbs somewhere outside the hotel as their world turns.

37

ENVOI

Miraculously, the article appears as promised. On my way to breakfast members of the staff who have hovered over the interview rush up, joyfully waving it in my face. Vietnamese at their best have the capacity to show delight with the open, spontaneous joy that we see only in the faces of children, beaming from one side of their face to another, bobbing and bowing, loose hands aflutter with Buddhist prayers like birds leaving a nest.

It is on the first page of the weekend edition featuring what seemed to be mostly local collective events, but then what did I know—it was in Vietnamese. The insert photograph is so grainy on the rough textured paper that I might as well be incognito. Little Tuy, the desk clerk, tries to interpret; something about the World Cup and how I am an American friend of Vietnam who is happy to be here and thinks soccer is a great thing for international understanding.

A few years before an article like this about a foreigner, particularly an American and his subversive thoughts, would have been sniffed and pawed over by the censors and seen as a threat to the State's obsession with political propriety.

In fact, relatively speaking, today's article, given the State's paranoia about the press, is amazing. While there are few remaining teeth in the jaws of the totalitarian tiger, the government's jealous control and stern censorship of any "un-official" expression can result in a sharp bite for the unwary.

Nevertheless, after the mudslide of post-war failures and the damage caused by self-imposed isolation and rejection by the rest of the world, some retreat from the remorseless lockdown of free expression became inevitable. As a result, Nguyen told me, non-ideological journalism has only recently started to blossom, expanding the scope of reportage to non-political areas such as art, literature and local events of popular interest.

So here I am, a picture on the front page of some weekend edition of a legally published paper in a city I almost did not dare myself to enter after thirty forbidden years. In this now harmless moment it is hard not to laugh out loud with the delicious irony of it all.

Believe it or not, when I arrive at The Golden Cock for my goodbye dinner I am treated like a Big Shot. One of the waiters has recognized me from the article, so I'm surprised when the Maitre D brings the menu and asks me about the evening's World Cup match and what team I was backing. "Croatia" I announced confidently, and accepted a complimentary drink. Emboldened, I declared that Italy and Brazil, but God forbid France, would beat England. I was so full of myself that I expansively order the lobster tail with a cold bottle of Sauvignon Blanc, breaking my sagging budget with self-indulgence.

Yes, the last day had been a great success: my survival on a moped, my masquerade as a foreign entrepreneur, and now a ten-second celebrity and surprising elevation to the status of favored customer of one of the city's best restaurants. My self-esteem experiences a momentary inflation.

But the truth is that I've been riding pretty close to empty since Ha Long Bay. The sense of being foreign does that. It fills you up and empties you out. At the end you are homeless, a cardboard cut out propped up by plastic credit cards and tucked away in hotel rooms. In short, it's time to go home.

Nguyen insists on picking me up at 5:30 a.m., rooster time, and even in down town Hanoi, that is literal. He wants to take me to a Pho shop that is famous for its old/traditional style "so you can see real Pho shop no tourist sees". He has lined up a friend who has borrowed a car to take me to the airport (a typical catch-as-catch-can arrangement that all three of them get part of the fare). It is gray and cool after a late night thunderstorm, but the restaurant is full. It is utilitarian and worn like a school cafeteria, all linoleum and iron folding chairs. Cigarette smoke is already so thick that you have to wave your hands to see the way ahead. With a show of authority Nguyen takes us to the second floor balcony and instructs the waitresses to arrange for a table so we have a view of the scene, "So you can see many important people in the morning crowd", and with that he greets and waves to almost all of them. Nguyen loves playing the host and guide, and he is good at it. The steaming Pho is quite wonderful as long as you don't have a problem with chicken-noodle soup for breakfast. It's a wondrous sight to watch the nimbleness of waiters wheeling around, holding steaming bowls aloft. The scene is so essentially Vietnamese that it would be clearly as preposterous for a foreigner to enter it alone as a clothed man to walk into a swimming pool. Nguyen watches me with his lop-sided grin, holding his cigarette high like a bandleader holding his baton, telling me with his eyes "This is the real Hanoi, and I am showing it to you, my friend."

Looking down from the plane I watch as Hanoi spins slowly in a lazy brown circle. Even though it was a surprisingly warm and receptive place, it hardly waves goodbye. At least I am departing

The last time I left Vietnam for Hong Kong it was Christmas Eve 1967, R&R 35 days before the infamous TET Offensive. It was an evening flight and the one thing that startled me after ten months of black out "In Country" was that it was lit up with galaxies of light as if there was no war on. The arrival was cold and windy for a guy in short sleeves traveling at the last minute with a hand bag after beginning the day coming out of a swamp in the western Mekong Delta. I managed to end up partying with a bunch of young Brits and Canadians at a place high up on a cliff-hanger high rise, posh and spacious, with an outside terrace that overlooked the famous harbor where ships from the U.S. Navy's 5th Fleet sat at anchor, dressed like Christmas trees.

From what I can remember then, today's Hong Kong looks like it has been on steroids. Arriving at the mammoth new airport says all there is to say about what is Third World and what isn't. Riding into Kowloon on a state of the art high-speed train seems to take me into another century, leaving Vietnam behind in time as well as space. From a park bench on the quay, the harbor scene is almost breathtaking. Gazing across at the Hong Kong side, I watch packed ferry boats scurry back and forth. Giant steel hulks stacked with tiers of containerized goods are prodded out to sea by teams of tugs through channels of glass and steel skyscrapers standing shoulder to shoulder glinting and glistening in their reflection off the water as if passing in review.

Proud and pompous on the mountain top, bustling and grasping in the downtown, Hong Kong is a citadel of the world with few peers, exuding the same inflated entrepreneurial panache that must have flushed the cheeks of the 15th Century Venetian and Genoese merchants in their ships and camels throughout their little known world. Against this parade of state of the art global opulence, Vietnam appears dwarfed, threadbare and in the world of today slightly, or maybe even largely, irrelevant.

I find the roll of Vietnamese *Dong* that I so carefully, then carelessly, stashed to give to Nguyen; about $100, not something to toss into the waste bin as a passing memory. With nothing else to do for the next 24 hours I think I'll find a money changer to cash it out. After all, Hong Kong is famous for its global financial heft. From where I am standing I can see as many neon signs advertising money changing as there are shrubs around the park.

The man behind the window shakes his head and points up and down the street. The rest of them do the same. With not much else to do I decide to go up-market and start on the banks along the Kowloon side. At least they go through the exercise of speaking. No, they have no exchange rate for Vietnamese currency and will not accept it, So Sorry, as they turn to better customers.

Across to Hong Kong on the ferry, I stride into its canyons of steel and glass and even to the top of one of them that announces the Royal Bank of Hong Kong Ltd. with carpeted offices and million dollar views. After patient inquiry and a polite wait a well dressed bank clerk with the flat oriental eyes some thousands of feet above ground zero confirms that there is no exchange available for Vietnamese currency.

It takes a rooftop restaurant with a world-class view and a fine Hong Kong brew before not considering this tail chase a personal affront. Behind me a regiment of Chinese office workers in their white shirts and ties enthusiastically attack their multi dish meals with chopsticks, waving to their accomplices and partners in keeping the world turning. None, I am sure, could have cared less about Vietnam, but I did.

Somewhere out there is a small, often forgotten country swollen with people whose sweat off their brow seemingly fails to earn interchangeable value in the international community. I thumb the roll of *Dong* that would have made Nguyen in Hanoi feel I had been a good investment and he, momentarily, a rich man, while several hundred miles away it cannot buy me a beer.

The people of Vietnam deserve more than they got, and from what I have seen much more than they are going to get in the near future. What, for instance, did they get from their War of Reunification if all that resulted was worse than they had before? The plow of the totalitarian authority over the last 30 years has turned over the timeless soils of inequality only to sow the same seeds that produce the revolving crops of the new rich on one side and enduring poverty on the other. Yesterday's socialist partisan is today's nouveau riche and visa-versa. By all accounts, even those among the ruling party, today's staggeringly insidious corruption and graft found in their midst threatens to produce the same venality and social injustice that led to national disintegration in the first place. It's effect is to turn the moral integrity of the idealistic tenets of socialism into a rusty bucket of empty rhetoric and tattered promises that none can believe in.

In economics, agricultural collectivism and State Owned Enterprises (SOEs), with their dogmatic price controls and incompetent management, have dragged the country's economy to the precipice of famine and national bankruptcy. In education, the state controlled curriculum still features Marxist-Leninism. In labor, the once admired "national human capital" in skilled motivated labor has been numbed by socialist disincentives, vitiating initiative, aspiration, and creativity. The blaring promises of universal human services and welfare safety nets have been discredited by persistent state insolvency. In health care, according to an American doctor, who is a frequent volunteer consultant on public health organization and policy issues, the system is in a shambles: physicians are paid below the poverty level, there is a woeful lack of trained staff, and services and supplies remain chronically undistributed, except in large urban centers where they are subject to rampant black market profiteering. And the list goes on.

The overall result is that notwithstanding the great "War of Reunification", there are again two very different Vietnam's. On the one side, there is the authoritarian State with a Politburo with a withering but tenacious grip on power while insulated from the reality around them. On the other, there are the people that, aside from being totally disenfranchised, simply make do on their own. The inhabitants of one pay little attention to the other, and each goes its own way, digging an ever-widening ditch in between.

While this is not exclusive to Vietnam, it presents the danger that the country will not find a way out of its dilemma. On the political front, the "Chinese solution" presents itself—the rationale that, in exchange for totalitarian control of the issues of legality and sovereignty, private capitalism and a market economy may be officially allowed to flourish and that the social and economic volcano created by this dualism will not blow its lid. But Vietnam is not China.

Without the economic heft of a China and its world markets Vietnam has little capacity for the necessary economic growth to sustain its 12% per year population increase. Stuck in the mud of ambivalence the State is simply beyond its depth in managing a conversion to a market economy abraded by runaway free enterprise while at the same time maintaining strict authoritarian control. Characteristically, knowing only the fist, the government opts for the latter. Meanwhile, the expectations of the successive generations entering the labor market portend pressures well beyond any anticipated projections of achievable growth.

As for a viable solution, there seems to be none, for two good reasons. First, there will not be any significant political change. The national trauma of the Civil War (never officially mentioned as such) remains too raw and brings shudders to rich and poor alike for any oppositional political challenge no matter how urgent. This fear factor is probably the only plebiscite on which the majority of the Vietnamese could agree. Secondly, since its military conquest, economic development under Communism in the sense of providing a staircase for prosperity has been such a complete failure that present and foreseeable national resources will be unable to provide it.

"So then what?" I ask myself thousands of miles away on top of a skyscraper high above the world. What will happen to them, the Vietnamese? I wonder as I walk past the window displays of shops selling luxury goods in a spanking new underground mall, its marble and soft pastel walls glowing with indirect lighting. Attractive, well-dressed people walk languorously about enjoying the seductive music or stare from shiny escalators into the scented air of unreality.

Here I am standing in some kind of fairyland, as if I have magically escaped from somewhere else, trying to remember the yesterday of the other part of it that isn't. In Vietnam there is no fairyland, just reality, where tomorrow seems fated to be little if nothing more than yesterday. I think back to all those people I have watched from every angle in every sequence for almost three weeks, passing by, brushing against them, observing from up close to far away, often as an invisible witness. None were "interviews", weighty conversations with personalities, or experts, a former this or that who might be of journalistic interest or use. They were simply people, but in each encounter I found shadows and echoes of experiences I thought I had forgotten, on which I could draw to understand the now and then. ·

Yes I thrilled at the sights and smells, the throngs and noise, the green of the land, the brown of the water and the blue of the sky. All provided the space, painted the scene and filled the ambience, but in the end, and when I look up to catch it in my mind all I really see are the people.

Bedeviled by the djinns of love and war: wrestling with the Taoist Yin and Yang, aspiring to the Buddhist spirit world and clothed in the complex rituals of Confucian mores each of them, all of them flash hot and cold, soft and hard, fragile and tough, romantic and tragic. Read their poetry of fate and destiny; listen to their songs of sorrow and yearning, clashing with cruelty and human indifference, unyielding and implacable. With such volatile elements brought together in one complex and ancient society, no wonder the people of Vietnam are unforgettable.

How can I forget: the hotel chauffeur who greeted me on arrival at Ton Son Nhut airport in (just say it!)"Ho Chi Minh City" in his thread bare gray suit, holding on to his dignity as tightly as the French Beret across his breast as a signal that if we had won the war he wouldn't be picking up tourists in a hand me down job after enduring two decades of "re-education" among nameless jungle hills for being "bourgeois" and watching others die.

Kim, the cheerful street survivor cyclo-driver pedaling through the pelting rain leaning over to me mocking the Communist regime in a low voice and chuckling at their hypocrisy.

Mai, the irrepressible child of the Conquerors with all the tools to make it plus the magic collateral of an American husband and a beautiful little baby-san dangling a blue passport with a "USA" stamped on it.

Houng, nervous companion, stoic driver, third son to a dying mother with a wife and two boys barely provided for, his gaze always defaulting to the sorrowful frown except when drinking beer; shame on the country to turn this meek, gentle man into a soldier.

Leave it instead to the militia man on the park bench watching the river of his thoughts along its wordless banks while smoking a "peace pipe" with someone better worth killing—if it had ever come to that—so many forgetful years ago.

The "lady of the manor" holding aloft into the morning sun the bright blaze of her prize rooster, tribute to a life friendship through the upheavals of war.

The Con Lai war orphan huddled there in the crooked pathway with her basket of sundries, frozen with the torment in her mongrel eyes and the slur of being "bu doi".

The little river girl Phanh Thuy laughing away the clouds, inflating a flagging heart for an afternoon on the wide brown waters of the Bassac and the deep cooling shades of her peasant world.

Trung, the Assistant Manager hoping for the advent of the better world he needs for his two sons who are working stoically up hill against the dead weight of government resistance.

Pham Loc, the soldier/artist painting the struggle with the same of colors of war, blood, mud and smoke and waiting for the sunshine to soften his horizon.

Nguyen the journalist, self-proclaimed ambassador and friend to foreigners who speak American making his way upstream into the future.

The school-girls at the "Birdcage" coffee shop, the hotel staffs who worried about me and all the others.

Will they survive, their lives finding hopes to fill them, overcome their worries, allay their fears, meet their needs and feed their wants? Yes and No. And what of the children everywhere and always so tenderly nurtured when they leave their nest of parental care and fly off. Will it be something better? I hope so.

My story is over. Not much is left out except various details unexpressed goings-on and scattered anecdotes. My journey has filled a journal of answered questions that had lain around its house of memory since I felt young 30 years before. Since then I often wonder whether I would go back again, but I doubt it. Why? I have trouble saying.

The commuting crowd is thick on the ferry back to Kowloon. The late afternoon sun flashes in gold off the wind-wrinkled water. From the stern deck, the red flag of China spirals and whips around the sternpost. The world has changed, new flags, new countries, not to mention more wars. I had been a part of one, a tiny piece on a remote square of the chessboard of World Order (or disorder). I would be dishonest not to confess my life's fascination with it. This is no paean to war's glory, just a clear eyed notion of its reality and force in life on earth. The poet's lament, the writer's critique, the professor's lecture, and the woman's disgust notwithstanding, it allowed me to grasp an understanding of the primacies of life's death and survival. Along with countless generations of young men before and those to follow inevitably after, I will have felt that beat in my chest and the quickening in my blood.

In my youth war had sent me far away to a distant place called Vietnam. There, great brown rivers uncoil out of green jungle mountains like dragon tails in the land where dragons were born.

0-595-31952-1